AN INTRODUCTION TO BIBLICAL LAW

An Introduction to Biblical Law

William S. Morrow

William B. Eerdmans Publishing Company
Grand Rapids, Michigan

Wm. B. Eerdmans Publishing Co.
2140 Oak Industrial Drive N.E., Grand Rapids, Michigan 49505
www.eerdmans.com

Published 2017
Printed in the United States of America

23 22 21 20 19 18 17 7 6 5 4 3 2 1

ISBN 978-0-8028-6865-7

Library of Congress Cataloging-in-Publication Data

Names: Morrow, William S. (William Sproull), 1953– author.
Title: An introduction to biblical law / William S. Morrow.
Description: Grand Rapids : Eerdmans Publishing Co., 2017. | Includes bibliographical references and index
Identifiers: LCCN 2016059253 | ISBN 9780802868657 (pbk. : alk. paper)
Subjects: LCSH: Jewish law. | Bible. Old Testament—Criticism, interpretation, etc.
Classification: LCC BM520.3 .M66 2017 | DDC 296.1/8—dc23
LC record available at https://lccn.loc.gov/2016059253

For my grandson, Curzon

Psalm 19:7–10

Contents

IV. ISRAEL IN THE COURTS OF THE LORD

V. ISRAEL IN THE CITY

List of Illustrations

INSETS

FIGURES

Preface

I have spent much of my professional career as a biblical scholar introducing the study of the Old Testament to theological students, most of them studying for ministries in the church. This textbook is a distillation of that experience. As such, it represents a particular approach to the study of biblical law. Of course, there are other ways of introducing and surveying a field as vast as legal discourse in the Bible. I have chosen this one because I have found it useful for theological students engaged in serious study of biblical law for the first time. A fuller rationale for the book is found in Chapter 1.

Through this book, I hope I can continue reaching theological students and other lay people interested in knowing more about the Old Testament. That hope has a certain poignancy, as the institution in which I taught theology as a professor of Hebrew Scriptures has now closed its doors. I will always be grateful to Queen's Theological College for the opportunities it gave me. While teaching there, I came to know the truth of the rabbinic proverb, "I have learned much from my teachers, more from my colleagues, and the most from my students."

This book has been formed by other academic relationships as well. I owe much to the Society of Biblical Literature's Biblical Law Section. Through it, I have had the privilege of meeting and learning from some of the top scholars in biblical and ancient Near Eastern law across the world. I am also grateful for the hospitality shown me by the Centre for Studies in Religion and Society at the University of Victoria. It was during my fellowship there in 2012 that the idea for this book first took shape. Finally, this manuscript came to completion during a sabbatical leave granted by Queen's University, for which I am most appreciative.

Many people have contributed their comments and questions in ways that brought my own thought to clearer expression. The parishes of St. Philip Oak Bay, Victoria, BC, and St. George's Cathedral, Kingston, ON, and the congregation of Edith Rankin Memorial United Church of Kingston hosted my series of talks called "Six Reasons Not to Read the Old Testament." It was a rewarding experience to workshop some of the material found in this book with these groups of enthusiastic and intelligent lay people and clergy.

A number of persons have read this manuscript in whole or in part. They include Herbert Basser, John Kessler, Debbie Sawczak, Mark Ward, and Bruce Wells. Their comments have helped me immeasurably. Special thanks are due to F. Rachel Magdalene for her thorough responses to this book in draft. My deepest gratitude goes to my wife Ruth, who believed in this project and constantly encouraged me. Of course, whatever errors remain in this book are solely my responsibility.

Abbreviations

AB	Anchor Bible
ABD	*Anchor Bible Dictionary* (1992)
AIL	Ancient Israel and Its Literature
AnBib	Analecta Biblica
ANEM	Ancient Near East Monographs
ANET	*Ancient Near Eastern Texts Relating to the Old Testament*, 3rd ed. (1969)
AOAT	Alter Orient und Altes Testament
AOTC	Abingdon Old Testament Commentaries
BA	*Biblical Archaeologist*
BASOR	*Bulletin of the American Schools of Oriental Research*
BBR	*Bulletin for Biblical Research*
BETL	Bibliotheca Ephemeridum Theologicarum Lovaniensium
Bib	*Biblica*
BibInt	*Biblical Interpretation*
BIW	The Bible in Its World
BJS	Brown Judaic Studies
BO	*Bibliotheca Orientalis*
BWANT	Beiträge zur Wissenschaft vom Alten und Neuen Testament
BZABR	Beihefte zur Zeitschrift für altorientalische und biblische Rechtsgeschichte
BZAW	Beihefte zur Zeitschrift für die alttestamentlische Wissenschaft
CahRB	Cahiers de la Revue biblique
CANE	*Civilizations of the Ancient Near East* (1995)
CBET	Contributions to Biblical Exegesis and Theology

CBQ	*Catholic Biblical Quarterly*
CBQMS	Catholic Biblical Quarterly Monograph Series
ChrCent	*Christian Century*
ConBOT	Coniectanea Biblica: Old Testament Series
COS	*The Context of Scripture* (2003)
CTJ	*Calvin Theological Journal*
CV	*Communio Viatorum*
DSD	*Dead Sea Discoveries*
ECC	Eerdmans Critical Commentary
EncJud	*Encyclopaedia Judaica* (1972)
ExAud	*Ex Auditu*
ExpTim	*Expository Times*
FAT	Forschungen zum Alten Testament
FAT/2	Forschungen zum Alten Testament (2nd ser.)
FRLANT	Forschungen zur Religion und Literatur des Alten und Neuen Testaments
GBS	Guides to Biblical Scholarship
HAR	*Hebrew Annual Review*
HCOT	Historical Commentary on the Old Testament
HdO	Handbuch der Orientalistik
HThKAT	Herders Theologischer Kommentar zum Alten Testament
HTR	*Harvard Theological Review*
HUCA	*Hebrew Union College Annual*
HvTSt	*Hervormde teologiese studies*
IDB	*The Interpreter's Dictionary of the Bible* (1962)
IEJ	*Israel Exploration Journal*
Int	*Interpretation*
JAOS	*Journal of the American Oriental Society*
JBL	*Journal of Biblical Literature*
JBS	Jerusalem Biblical Studies
JFSR	*Journal of Feminist Studies in Religion*
JHebS	*Journal of Hebrew Scriptures*
JNES	*Journal of Near Eastern Studies*
JSOT	*Journal for the Study of the Old Testament*
JSOTSup	Journal for the Study of the Old Testament Supplement Series
JSQ	*Jewish Studies Quarterly*
JSS	*Journal of Semitic Studies*
LAI	Library of Ancient Israel
LHBOTS	The Library of Hebrew Bible/Old Testament Studies

NCB	New Century Bible
NEchtB	Neue Echter Bibel
NIBCNT	New International Biblical Commentary on the New Testament
NIBCOT	New International Biblical Commentary on the Old Testament
NovTSup	Supplements to Novum Testamentum
NTS	*New Testament Studies*
OBO	Orbis Biblicus et Orientalis
OBT	Overtures to Biblical Theology
OTL	Old Testament Library
PRSt	*Perspectives in Religious Studies*
RBS	Resources for Biblical Study
RelS	*Religious Studies*
RIDA	*Revue internationale des droits de l'antiquité*
SAA	State Archives of Assyria
SANT	Studien zum Alten und Neuen Testaments
SBL	Society of Biblical Literature
SBLDS	Society of Biblical Literature Dissertation Series
SBLMS	Society of Biblical Literature Monograph Series
SBLStBL	Society of Biblical Literature Studies in Biblical Literature
SBT	Studies in Biblical Theology
ScrHier	Scripta Hierosolymitana
SJLA	Studies in Judaism in Late Antiquity
SR	*Studies in Religion*
StudBib	*Studia Biblica*
SymS	Symposium Series
TAPS	Transactions of the American Philosophical Society
TDOT	*Theological Dictionary of the Old Testament* (1974–).
VT	*Vetus Testamentum*
VTSup	Supplements to Vetus Testamentum
WAW	Writings from the Ancient World
WAWSup	Writings from the Ancient World Supplement Series
WBC	Word Biblical Commentary
WMANT	Wissenschaftliche Monographien zum Alten und Neuen Testament
ZABR	*Zeitschrift für altorientalische und biblische Rechtsgeschichte*
ZAW	*Zeitschrift für die alttestamentlische Wissenschaft*

PART ONE

Thinking about Biblical Law

CHAPTER 1

Introduction: Water from Sinai

listen: there is a hell of a good universe next door; let's go

e. e. cummings, "pity this monster, mankind"

The quotation from e. e. cummings ends a poem that protests the way modern society defines itself. The stories of Israel's desert wanderings also portray a people in a crisis of self-definition. Time and again, they confront the harshness of life in the desert with complaints and regrets: "If only we had never left Egypt!" (e.g., Exod 15:24; Num 14:1–4). The issue comes to a head in Exod 17:1–7, when Moses strikes a mountainside to give water to his thirsty people at the behest of YHWH.

How This Book Refers to God

This book uses two terms to refer to the biblical divinity: God and YHWH. References to God use gender-neutral language whenever possible. For references to YHWH, Hebrew usage takes precedence; the personal name of Israel's deity is a masculine noun.

The account in Exodus 17 contains irony, however. The stories about Israel complaining in the desert were written with an eye to the impending revelation of YHWH's *torah* (covenant instructions).[1] Notice where God tells Moses to stand to strike the rock:

1. *Torah* is a transliteration of a Hebrew word that has rich meanings in Judaism. While it originally meant "instruction" or "teaching," *torah* came to mean the sum total of teachings that stem from Israel's encounter with God.

> The LORD said to Moses, "Go on ahead of the people, and take some of the elders of Israel with you; take in your hand the staff with which you struck the Nile, and go. I will be standing there in front of you on the rock at Horeb. Strike the rock, and water will come out of it, so that the people may drink." (Exod 17:5–6)

Horeb is one of the names the Bible gives to the mountain where tradition says God revealed *torah* to Israel. As Exodus 17 begins, the people are literally camping on the backside of the mountain of God. There, on the other side of the mountain, divine instruction will constitute forms of social organization that Walter Brueggemann calls "the alternative community of Moses."[2] On Mount Sinai/Horeb, Israel will be given a new sense of self.

In Jewish tradition, water became a symbol for *torah*. Exodus 17 hints that Israel was unaware of the kind of water it really needed. All the people could imagine is life as it had been for them; all they knew was Egypt. They didn't understand that when they left Egypt they would be changing the very way they defined themselves. While they camp on the backside of Mount Sinai, Israel is unaware that there is an amazing universe just next door!

The story in Exod 17:1–7 provides a parable for the way biblical law is often ignored in Christian churches. The problem can be illustrated with reference to the Revised Common Lectionary, a liturgical resource used by many denominations. The following is a list of the readings from Exodus–Deuteronomy the lectionary recommends over a three-year cycle:

Readings from the Revised Common Lectionary[3]

Exod	1:8–2:10	16:2–15
	3:1–15	16:2–4, 9–15
	12:1–4 (5–10), 11–14	17:1–7
	14:10–31; 15:20–21	19:2–8a
	14:19–31	20:1–17
	15:1b–11, 20–21	20:1–4, 7–9, 12–20
	15:1b–13, 17–18	24:12–18

2. Walter Brueggemann, *The Prophetic Imagination*, 2nd ed. (Minneapolis: Fortress, 2001), 1–19.

3. "The Revised Common Lectionary," Vanderbilt Divinity Library. http://lectionary.library.vanderbilt.edu/.

Exod	32:1–14	Deut	4:1–2, 6–9
	32:7–14		5:12–15
	32:12–23		6:1–9
	33:12–23		8:7–18
	34:29–35		11:18–21, 26–28
Lev	19:1–2, 9–18		18:15–20
	19:1–2, 15–18		26:1–11
Num	6:22–27		30:9–14
	11:4–6, 10–16, 24–29		30:15–20
	11:24–30		34:1–12

Evidently, there is nothing of value in Leviticus except the well-known "love your neighbor as yourself." Also, it is apparently sufficient to read the Ten Commandments while most of the other legal traditions in Exodus and Deuteronomy are overlooked. Numbers, we see, is only good for mining a few choice pieces of narrative.

Of course the contents of biblical law can pose significant hermeneutical (interpretative) challenges to contemporary readers. Women's rights, queer sexuality, and religious pluralism (to name just a few "hot-button" issues) are important concerns that seem to be ignored or challenged in the Bible's legal discourses. Nevertheless, when readers confine themselves to the narratives of Exodus–Deuteronomy, they are missing the possibility of entering an amazing universe—just next door. Something life-sustaining and nourishing still flows from ancient Israel's legal literature. Hence the subtitle of this chapter: *Water from Sinai.*

Approaching Biblical Law

This book focuses on the law collections in the Bible for several reasons. First, many theology students are less familiar with the law in the Pentateuch than with its narratives. This book is an attempt to redress that imbalance. Second, collections of biblical law deserve to be studied as a meaningful genre of biblical literature. Just as important, law represents a significant way in which ancient Israel did theology.[4] The legal collections surveyed in this

4. This claim is more contentious than it may appear, as biblical scholarship has wrestled with the question about whether it is legitimate to read the writings of the Old Testament

textbook articulate visions of a human community that can respond to the divine reality with integrity.

The major collections of biblical law are found in the first five books of the Bible. Jewish tradition thinks of Genesis, Exodus, Leviticus, Numbers, and Deuteronomy as the Torah *par excellence*. As a synonym for Torah this book uses the word "Pentateuch," a traditional term derived from ancient Greek meaning "the fivefold book."

The writings in the Pentateuch are the spiritual patrimony of both Jews and Christians. It is important, therefore, to find terms that recognize their canonical status in the scriptural traditions of both Judaism and Christianity. This book uses the term "Tanakh" as a synonym for the Old Testament. Jewish usage often refers to this body of sacred writings by an acronym formed from the words that describe its three major literary divisions: *Tôrâ* (Torah), *Nəbîʾîm* (Prophets), and *Kətûbîm* (Writings), thus Tanakh.

A reminder of the status of the Torah or Pentateuch as Scripture in both Christianity and Judaism points to an emphasis of this introductory text. It is interested in introducing the major collections of biblical law as efforts at self-definition. At Sinai, Israel received its identity as the people of God; yet the identity that YHWH graciously bestows on his people is also a vocation. This observation is not new;[5] but it underscores one of the primary interests of legal discourse in the Old Testament. Indeed, it would not go too far to claim that underlying the intent of biblical law is the desire for incarnation: to embody the spirit of God in human community.

Meanings of "Israel"

The word "Israel" can have three different points of reference:

1. Geographical: as a name for a region of land in the Middle East
2. Political: as a name for an ancient kingdom and a modern state

---

as expressions of what the contemporary church has come to think of as theology. My claim finds justification not only in the attempts by past generations to write theologies of the Old Testament but also in recent studies such as that of Konrad Schmid, *Is There Theology in the Hebrew Bible?* (Critical Studies in the Hebrew Bible 4; Winona Lake: Eisenbrauns, 2015), 114–19.

5. See, e.g., Walter Zimmerli, *Old Testament Theology in Outline* (Atlanta: John Knox, 1978), 109; Dale Patrick, *The Rhetoric of Revelation in the Hebrew Bible* (OBT; Minneapolis: Fortress, 1999), 80.

3. Religious: a name for a faith community that has had various configurations over time

Although all three reference points have their value, when this book uses "Israel" without qualification, it usually has a religious connotation.

My perspective is connected to an exegetical method known as canonical criticism. It has been influenced by observations that James Sanders has made about the dynamics that brought individual books and traditions into the standardized (canonical) form called Scripture. These include claims that:[6]

1. Canon and community are inextricably bound.
2. Scripture contains a plurality of voices.
3. Scripture allows for both community stability and adaptability.
4. The underlying purpose of Scripture is to enable communities to *monotheize* in a particular time and place.

These perspectives provide valuable ways to understand what is going on in biblical law:

1) Canonical criticism makes the claim that there is a reciprocal relationship between the written standards called Scripture and the community that knows itself through them. When we read a collection of biblical law we can ask ourselves, "How does this collection of instructions convey a vision of community, of collective self-definition?"
2) In this book, we will discover that the social and theological perspectives that motivated the composition of the Covenant Code (Exod 20:22–23:19), collections of Priestly instruction, and the laws of Deuteronomy are formed around different metaphors for the character of the community. A remarkable feature about the Pentateuch is that these differing perspectives are allowed to stand side by side. To some degree, of course, they have also blended with each other. This can be

6. This list is mine. It is based on James A. Sanders, "The Bible as Canon," *ChrCent* 98 (2 December 1981): 1250–55; *Canon and Community: A Guide to Canonical Criticism* (GBS; Philadelphia: Fortress, 1984); and *From Sacred Story to Sacred Text: Canon as Paradigm* (Philadelphia: Fortress, 1987).

seen, e.g., in what appears to be Priestly editing of one version of the Ten Commandments (Exod 20:11; cf. Deut 5:15). Nevertheless, these voices resolve themselves into different social metaphors out of which the Mosaic tradition is expressed. What might it mean that the Bible allows a plurality of voices in its legal collections?

3) Collections of biblical law are capable of revising and, in some cases, challenging other perspectives now found in the canon. In fact, biblical law negotiates the need for both *stability* in the communities that know themselves in relationship to the Mosaic tradition and *adaptability*. Differing perspectives and different historical contexts dictate not only the preservation of past traditions but also their modification.
4) Fidelity to the Mosaic tradition required Israel's thinkers to *monotheize*. According to Sanders, the human tendency is to compartmentalize, to let God have sovereignty over some of life but to leave other parts open to the domination of other powers/deities. Israel's thinkers were constrained, however, to bring all of their experiences of life under the purview of YHWH.[7]

One of the inferences of this book's approach is that biblical law represents a dynamic system of thought. It is capable of both innovation and conservatism, of stabilizing a religious community while also helping it adapt to new cultural exigencies. Modern readers of the Old Testament, no less than ancient ones, have to negotiate the tension between finding stability with tradition and adapting to new and often unprecedented situations.

It is my opinion that the dynamism which generated collections of biblical law can also energize contemporary communities of faith. Nevertheless, this book stops short of telling modern readers what to derive from encountering the community-making tactics of biblical law. As one might expect, contemporary attitudes vary significantly with regard to the relevance of the collections of rules and rituals this book seeks to introduce. Some would assert that the Bible's criminal law remains completely applicable to the modern state.[8] Others want to privilege key texts such as the Ten Commandments, while ignoring most of the rest. There has also been extensive debate about the continuing relevance of biblical law to debates

7. Sanders, "The Bible as Canon," 1255.

8. E.g., the "dominion theology" movement represented by R. J. Rushdoony, *The Institutes of Biblical Law,* vol. 1 (Phillipsburg: P & R, 1973).

about capital punishment, gender roles, and environmental ethics—to name only a few prominent examples.[9]

As important as these discussions are, this book will not engage with them directly. Rather, it seeks to prepare the groundwork for contemporary interactions with biblical law by asking about the concept of community that a given law collection promotes or assumes. What might such visions mean for contemporary faith communities seeking to know themselves as heirs of the Mosaic tradition? A particular goal is that this book will be useful to students in seminaries and lay people in the church. Therefore, many chapters of this *Introduction to Biblical Law* inquire about the fate or development of the Torah's legal traditions in New Testament times. These discussions can be found at the end of chapters 5–22 under the heading "Developments."

Obviously, there are hazards in writing on developments in the first century CE (Common Era).[10] In many cases, interactions with the legal patrimony of the Pentateuch at the beginning of the Common Era deserve their own full, book-length discussions. Even so, the analyses are kept brief in order to keep attention fixed on interpretation of the biblical law collections themselves.

Another risk of mentioning first-century CE developments is that these discussions might play into the hands of Christian inclinations towards "supersessionism," a doctrine that contends Christianity has superseded Judaism as the legitimate heir of the biblical tradition. As a guard against the rhetoric of supersessionism, this book refers to the Scriptures shared between church and synagogue as the Tanakh as well as the Old Testament.

A further emphasis is that the first Christians thought of themselves as Jews. This is not to claim that Jewish self-definition in the first century CE was monolithic. On the contrary, this historical era was one of extraordinary creativity.[11] The early church emerged at the time when a number of Jewish groups were actively addressing problems of adaptation and stability as the

9. See, e.g., the discussions on the continuing relevance of biblical law in Joe M. Sprinkle, *Biblical Law and Its Relevance: A Christian Understanding and Ethical Application for Today of the Mosaic Regulations* (Lanham: University Press of America, 2006); Cheryl B. Anderson, *Ancient Laws & Contemporary Controversies: The Need for Inclusive Biblical Interpretation* (New York: Oxford University Press, 2009); and Richard E. Friedman and Shawna Dolansky, *The Bible Now* (New York: Oxford University Press, 2011).

10. Current biblical scholarship frequently uses the abbreviations BCE ("before the Common Era") and CE ("Common Era") to be more inclusive of Jewish perspectives, rather than BC ("before Christ") and AD (for *anno domini*, "the year of our Lord").

11. Donald H. Akenson, *Surpassing Wonder: The Invention of the Bible and the Talmuds* (Montreal: McGill-Queen's, 1998), 107–207.

people of Israel. Among its rivals and coreligionists were the protorabbinic movement (represented, e.g., by the Pharisees) and the Dead Sea Scroll sect at Qumran. All of these groups lived in substantial dialogue with the spirituality and community-making tactics of biblical law, even as they sought to create viable expressions of the Mosaic tradition for their own time. The sections on "Developments" seek to demonstrate that those who created the early church were making Jewish choices—not necessarily ones that led to normative Judaism, but Jewish in inspiration nonetheless.[12]

What This Book Is Not

This book is not a comprehensive introduction to biblical law. It is illustrative but not exhaustive. Some excellent surveys of biblical law are available that are quite technical and thorough; this book will not duplicate their efforts.[13] At the end of each part I provide a reading list of some of the more major works on each specific subject, and at the end of the book I provide a select bibliography of more general surveys of biblical law and books exploring biblical law and religion. Those seeking a comprehensive guide to scholarship in biblical law should consult John Welch's "Biblical Law Cumulative Bibliography."[14]

In fact, a variety of specialized kinds of learning are required to fully study collections of biblical law. Many of these approaches will be used in the following chapters; but readers wanting to be fully informed by them will have to look elsewhere. These disciplines include:

- familiarity with the literary forms and techniques used by ancient scribes;
- a knowledge of legal process and legal history;
- expertise in the literatures of surrounding cultures, especially texts from ancient Mesopotamia;

12. For descriptions of how New Testament writers were engaged with their Jewish heritage and thought patterns, see *The Jewish Annotated New Testament*, edited by Amy-Jill Levine and Marc Zvi Brettler (New York: Oxford University Press, 2011).

13. Brent Strawn, ed., *The Oxford Encyclopedia of Bible and Law* (New York: Oxford University Press, 2015); Pamela Barmash, ed., *The Oxford Handbook of Biblical Law* (New York: Oxford University Press, 2017).

14. "Biblical Law Cumulative Bibliography." The Ancient World Online: Institute for the Study of the Ancient World, 2014.

- the history and archaeology of the societies mentioned in the Bible;
- the use and interpretation of biblical law in postbiblical times;
- the ability to appropriate biblical scholarship in a number of modern languages.

The last point in this list bears special attention. The literature devoted to the study of biblical law is extensive and it has been produced by scholars in many different countries. As this textbook has been written with an English-speaking audience in mind, most of its references are in English. Nevertheless, readers will find a representative number of references in French, German, and Modern Hebrew. While important in their own right, these notes also signal a significant dimension of the study of biblical law. Students hoping to specialize in this field need to recognize that many important studies are not translated into English.

This book is not an exegetical handbook. Careful study of a text through close readings of its structure, form, historical background, etc. reward the reader with significant insights into a passage's meaning. Close reading involves, therefore, what scholars refer to as "exegetical method."[15] While various exegetical operations will be used in this book, its interest lies elsewhere than laying out a full methodology for the interpretation of biblical law.

Finally, this book is not intended to be a history of biblical law. Of necessity, students ought to be aware of some of the problems and solutions available to account for the development of a particular legal collection into its canonical form. These are briefly surveyed in the introductions to each of the law collections this book discusses. It is hoped that some students will be inspired by these short surveys to undertake the specialized training and research needed to address problems involved in the historical development of the Bible's legal traditions in depth.

What This Book Is

Central to this book is the idea that what is conventionally called "biblical law" is not a monolith but is made up of various voices or perspectives. The

15. A number of books introduce exegetical method for biblical study, e.g., John H. Hayes and Carl A. Holladay, *Biblical Exegesis: A Beginner's Handbook*, 3rd ed. (Louisville: Westminster John Knox, 2007); Michael Gorman, *Elements of Biblical Exegesis: A Basic Guide for Students and Ministers*, rev. ed. (Peabody, MA: Hendrickson, 2008); Douglas Stuart, *Old Testament Exegesis: A Handbook for Students and Pastors*, 4th ed. (Louisville: Westminster John Knox, 2009).

sections that follow will describe four different social contexts out of which biblical law was articulated:[16]

1. Israel at the holy mountain (Chapters 5–6). These chapters deal with the Ten Commandments.
2. Israel in the village assembly (Chapters 7–9). These chapters discuss the laws in Exod 20:22–23:19.
3. Israel in the courts of the Lord (Chapters 10–17). Here, Priestly and Holiness law found in Exodus, Leviticus, and Numbers are examined.
4. Law in the city (Chapters 18–22). The focus of these chapters is on the book of Deuteronomy.

Each of these four sections contains an introductory chapter followed by studies of representative laws in order to portray their community-making dynamics at work. In describing them, the discussion will not shy away from controversy. The Torah's law collections touch on themes such as slavery, revenge, sacrifice, ritual purity, gender inequality, and religious intolerance. Although this book intends to read biblical law sympathetically, it will not explain away material that may offend or puzzle modern sensibilities. Rather, it seeks to understand the witness of these instructions and regulations in an effort to make a viable community of faith.

The book begins with methodological considerations relevant to reading legal material. Chapters 2–4 introduce students to aspects important in approaching the study of biblical law.

- Since historical references are important, Chapter 2 sets out basic terminology related to biblical history.
- Chapter 3 addresses important questions about the relationship between the meaning of Moses as a mediator of Israel's legal traditions and the Moses of history. It will become clear that all of the collections of biblical law studied here owe their canonical form to processes of Scripture formation which came to fruition in the Persian period, perhaps 750–950 years after the time of the Exodus. What can it possibly mean to refer to Mosaic law under such circumstances?

16. In his work on the ideology of biblical law, Douglas Knight (*Law, Power, and Justice in Ancient Israel* [LAI; Louisville: Westminster John Knox, 2011], 4) identified three perspectives that characterize different collections of biblical law: a village perspective (the Covenant Code), a temple-centered perspective (Priestly law), and a nationalist perspective (found in Deuteronomy). This textbook both reflects Knight's social distinctions and modifies them.

- Chapter 4 describes various approaches that biblical scholars have employed to investigate biblical law. This includes different kinds of legal theory, comparative approaches drawing on the literature of the ancient Near East, and the study of law as literature.

Beginning with Chapter 5, the book examines the community-making dynamics of biblical law using the perspectives listed above. A summary chapter concludes the book.

Verse References and Translation

The standard edition of the Old Testament in Hebrew is called the Masoretic Text (MT). Occasionally, the chapter and verse divisions of MT differ from the tradition used in most English translations. For example, Exod 21:37 in the MT is Exod 22:1 in the New Revised Standard Version (NRSV). In these cases, verse references follow the tradition used in the NRSV. Readers familiar with the Hebrew will be able to make the necessary adjustments. Unless otherwise noted, biblical translations follow the NRSV.

CHAPTER 2

The Laws in Scripture: Dates and Origins

Although this book focuses on the canonical forms of biblical law collections, it cannot ignore the fact that each of them has a history of composition.

Often, it will be necessary to refer to various eras in biblical history in which some of the processes that formed the laws must be located. Different kinds of dating systems are used by biblical scholars. Three different kinds of dating systems can be distinguished, all of which are used in the chapters that follow. One is based on archaeological criteria, a second on historical eras, and a third on literary developments leading to the canon of the Old Testament. This chapter will indicate how the development of the biblical law collections is implicated in these chronological patterns.

Dating events in the ancient past is not easy, especially as they get further back in time. Equally difficult is to how to refer to the various geographical and political entities involved. Students interested in locating geographical references used in this book would be well served by referring to the maps published in standard Bible dictionaries and reference works.[1]

An Archaeological Timeline[2]

LATE BRONZE AGE ca. 1500–1200 BCE

1. David Noel Freedman, ed., *Eerdmans Dictionary of the Bible* (Grand Rapids: Eerdmans, 2000); Gordon Fee and Robert L. Hubbard Jr., eds., *The Eerdmans Companion to the Bible* (Grand Rapids: Eerdmans, 2011).

2. The timeline presented here is widely used, but there are alternatives. See Amihai Mazar, "The Debate over the Chronology of the Iron Age in the Southern Levant," in *The Bible*

IRON AGE	ca. 1200–539
IRON I	ca. 1200–1000 (premonarchical period)
IRON IIA	ca. 1000–925 (united monarchy of David and Solomon)
IRON IIB	ca. 925–720 (divided monarchies of Israel and Judah)
IRON IIC	ca. 720–587/6 (kingdom of Judah)
IRON III	ca. 587/6–539

The Late Bronze Age

Politically, Canaan in the Late Bronze Age was divided into a number of small city-states controlled in the south by Egypt and in the north by the Hittite Empire (centered in Asia Minor). This changed at the end of the Bronze Age: the Hittite Empire fell, and at the same time the Egyptians lost control of southern Canaan. In addition, many of the city-states were either destroyed or lost power. Out of this period of deurbanization and social shifts emerged new forms of political organization, some of which were the direct antecedents of the kingdoms of Israel and Judah.

It is probable that the Exodus took place during the end of the Late Bronze Age or at the beginning of the Iron I period (see Chapter 3). For ease of reference regarding the Bronze Age, the terms "Canaan" or "the Levant" will be used to refer to the whole area now divided between modern Lebanon, Israel, the Gaza Strip, and western Syria. No materials in the Pentateuch's legal collections can be reliably dated to the Late Bronze Age.

The Iron Age

Around 1200 BCE, a major technological change came about because iron was increasingly used to make weapons. This contributed to important shifts in political organization and material culture in the Levant. The Iron Age in biblical history can be divided into two main parts: Iron I, a premonarchical period remembered in the books of Joshua and Judges, and Iron II, the period when ancient Israel was ruled by kings.

Changes in history and material culture are used to distinguish Iron

---

and Radiocarbon Dating, edited by Thomas E. Levy and Thomas Higham (Sheffield: Equinox, 2005), 13–15.

IIA, the period of the united monarchy; Iron IIB, the period of the divided monarchies; and Iron IIC, the period when only Judah remained as an independent state, after the fall of the northern kingdom. Some archaeologists also distinguish an Iron III period, which describes the material culture of the land of Judah when it was dominated by the Neo-Babylonian Empire (587/6–539 BCE). The Iron II period is that in which the materials that formed the bases of the collections of law in the Torah were first composed and collected.

A Historical Timeline

PREEXILIC PERIOD	ca. 1200–597	
Premonarchical period	ca. 1200–1000	
Monarchical period	ca. 1000–587/6	
United monarchy	ca. 1000–925	**First Temple period**
Divided monarchy	ca. 925–720	**ca. 960–587/6**
Kingdom of Judah	ca. 720–587/6	
EXILIC PERIOD	ca. 597–539/20	
POSTEXILIC PERIOD	ca. 520 BCE–70/135 CE	
Persian Period	ca. 539–333	**Second Temple period**
Hellenistic Period	333–63	**ca. 520 BCE–70 CE**
Roman Period	63 BCE–635 CE	

The Preexilic Period

Historically, the single most important date for the composition of the Tanakh is the destruction of the First Temple by the Babylonians. This catastrophe marked the end of the monarchy in Judah. It also propelled the survivors of the destruction of the kingdom of Judah into a process of reflection and self-definition that had far-reaching effects. It is so important that biblical scholars often distinguish between a preexilic, an exilic, and a postexilic period in Israel's history.

The Monarchical Period

While there seem to have been earlier experiments with monarchy (e.g., the attempt to make Gideon king in Judg 8:22), a stable dynasty was first established in Jerusalem during the time of David. Hence the monarchical period is often dated from the beginning of David's reign. The monarchical period lasted until the destruction of Jerusalem by the Babylonians. As scholars differ on whether the First Temple was destroyed in 587 or 586, the timeline above dates the end of the monarchical period to 587/6 BCE.[3]

According to the biblical record, the monarchical period can be divided into three phases. The monarchy of David and Solomon ruled ethnically-related but disunited tribes in the hill countries of Judah and Israel. This tenuous federation did not last after the reign of Solomon. From the end of the tenth century to the end of the eighth century BCE, the land of Israel was divided into two competing monarchies.

The northern kingdom was ruled by a succession of different dynasties. It was finally destroyed around 720 BCE, when it was completely absorbed into the Neo-Assyrian province system. The southern kingdom of Judah was ruled by a single dynasty (the house of David) until it was destroyed in 587/6. At that time, Judah became absorbed into the province system of the Neo-Babylonian Empire (the Babylonians succeeded the Assyrians and took over their imperial structure). Judah would never regain its independence except for a hundred-year period between c. 160 and c. 63 BCE, when it was ruled by a dynasty of non-Davidic rulers called the Hasmoneans.

All the documents we now have in the Bible were written or received their final shape in a way that reflects the interests of the southern kingdom of Judah and its successor communities. This situation is relevant to attempts to reconstruct legal history in the monarchical period. It is difficult to recover legal traditions that belonged to the northern kingdom.

The First Temple Period

Scholars debate the nature of the monarchies of David and Solomon and the extent to which this era can be reconstructed on the basis of biblical materials. Be that as it may, there is little reason to doubt that early in his reign Solomon built a temple in Jerusalem. This temple became the foremost and, at some point in time, the only legitimate place to worship YHWH, the

3. For the date 587, see Rainer Albertz, *Israel in Exile: The History and Literature of the Sixth Century B.C.E.* (SBLStBL 3; Atlanta: Society of Biblical Literature, 2003), 78–81. For the date 586, see J. Maxwell Miller and John H. Hayes, *A History of Ancient Israel and Judah,* 2nd ed. (Louisville: Westminster John Knox, 2006), 468–69.

god of Israel, with sacrificial offerings. As a result of its destruction by the Babylonians in 587/6 BCE, the monarchical period more or less overlaps with another key way of dividing Israel's history into important eras: we can refer to the period from ca. 960 to 587/6 as the First Temple period.

Most scholars think that some of the material found in collections of biblical law can be dated to the First Temple period. It is unlikely, however, that the books of the Pentateuch obtained anything close to their canonical form during this era. In fact, the very idea of Scripture does not appear to belong to the First Temple period. That is not to say that there were no authoritative documents used in palace and temple administration; but there is no evidence that Israel as a faith community fundamentally oriented itself or discovered its identity by reference to a written text.

Proof of this comes from a survey of the words of the prophets who operated during the First Temple era. These spokespersons for YHWH were intellectual and religious thinkers of the highest caliber. Yet a survey of whatever words can be credibly ascribed to Amos, Hosea, Micah, Isaiah of Jerusalem, Zephaniah, Nahum, and Jeremiah shows that they did not primarily justify their messages with reference to religiously authoritative documents. That is, there seems to have been no body of Scripture with which the prophets expected their audiences to be familiar.

The Exilic Period

About ten years before the end of the First Temple/monarchical period, when Babylon had made Judah a vassal kingdom, the Babylonians stamped out an abortive rebellion there. In 597 the young Davidic ruler Jehoiachin and many of Jerusalem's leading citizens, priests, military officers, and artisans were forcibly deported to southern Mesopotamia together with their families. This measure was used to undermine Judah's capacity to rebel against its foreign overlord. A puppet king, Zedekiah (the uncle of the exiled Jehoiachin), was placed on the throne, and Judah retained nominal independence within the Neo-Babylonian Empire.

Zedekiah, however, also rebelled. The Babylonian reaction was harsh and punitive. In 587/6 the city of Jerusalem was burned to the ground, the temple of Solomon destroyed, and more people deported to Mesopotamia. These events represent the end of Judah as a monarchy. From 587/6 on, Judah was absorbed into the Babylonian province system, a status that continued when the ancient Near East was subsequently dominated by Persian and

Hellenistic powers. Most biblical scholars date the end of the exilic period to the the early Persian Empire when various deported peoples were given permission to return to their ancestral homelands from Mesopotamia (539 BCE). This permission is represented as being specifically directed to the exiled citizens of Judah in Ezra 1.

From the perspective of this book, the exilic period is extremely important. It was during this time that efforts were made to organize previously-existing historical, legal, and religious documents and traditions and mold them into works that could be read in order to maintain a distinct sense of identity and faith community in the Babylonian melting pot. This formative period allowed for not only recollection but also adaptation to new circumstances and new challenges; that is, legal traditions were not only being remembered, they were also being reinterpreted and created to respond to the exilic situation. This fact poses a constant problem to scholars trying to describe the intellectual history of ancient Israel. To what extent was the past remembered the way it actually happened, and to what extent was it remembered the way Scripture writers wanted it to be?

The Second Temple/Postexilic Period

Following the exilic period is, of course, the postexilic period. Determining when that period ended, however, involves a number of different perspectives. Was it with the emergence of rabbinic Judaism? With the Christ event? With the formation of the modern state of Israel? Has it ever ended? Because these questions are so contentious, scholars tend to use the adjective "postexilic" simply to indicate developments that took place after the end of the exile. When this book refers to the postexilic era, it effectively means the Second Temple period in the history of biblical literature.

The foundation for the Second Temple was laid in 520 BCE, and the temple was dedicated in 515. It stood until 70 CE, when it was captured and burned by the Romans. Jews hoped that the Second Temple could be restored, but these dreams were cruelly dashed when Rome crushed the Bar Kokhba revolt in 135 CE. Thereafter, Jerusalem was turned into a Hellenistic city in which Jews were forbidden to set foot.

Critical scholarship has concluded that all of the books in the Pentateuch came into something close to their canonical forms during Second Temple times, although the processes involved continue to be a matter of debate.[4] We can reasonably say that the idea of using written documents to create and maintain a sense of community (i.e., Scripture) was an innovation that firmly established itself in the Second Temple era. It was during that time period that early Judaism first knew itself as "the people of the book."[5] It is likely that the five books of Moses were more or less complete by the late Persian period (ca. 400 BCE), although signs suggest that small changes continued to be made into the Hellenistic era.[6]

A Literary Timeline

Midmonarchical era
- Pre-Deuteronomic law (Non-P materials)
- Early Priestly law (P)

Late monarchical era
- First version of Deuteronomy (D)
- Laws from the Holiness School (H)

Exilic and postexilic eras
- Development towards canonical forms of the Covenant Code, P and H, and Deuteronomy

Different theories exist about the development of biblical literature. The most significant has been the Documentary Hypothesis, associated with the work of the great German biblical scholar Julius Wellhausen (1844–1918). Since accounts of the Documentary Hypothesis and its influence on biblical scholarship are available in any number of introductions and reference works, only a few aspects of this influential current of thought will be addressed here.

In its classical formulation, this theory proposed that the Pentateuch is an amalgam of four written sources (documents). The earliest was a nar-

4. For recent reconstructions of the development of the Old Testament, see David M. Carr, *The Formation of the Hebrew Bible: A New Reconstruction* (New York: Oxford University Press, 2011); Konrad Schmid, *The Old Testament: A Literary History* (Minneapolis: Fortress, 2012).

5. William M. Schniedewind, *How the Bible Became a Book: The Textualization of Ancient Israel* (New York: Cambridge University Press, 2004), 183–87.

6. E.g., there is evidence that the time frame used in the Pentateuch was given its canonical form during Maccabean times; see J. Maxwell Miller, *The Old Testament and the Historian* (GBS; Philadelphia: Fortress, 1976), 70–76.

rative of Israel's foundation stories thought to favor the name Yahweh when referring to God. It is often referred to as the Yahwist source (abbreviated as J, following German usage). The J source was supposed to have been written in the ninth century in Judah. A slightly younger and competing narrative of Israel's origins favored a common Hebrew word for God, Elohîm, and was called the Elohist source (abbreviated to E). The E source was thought to have been written in the northern kingdom of Israel. J and E were believed to have been brought together after the collapse of the northern kingdom in the late eighth century. The editors of this document were influenced by the theology and rhetoric of the book of Deuteronomy, known as the D source. Finally, in the exilic or postexilic period, the combined J-E-D document was extensively supplemented by Priestly writers drawing on narrative traditions preserved in their circles (the P source).

Although the Documentary Hypothesis retains currency in some circles, critical scholarship has now cast doubt on many of its premises. Nevertheless, there is a consensus that an extensive Pentateuchal narrative corresponding basically to the J-E material can be separated from writings in the Priestly style, reconstructed as a non-P history made up of preexisting sources and traditions.[7] In fact, the Documentary Hypothesis did not provide a very convincing account of the origins of biblical law, as many of the collections of biblical law do not fit very well within the literary distinctions it made.

This book recognizes three distinct styles of law within the Pentateuch. The first is material written in the non-P style, a good example being the Covenant Code (see Chapter 7). The fact that some of its laws were adapted by Deuteronomy shows that non-P law must have been in circulation by the mid-monarchical period. A second style is found in the book of Deuteronomy (D). While the earliest form of Deuteronomy probably comes from the late monarchy (see Chapter 18), law continued to be written in the D style through the exilic and postexilic eras. Another source of law that probably begins in the late monarchical period comes from the Holiness School (H; see Chapter 10). Some of this Holiness material reworks earlier Priestly law (P). Therefore, there is a good case for seeing some P materials as preexilic in origin.

All of these styles of legal composition may have had very long lifespans. For this reason, the attempt made here to isolate and date various

7. David M. Carr, *Reading the Fractures of Genesis: Historical and Literary Approaches* (Louisville: Westminster John Knox, 1996), 44–45. See, e.g., the essays in Thomas B. Dozeman and Konrad Schmid, *A Farewell to the Yahwist? The Composition of the Pentateuch in Recent European Interpretation* (SymS 34; Atlanta: Society of Biblical Literature, 2006).

styles of biblical law is rudimentary and intentionally incomplete. Rather than reconstructing this history of composition in detail, the focus here remains on the collections of biblical law in their canonical forms.

In one respect, this book stands in clear opposition to the historical reconstruction of Israel's laws articulated by Wellhausen. It was his opinion that the canonization of biblical law was the result of a consolidation of Israel's religion that postdated the prophetic experience and represented the hardening of Israel's theological categories into a religion of legalism and formalism.[8] The anti-Semitic implications of this view of the development of biblical religion should not be overlooked. In early modernity, they allowed Christian scholarship to claim the legacy of the prophets while portraying Judaism as a fossilized and regressive expression of ancient Israel's religious experience.

On the contrary, law in the Bible is in many instances just as radical as the pronouncements of prophets of the stature of Hosea, Isaiah of Jerusalem, Jeremiah, and Ezekiel. In this study we will find numerous examples of the profound ways in which biblical law challenged social conventions and articulated a countercultural vision paralleling the prophetic imagination. Biblical law, no less than the prophets, was concerned to articulate "the alternative community of Moses."[9]

8. Julius Wellhausen, *Prolegomenon to the History of Ancient Israel* (Cleveland: World, 1965), 422–25.

9. The term "prophetic imagination," like the idea of "the alternative community of Moses," comes from Walter Brueggemann, *The Prophetic Imagination*, 2nd ed. (Minneapolis: Fortress, 2001).

CHAPTER 3

Biblical Law: Mosaic or a Mosaic?

The word "Mosaic" refers to actions, texts, and traditions associated with the person called Moses, who led Israel out of Egypt and had primary responsibility for giving God's laws to the people. His story is recorded in the books of Exodus, Leviticus, Numbers, and Deuteronomy. A mosaic, of course, is a piece of art composed of small stones that make up a pattern or design. Usually the stones are of different colors and origins. By arranging them carefully, an artist can produce a picture, sometimes quite elaborate and large, which may cover part of a floor or a wall.

The difference in meaning between the two words highlights a key problem in reading biblical law. For roughly two hundred years, the Bible has been subject to close scrutiny through the methods of modern historical-literary criticism. The results of those studies are used in this book; but, these studies conclude that the books of Exodus, Leviticus, Numbers, and Deuteronomy are best regarded as a *mosaic* of different writers and texts, coming from various time periods in biblical history, rather than as *Mosaic* in origin. For many biblical scholars, this is true even of the Ten Commandments.

The inability of modern critical study to identify the contributions of a historical Moses to the composition and transmission of biblical law often comes as a shock to students of the Bible. It can be felt as a direct challenge to cherished notions of biblical authority and the truth claims of Holy Scripture. These are weighty issues and this book certainly will not solve them; but it is important that readers know how this book intends to manage the conflict between reading biblical law as Mosaic and reading it as a mosaic.

Figure 1. A mosaic picturing Moses, on display at the Basilica Church of St. Louis, Missouri. Wikimedia (https://commons.wikimedia.org/wiki/File:MosesMosaic.jpg)

Moses in History

Any approach to finding Moses in history has to grapple with the question of when the Exodus took place, because this is the primary event with which he is associated. In fact, three models for dating the Exodus can be derived from biblical data:[1]

1. The possibilities listed here have the most biblical data to support them; see Gary Rendsburg, "The Date of the Exodus and the Conquest/Settlement: The Case for the 1100s," *VT* 42 (1992): 510–27. In fact, a wide range of dates for the Exodus have been suggested; see Law-

1. *Evidence for a Fifteenth-Century Date*

- 1 Kgs 6:1 (ca. 960 BCE + 480 years = ca. 1440 BCE)
- Expulsion of Hyksos as background to Exod 1:8
- References to the *ḫāpiru/ḫābiru* in the Amarna letters (14th century)

Assuming that the First Temple was dedicated by Solomon ca. 960 BCE, Model 1 is based on a literal reading of 1 Kgs 6:1. Tracing the Exodus back 12 generations of forty years each places the Exodus in the mid-fifteenth century, when Egypt's New Kingdom was beginning its expansion into southern Canaan. On this reading, the Pharaoh who did not know Joseph (Exod 1:8) developed a hostility towards the Israelites after driving out a Semitic people called the Hyksos, who had temporarily controlled the Nile Delta in the sixteenth century.[2] As Egypt attempted to expand and secure its empire in southern Canaan, its governors and vassals often reported their troubles with a refractory and somewhat unsettled group of people called the *ḫāpiru/ḫābiru* during the fourteenth century.[3] The coincidence between *ḫāpiru/ḫābiru* and the ethnic term Hebrew (*ʿibrî*) is suggestive.

2. *Evidence for a Thirteenth-Century Date*

- Exod 1:11 mentions the cities of Pithom and Rameses
- Merneptah Stele ca. 1208 BCE
- Genealogy of the Levites has about 12 generations between the time of Moses and the First Temple (1 Chr 6:1–10)

Model 2 takes a more pragmatic view of the meaning of 1 Kgs 6:1. If a generation is more like 25 years than 40, then 12 x 25 would yield about 300 years. In fact, the weight of critical scholarship has favored a date in the mid-thirteenth century for the historical core of the Exodus experience.[4] The

---

rence T. Geraty, "Exodus Dates and Theories," in *Israel's Exodus in Transdisciplinary Perspective: Text, Archaeology, Culture, and Geoscience*, edited by Thomas E. Levi, Thomas Schneider, and William H. C. Propp (New York: Springer, 2015), 55–64.

2. Bernhard W. Anderson, *Understanding the Old Testament*, 4th ed. (Englewood Cliffs: Prentice-Hall, 1986), 47–48.

3. E.g., "Letter of Lab'ayu of Shechem (Šakmu)," trans. William Moran (*COS* 3.92:242–43).

4. Geraty, "Exodus Dates and Theories," 55.

number 12 can find some justification from the genealogy of the Levites, the tribe in Israel with the most Egyptian-sounding names. The construction of a storage city named Rameses in the Nile Delta (Exod 1:11) fits comfortably with what is known about building activities in Egypt's Nineteenth Dynasty (ca. 1292–1187 BCE).[5] Moreover, this date would place Israel in the land of Canaan somewhat prior to the first extrabiblical mention of the people of Israel, found in the stela of King Merneptah of Egypt (ca. 1208).[6]

3. *Evidence for a Twelfth-Century Date*

- Genealogies in Ruth 4:18–22 and 1 Chr 2:10–15
- Decline of Egyptian political domination in Canaan

Model 3 dates the Exodus to the first half of the twelfth century. By that time, Egypt's power in Canaan was definitely waning; we know of reports of slaves escaping across the border into Egypt during this era.[7] Moreover, the genealogy of Naḥshon, a descendant of Judah and ancestor of David, is suggestive.[8] Biblical genealogy puts Naḥshon five generations prior to the birth of David (ca. 1030?). The canonical form of the Exodus story insists on the presence of Naḥshon, prince of Judah, during the Exodus (e.g., Exod 6:23; Num 10:14). While one can legitimately question whether the tribe of Judah participated in the Exodus, the association of Naḥshon's genealogy with the Exodus may indicate that Judah's scribes had a tradition that dated this event to the early Iron I period.

Of these three solutions, the most unlikely is the most literal. Model 1 is not generally followed in critical scholarship. The date of 480 years is a product of two numbers with symbolic value in the biblical imagination (12 × 40). Moreover, a date ca. 1440 places the Exodus in an era when Egypt's control over Canaan was increasing, which ill accords with the traditions of Joshua and Judges. Finally, while suggestive, there appears to be no direct link between the *ḫāpiru/ḫābiru* and the Israelites of the premonarchical era.[9] Of

5. J. Maxwell Miller and John H. Hayes, *A History of Ancient Israel and Judah*, 2nd ed. (Louisville: Westminster John Knox, 2006), 53.

6. "The (Israel) Stela of Merneptah," trans. James K. Hoffmeier (*COS* 2.6:40–41).

7. "A Report of Escaped Laborers," trans. James P. Allen (*COS* 3.4:16).

8. Rendsburg, "The Date of the Exodus," 532.

9. Nadav Na'aman, "Habiru and Hebrews: The Transfer of a Social Term to the Literary Sphere," *JNES* 45 (1986): 278.

course, both Models 2 and 3 also have their problems. In the case of Model 2, the southern Canaan that Israel would have entered in the mid-thirteenth century remained under the control of Egypt, and this is not remembered in Israel's narratives of conquest. Model 3 runs into difficulty because the relationship of the tribe of Judah to the Exodus tradition is less certain than for tribes such as Levi. Also, it least agrees with the dating formula in 1 Kgs 6:1.

We can only conclude that any historical events the Exodus tradition recalls must have taken place either in the Late Bronze Age or in the early Iron 1 period. This imprecision accords with other results from modern scholarship indicating that the emergence of Israel as an identifiable political and ethnic entity was the result of a complex set of developments that took place in Canaan during the end of the Bronze Age and the beginning of the Iron Age.

In particular, modern scholarship does not support the viewpoint of Joshua 1–12, that Israel entered the land through a swift military action that exterminated the Canaanite peoples. There are grounds for thinking that the backbone of Israel and Judah's traditional territory was largely unoccupied at the end of the Bronze Age. Israel's central hill country was not settled exclusively or even mainly through a process of military conquest.[10] Whatever their fate, to the extent that there were elements of Amorites, Hivvites, Jebusites, and others vying with ancient Israel for the possession of the land of Canaan, their disappearance from the historical record cannot be ascribed to genocide. The wholesale destruction of the Canaanites described in the book of Joshua and foreshadowed in the book of Deuteronomy must be considered a fiction.[11]

The archaeologist William Dever gives a plausible description of the contribution of the Exodus story to the foundation of Israel at the end of the Bronze Age. Most likely, the Exodus tradition reflects the experience of a relatively small number of Israelites who had escaped from Egypt in some unexpected or unprecedented way. They brought their Exodus story with them into a culture that was already experimenting with forms of settlement

10. William G. Dever, *Who Were the Early Israelites and Where Did They Come From?* (Grand Rapids: Eerdmans, 2003), 220–21; Miller and Hayes, *History of Ancient Israel and Judah*, 55.

11. Moshe Weinfeld, "The Ban on the Canaanites in the Biblical Codes and Its Historical Development," in *History and Traditions of Early Israel: Studies Presented to Eduard Nielsen*, edited by André Lemaire and Benedikt Otzen (VTSup 50; Leiden: Brill, 1993), 153–54; Jeffrey H. Tigay, *Deuteronomy* (JPS Torah Commentary; Philadelphia: Jewish Publication Society, 1996), 471–72.

patterns different from those that had predominated in Late Bronze Age Canaan. This involved the establishment of hundreds of small, mainly unfortified subsistence-farming villages on virgin soil in the central hill country of Canaan: the same territory that would later become the backbone of the kingdoms of Israel and Judah.[12]

The form of agriculture and social organization typical of these small Late Bronze-Iron I villages resembles a type of society that does not require monarchical organization. As Dever notes, this is "an astonishingly accurate portrait of early Israel, whose only sovereign was Yahweh."[13] The Exodus story may have given the peoples establishing themselves in the Israelite hill country a sort of ideological "glue" to support the kind of society they were developing. Groups informed by the Exodus story could appropriate this motif to express their mutual commitment to political self-determination. They were forming a society not subject to the kind of despotic rulers symbolized by Pharaoh. Such tyranny would have been evident both in Egypt and in the city-states of Late Bronze Age Canaan.

It is probable that a historical Moses lived and functioned as a charismatic leader of a small but significant part of nascent Israel during the Late Bronze or early Iron I Ages. He was remembered as the political genius responsible for the Exodus. The next section will argue for the possibility that he could have played a vital part in imparting the covenantal concept to early Israel.

Moses and the Covenant Concept

According to the biblical record, Israel bound itself to its God by oaths that were ratified ceremonially (e.g., Exod 24:3–8; Deuteronomy 27; see Chapter 18). Moses is said to have mediated these agreements between God and Israel. Biblical scholarship often refers to these agreements as covenants. A covenant is a promissory agreement guaranteed by a solemn oath; it is, in fact, a contract.

Biblical covenants can have different forms. One that is particularly important in biblical law uses a paradigm taken from the world of ancient Near Eastern politics. In the Torah, Israel's covenant with God is expressed in literary structures similar to political agreements called vassal treaties and

12. Dever, *Who Were the Early Israelites?* 223–37.

13. William G. Dever, "Archaeology and the Israelite 'Conquest,'" *ABD* 3:551.

loyalty oaths.[14] A vassal treaty is an agreement made between a king and a lesser ruler. In most vassal treaties, a subject ruler promises certain kinds of military aid, tribute, and support in exchange for being allowed to remain on the throne of his country. The duties of the vassal are set down as a list of instructions that he has to follow. Loyalty oaths are made by persons living inside a state to support the ruler and his dynasty; they also set out the people's duties in instructional form.[15]

Both vassal treaties and loyalty oaths called on deities to witness the agreement; the parties bound themselves by sacred oaths in the presence of the gods. These contracts were especially binding on the vassal or the king's subjects. If the subordinate party broke the covenant, it was assumed that the gods would punish the offender.

In the ancient Near East, covenants or treaties were usually made between human beings. At some point in time, however, Israel used the treaty form to express its fidelity to YHWH, its God. Just when it did so is a big question with respect to the development of the covenant idea.[16] One opinion is that the covenant idea must be a fairly late development in Israelite religion, because its literary expressions use treaty forms that must be dated to the late monarchical period.[17] However, the concept of covenant could well go back to earlier times, because it is possible to distinguish between the covenant idea in ancient Israel and its literary expressions in the treaty form.

At the origin of the covenant idea is a sense of obligation. In the ancient Near East the idea of obligating oneself to a god by making a vow is very old.[18]

14. See Dennis J. McCarthy, *Treaty and Covenant: A Study in Form in the Ancient Oriental Documents and in the Old Testament,* 2nd ed. (AnBib 21A; Rome: Biblical Institute, 1978), 277–98; Noel Weeks, *Admonition and Curse: The Ancient Near Eastern Treaty/Covenant Form as a Problem in Inter-Cultural Relationships* (JSOTSup 407; London: T. & T. Clark, 2004), 134–73.

15. Moshe Weinfeld, "The Origin of the Apodictic Law: An Overlooked Source," *VT* 23 (1973): 63–75.

16. For the history of the covenantal idea in biblical scholarship, see Robert A. Oden, "The Place of Covenant in the Religion of Israel," in *Ancient Israelite Religion: Essays in Honor of Frank Moore Cross,* edited by Patrick D. Miller Jr., Paul D. Hanson, and S. Dean McBride (Philadelphia: Fortress, 1987), 429–47.

17. E.g., Eckart Otto, *Das Deuteronomium: Politische Theologie und Rechtsreform in Juda und Assyrien* (BZAW 284; Berlin: de Gruyter, 1999), 79–88; Christoph Koch, *Vertrag, Treueid und Bund: Studien zur Rezeption des altorientalischen Vertragrechts im Deuteronomium und zur Ausbildung der Bundestheologie im Alten Testament* (BZAW 383; Berlin: de Gruyter, 2008), 250–51; Richard J. Thompson, *Terror of the Radiance: Aššur Covenant to Yahweh Covenant* (OBO 258; Fribourg/Göttingen: Academic/Vandenhoeck & Ruprecht, 2013), 189–229.

18. Adrian Schenker, "L'origine de l'idée d'une alliance entre Dieu et Israël dans l'Ancien

Conceptually, covenants and vows are not far removed from each other. The question of the origin of the covenant idea, therefore, involves (at least) two different facets:

- How old is the idea of Israel's sense of obligation to YHWH for its life and land?
- When was this sense of obligation expressed as a kind of vow or oath?

Some of the earliest materials in the Tanakh that can be reliably dated come from the writings of the eighth-century prophets. This includes sayings and stories of Amos and Hosea preserved in the books that bear their names. These religious thinkers assumed that Israel and YHWH were in a committed relationship: Israel had obligations to YHWH if it was to live at peace in the land (see, e.g., early material in Hosea 4 or Amos 5). These prophets would have had little credibility if they were not able to draw on religious understandings shared with their contemporaries. For their appeal to work, therefore, the idea that God and Israel were in a committed relationship must already have been in Israel's consciousness—perhaps centuries—before the prophecies of Amos and Hosea.

Even if the formalization of the covenant concept by the treaty metaphor is late, the sentiment that gave rise to it belonged to ancient tradition. Israel's thinkers grounded their feeling of obligation to YHWH in the experience of the Exodus and the emergence of Israel in the land of Canaan (e.g., Hos 11:1; 12:13; Amos 2:9–11; 5:25–26). It is not surprising, therefore, to find the covenant motif connected with the leader of the Exodus group, Moses. Nor is it beyond possibility that, under his leadership, the Exodus group bound itself to its God and to each other by an oath or vow.

Moses as Metaphor

Despite the observations above, the content of the legal collections that now appear in the Bible cannot be reliably traced to Moses' time (see Chapter 2). The various collections of biblical law reached something close to their canonical forms only in the Persian era (ca. 539–333 BCE). Each is, therefore, the result of a lengthy process in which generations of thinkers had to

---

Testament," in *Recht und Kult im Alten Testament* (OBO 172; Freiburg: Universitätsverlag Freiburg), 67–76.

grapple with the significance of Israel's obligations to YHWH. They did this, in part, by the ways they developed and reworked the Mosaic tradition.

From this perspective, the biblical Moses is less a historical figure than a metaphor. His memory was the inspiration and justification for a number of movements that used law as a way to define Israel's relationship with YHWH. In a sense, the story of legal developments in Exodus to Deuteronomy is not only *about* Moses, it *is* a sort of Moses itself—leading readers deeper and deeper into an understanding of what it meant to know YHWH and their identity as the people of God. The Mosaic memory was, therefore, not only a metaphor but also a mandate: a requirement to wrestle with the meanings of Israel's obligations to YHWH through time.

A rabbinic proverb puts it like this: "What is Torah? It is the study of Torah." In other words, Jewish tradition assumes that the Mosaic metaphor continues to possess force in later eras. This dynamic is observable in the Tanakh itself: faced with changing social and geographical circumstances, groups in ancient Israel claiming continuity with the Mosaic tradition felt the necessity of developing workable expressions of their relationship to the God of the Exodus. This is apparent, for example, in the ways that Deuteronomic thinkers adapted contents of the Covenant Code (see Chapter 20). In fact, Deuteronomy presents Moses as both a commentator on and developer of preexisting legal traditions.

Another sign of the reference value of Moses appears in Priestly literature. Various sections of biblical law are punctuated by statements such as, "The Lord spoke to Moses saying . . ." (e.g., Lev 4:1; 6:1; 12:1; 18:1; 19:1; 20:1; 27:1; Num 15:1; 18:25). According to critical scholarship, these phrases introduce laws that originated at various times in Israel's history. They express the writers' conviction that they were themselves authentic and authoritative representatives of the Mosaic tradition.

A remarkable indication that Priestly thinkers had a role in developing and revising preexisting legal tradition occurs at the end of the story about the deaths of Aaron's sons in Lev 10:16–20. Moses takes exception to the fact that, after their deaths, Aaron did not eat the purification offering (NRSV "sin offering") as he ought to have done. Instead, it was burned entirely on the altar. Aaron protests, however, that the day's events made eating the offering in sacred space inappropriate. Moses concurred. Behind this story, we can detect a claim by Priestly thinkers to the right to examine and revise cultic practices without violating the Mosaic tradition.[19]

19. Eckart Otto, *Das Gesetz des Mose* (Darmstadt: WBG, 2007), 64.

A modern analogy might illustrate the motivation for these developments. It has been common in certain church circles to wear wristbands and drink from coffee cups with the initials WWJD, which abbreviate the slogan "What Would Jesus Do?" This abbreviation serves as an inspiration to resolve various ethical and social dilemmas by thinking about what Jesus would do if faced with the same situation; it is an invitation to work out how his teachings can be faithfully implemented in contemporary contexts. Perhaps one should read biblical law as if its various collections had the abbreviation WWMD written over them in invisible ink. For centuries biblical law was being articulated, supplemented, revised, and transmitted by Israel's intellectuals. As they did so, they were asking, "What Would Moses Do?" in the challenging and unprecedented situations in which they found themselves.

First-century Jewish faith communities continued that same task. They pondered what it meant to appropriate the Mosaic tradition, to work out their obligations to the God of Israel, in the cultural contexts in which they lived. Illustrations of this process appear not only in the developing oral law codified in the Mishnah, but also in sectarian material such as the Dead Sea Scrolls.[20] A good example of WWMD in the New Testament appears in the Sermon on the Mount, where Jesus acts as a kind of second Moses, proclaiming law from the mountain top.[21]

Posing the question WWMD might also inform the present. What does it mean to carry on the Mosaic tradition in contemporary times? Something can be learned by seeing how the same question was addressed by the various groups responsible for the development of biblical law.

20. See, e.g., the Dead Sea Scroll texts discussed in Robert A. Kugler, "Rewriting Rubrics: Sacrifice and the Religion of Qumran," in *Religion in the Dead Sea Scrolls*, edited by John J. Collins and Robert A. Kugler (SDSSRL; Grand Rapids: Eerdmans, 2000), 90–112; Bernard M. Levinson, *A More Perfect Torah: At the Intersection of Philology and Hermeneutics in Deuteronomy and the Temple Scroll* (Critical Studies in the Hebrew Bible 1; Winona Lake: Eisenbrauns, 2013).

21. Dale C. Allison, "Jesus and Moses (Mt 5:1–2)," *ExpTim* 98.7 (1987): 203–5.

CHAPTER 4

Approaches to the Law: Text and Context

The corpus of biblical law (spanning much of Exodus–Deuteronomy) is made up of various components. These include ethical admonitions, instructions for sacrificial rituals, ceremonies for covenant ratification, rules for adjudicating civil damages, stories about legal processes, and criminal law. Discerning how these various concerns cohere is not easy.

This textbook concentrates on just one of a number of approaches that could be taken to the description and analysis of biblical law. It is an attempt to describe major expressions of legal discourse as visions of community and focuses on the fact that, in their canonical form, the various collections are all considered to be Torah. George Foot Moore clarifies the meaning of Torah thus:

> It is a source of manifold misconceptions that [Torah] is customarily translated "Law," though it is not easy to suggest any one English word by which it would be better rendered. "Law" must, however, not be understood in the restricted sense of legislation, but must be taken to include the whole of revelation—all that God has made known of his nature, character and purpose, and what he would have [human beings] be and do.[1]

An introduction to biblical law would be remiss, however, if it failed to observe that there are many ways of grasping the complexities of this subject. Three different trends in the contemporary study of biblical law are described below, along with a brief account of how this book relates to each one:

1. George F. Moore, *Judaism in the First Centuries of the Christian Era*, 2 vols. (New York: Schocken, 1971), 1:263.

- studies using modern legal theory
- comparisons with ancient Near Eastern legal and ritual practices
- law as literature

All are well worth pursuing in their own right.

Studies Using Modern Legal Theory[2]

Modern legal science has generated sophisticated ways of thinking about law. The following are two different trends in contemporary jurisprudence that have made themselves felt in the study of biblical law.

Positive Law Theory

In their book *Everyday Law in Biblical Israel,* Raymond Westbrook and Bruce Wells define their focus as

> law understood by jurists. It comprises those rules that regulate relationships between humans who are the members of a society in the conduct of their everyday lives, protecting their economic, social, corporal, and psychological interests. Those rules establish rights and duties that can be enforced in a court of law.[3]

This is a description of biblical law from the perspective of theories of "positive law": rules and regulations subject to administration by systems of sanctions and adjudication involving judicial or quasi-judicial processes.[4] Think of courts and magistrates.

It is important to know that there are categories of modern jurisprudence that can be used to analyze ancient texts, because by far the majority of those who come to biblical studies have no legal training. For example, it

2. My discussion is based on F. Rachel Magdalene, "Legal Science Then and Now: Theory and Method in the Work of Raymond Westbrook," *Maarav* 18 (2013): 25–29.

3. Raymond Westbrook and Bruce Wells, *Everyday Law in Biblical Israel: An Introduction* (Louisville: Westminster John Knox, 2009), 1.

4. Bryan A. Garner, ed., *Black's Law Dictionary,* 10th ed. (St. Paul: Thomson Reuters, 2014), 1350. For the use of positive legal theory in the works of Raymond Westbrook, see Magdalene, "Legal Science Then and Now," 29–32.

is useful to be able to distinguish between "crimes" and "delicts," even if these categories do not manifest themselves in the same way in ancient Israel as they do today. Similarly, Westbrook and Wells's chapter on contracts gives students helpful distinctions between different varieties of legal agreements.[5]

Everyday Law in Biblical Israel reflects a history of scholarship that has brought modern principles of legal reasoning to the interpretation of ancient Near Eastern and biblical law.[6] The present book's approach to the description of biblical law differs from that of Westbrook and Wells for two reasons. First, it is evident that positive legal traditions form only a part of the biblical law collections that contain them. Second, the record of positive law traditions in ancient Israel is incomplete, as it is in the case of other cultures of the ancient Near East.

The approach of Westbrook and Wells has its limits as a description of the dynamics of the biblical law collections. In fact, these scholars are prepared to regard only about 60 out of the traditional rabbinical count of 613 Pentateuchal laws as "everyday law."[7] Whether the rabbinic tradition is accurate or not, a large amount of instructional material in the Torah remains unaddressed by an approach that limits itself to the principles of positive law. The present book seeks a more comprehensive approach to the canonical form of biblical law collections, while appropriating some of the results of applying positive legal theory to the interpretation of their contents.

In addition, the positive law found in the Bible only partially addresses concerns proper to the domain of this kind of legal thinking. For example, despite their importance, there are no laws in the Bible covering adoption or property rental, although these concerns are addressed by other ancient Near Eastern legal collections. These absences can be explained, however, by the hypothesis that the application of positive law in ancient Israel functioned within a system of common or customary law. In common law, the application of law by judges and other legal decision makers is guided by a knowledge of legal precedents and broad principles rather than strictly by legislation.

The legal principles relevant to ancient Israel were probably not embodied exclusively in collections of instructions. They were also contained in stories and conveyed through oral tradition. To some extent, the bibli-

5. Westbrook and Wells, *Everyday Law in Ancient Israel*, 107–27.

6. E.g., Ze'ev W. Falk, *Hebrew Law in Biblical Times: An Introduction*, 2nd ed. (Provo: Brigham Young University and Winona Lake: Eisenbrauns, 2001); and Raymond Westbrook, ed., *A History of Ancient Near Eastern Law*, 2 vols. (HdO 72; Leiden: Brill, 2003).

7. Westbrook and Wells, *Everyday Law in Ancient Israel*, 11.

cal evidence can be augmented by later rabbinical literature. There is reason to think that a number of ancient Near Eastern legal conventions were preserved unchanged in early Jewish jurisprudence. These were probably operative in biblical times, although they are not set down in biblical law collections.[8] In other words, biblical material allows only partial reconstruction of the positive legal system(s) at work in ancient Israel.

Note that throughout, this book avoids the word "code" to refer to collections of laws either in the Pentateuch or the ancient Near East (with the exception of the conventional terms "Covenant Code" and "Holiness Code"). "Law code" implies a kind of comprehensive legal document that regulated society in a systematic way. No such documents were produced in biblical Israel or in the cultures that surrounded it.

Critical Legal Theory

Critical legal theory regards law as a socially constructed category that is political and ideological by nature. It is skeptical about the claim that legal decisions are made by autonomous individuals; instead, agents in the legal context are considered to be acting out of complex constructs of gender, race/ethnicity, and socioeconomic class.[9] Critical legal theory, therefore, brings a "hermeneutic of suspicion" to the description of biblical law. It supposes, rightly, that the collections of law found in the Bible were transmitted by highly trained scribes. Consequently, the various ritual and legal institutions preserved in biblical law frequently reflect their biases and interests.[10]

A number of recent studies of biblical law are based on critical legal theory,[11] and much can be learned from that perspective about significant relations between law and the distribution of social power. The ways in

8. Samuel Greengus, *Laws in the Bible and in Early Rabbinic Collections* (Eugene: Cascade, 2011), 282–83.

9. Magdalene, "Legal Science Then and Now," 28–29.

10. Douglas A. Knight, *Law, Power, and Justice in Ancient Israel* (Louisville: Westminster John Knox, 2011), 82–86.

11. See, e.g., the methodology used in Harold V. Bennett, *Injustice Made Legal: Deuteronomic Law and the Plight of Widows, Strangers, and Orphans in Ancient Israel* (BIW; Grand Rapids: Eerdmans, 2002); Cheryl B. Anderson, *Women, Ideology, and Violence: Critical Theory and the Construction of Gender in the Book of the Covenant and the Deuteronomic Law* (JSOTSup 394; London: T. & T. Clark, 2004); and Knight, *Law, Power, and Justice.*

which biblical law addresses such questions will be one of the concerns of this book.

An approach that uses critical legal theory will find situations in which biblical law calls into radical question the conventional constructions of social power. There are also legal situations in which the biblical writers vacillate between affirming social conventions and challenging them. In addition, there are relationships of asymmetrical power distribution that are never called into question. For example, biblical law is formulated in ways that express suspicion of the virtues of monarchy as a form of social organization. On the other hand, while writers of biblical law frequently set out provisions that show sympathy for debt slaves, they fall short of calling into question the institution of slavery itself. Finally, certain concerns of the modern discourse on human rights, such as the rights of children, are more or less ignored in biblical law.

Comparisons with Ancient Near Eastern Legal and Ritual Practices

Part of the challenge in studying the Tanakh arises from the fact that there is not that much material to work with. Fortunately, research on the civilizations of the ancient Near East has unearthed many documents and inscriptions that can be used to augment the study of the Old Testament. For this reason, the reading of texts produced by ancient Aramaean, Assyrian, Babylonian, Canaanite, Egyptian, Hittite, Persian, and Sumerian peoples is *de rigueur* in introductory courses on the Hebrew Bible.[12] This textbook will also refer to written materials produced by ancient Near Eastern peoples as it discusses various facets of biblical law.

Many useful comparisons can be made between such materials and the contents of biblical law, whether concerning civil, criminal, or international law, or the vast world of ritual practices. At the same time, one must respect the limits of the comparative enterprise. More than one scholar has expressed dismay at what can be called "parallelomania," the drive to find a comparable idea or institution in ancient Near Eastern culture for every biblical one. Biblical thinkers shared a number of legal and ritual conventions with their cultural neighbors, adapted or reacted to others, and in still other cases displayed unique perspectives independent of their wider social

12. E.g., *ANET; COS;* and Kenton L. Sparks, *Ancient Texts for the Study of the Hebrew Bible: A Guide to the Background Literature* (Peabody: Hendrickson, 2005).

environment. Careful use of comparative material will identify all of these possibilities in biblical law.

The following chart lists collections of law that have been discovered in the ancient Near East:[13]

Law Collections of the Ancient Near East

Sumerian	Laws of Ur-Namma (ca. 2100 BCE) Laws of Lipit-Ishtar (ca. 1930)
Akkadian	Laws of Eshnunna (ca. 1770) Laws of Hammurabi (ca. 1750) Middle Assyrian Laws (ca. 1075) Neo-Babylonian Laws (ca. 700–600)
Hittite	The Hittite Laws (Late Bronze Age)
Greek	The Laws of Gortyn (5th century BCE)

Although ancient Near Eastern legal collections provide a useful point of comparison with materials in biblical law, they point to a problem that is equally relevant to the interpretation of both bodies of legal discourse: How were these texts meant to be used? What was their connection to the day-to-day practice of law in the societies in which they were found? Were these collections ever regarded as actual law?

These questions indicate that legal discourse can be viewed in various ways. By and large, scholars differ in their emphasis on three approaches to interpreting collections of ancient Near Eastern law:[14]

1. They are codifications of existing practice, written down to provide guidance to judges in making legal decisions.
2. They are scholarly treatises meant primarily for training scribes in legal reasoning (the predominant view in recent decades).
3. They are forms of royal propaganda intended to enhance the reputation of a king as a sponsor of justice.

13. Collected and translated in Martha T. Roth, *Law Collections from Mesopotamia and Asia Minor*, 2nd ed. (WAW 6; Atlanta: Scholars, 1997).

14. Roth, *Law Collections from Mesopotamia and Asia Minor*, 4.

Probably all three of these concepts are justified to some degree, and they can be applied analogously to the interpretation of biblical law:

1) It would be surprising if there were no connection between the collections of biblical law and ancient Israelite legal practices.[15] At least some biblical law was intended to be implemented.
2) Some biblical law seems to exist more in the area of theory than practicality. The laws about the Jubilee are a case in point (see Chapter 17). Biblical law was also a place for scribes to engage legal problems intellectually and to think speculatively about jurisprudence. Consequently, one cannot assume a one-to-one relationship between biblical law and the day-to-day life of ancient Israel.
3) The collections of biblical law have their own propaganda value. They exist partly to promote and enhance the image of the divine king who is their source (cf. Deut 4:5–8).

While there are important similarities between biblical law and ancient Near Eastern law codes, there are also some significant differences:

1. ancient Israel and Mesopotamia only partially shared a common legal culture
2. the scope of biblical law
3. authorship of biblical law

1) Common legal culture

An important problem concerns the extent to which Israel shared a common legal culture with the rest of the ancient Near East. Various scholars take different positions on the degree of similarity,[16] but there can be no doubt that ancient Israel held a large number of presuppositions and practices in common with its neighbors. Good examples of this come from the realm of

15. Bruce Wells, "What Is Biblical Law? A Look at Pentateuchal Rules and Near Eastern Practice," *CBQ* 70 (2008): 242.

16. Raymond Westbrook is a notable representative of the view that Israel shared a common legal culture with other cultures in the ancient Near East; e.g., Westbrook, *History of Ancient Near Eastern Law,* 1:2–4. The merits and limits of Westbrook's position are assessed in Anselm Hagedorn, "How Far Does a Legal Koine Extend? Remarks on Raymond Westbrook's 'Common Law' in the Mediterranean," *Maarav* 18 (2013): 63–77.

contracts, including treaties. Documents from the cuneiform legal tradition covering a range of different time periods help to explain practices attested in the Bible.

Nevertheless, comparisons with Israel's ancient Near Eastern context must consider economic aspects of these civilizations as well as ideological parallels, because there is a connection between a culture's economic development and its legal practices.[17] Although ancient Israel shared a number of cultural institutions with ancient Mesopotamia, its economic circumstances differed to some degree, a fact which can be expected to lead to certain differences in the construction of legal processes.[18]

2) The scope of biblical law

Unlike the ancient Near Eastern law collections listed above, biblical law routinely combines matters of positive law with ritual instructions and ethical teachings. The relationship between these interests has been the subject of much debate. One can certainly show that a number of rules in the Pentateuch have parallels in other ancient Near Eastern law collections;[19] but what is their force when transmitted in the context of Torah? In other words, how are they to be interpreted when they are framed in religious discourses unparalleled in ancient Near Eastern sources?

The ancient Near Eastern collection showing the closest analogy to the range of concerns found in biblical law is the Hittite instructions.[20] In the Hittite Empire, various temple officials, military officers, and other personnel had their duties spelled out to them under oath.[21] Not even the Hittite instructions, however, combine all the genres found in biblical law. For example, they do not contain extensive collections of third-person case law such as found in the middle of the Covenant Code (Exod 21:18–22:17). Biblical law

17. A. S. Diamond, *Primitive Law, Past and Present* (London: Methuen, 1971), 4–5.

18. H. J. Boecker, *Law and the Administration of Justice in the Old Testament and Ancient Near East* (Minneapolis: Fortress, 1980), 166–67; J. W. Marshall, *Israel and the Book of the Covenant: An Anthropological Approach to Biblical Law* (SBLDS 140: Atlanta: Scholars 1993), 177–80.

19. See, e.g., the comparative list in Shalom M. Paul, *Studies in the Book of the Covenant in the Light of Cuneiform and Biblical Law* (Eugene: Wipf & Stock, 2006), 102–4.

20. Moshe Weinfeld, "The Origin of the Apodictic Law: An Overlooked Source," *VT* 23 (1973): 63–75.

21. Collected and translated in Jared L. Miller, *Royal Hittite Instructions and Related Administrative Texts* (WAW 31; Atlanta: Society of Biblical Literature, 2013).

seems to be unique, therefore, in terms of the breadth of the social vision its legal materials seek to convey.

3) Authorship of biblical law

Another striking divergence between biblical law and other law collections in the ancient Near East is found in the ascription of authorship. Ancient Near Eastern law typically comes from the king. A good example can be found on the stela containing the laws of Hammurabi. At its top, the god Shamash is depicted giving Hammurabi the authority to rule, but the text makes clear that its laws originate with the king himself. The situation is different for biblical law. For the most part, biblical law has its source in pronouncements by Israel's deity.[22] What is the relationship between their comprehensive social vision and their claim to divine origin? This is a question that this book seeks to answer. Part of the answer, however, has already been anticipated in the opening chapter. In the Torah, law seeks to articulate the meaning of the relationship that YHWH has established with Israel.

Law as Literature

Recognition of the literary dimensions of law has made itself felt in contemporary legal interpretation.[23] In recent times, exegetical approaches informed by literary theory have also been applied to the interpretation of biblical law and to legal motifs in biblical narratives.[24] For example, there are stories about legal processes related to the purchase of land in Genesis 23, Ruth, and Jeremiah 32; and the book of Job is replete with allusions to legal processes.[25]

22. Paul Heger, "Source of Law in Biblical and Mesopotamian Law Collections," *Bib* 86 (2005): 325–27.

23. E.g., Michael Freeman and Andrew D. E. Lewis, eds., *Law and Literature* (Current Legal Issues 2; New York: Oxford University Press, 1999).

24. E.g., Joe M. Sprinkle, *The Book of the Covenant: A Narrative Approach* (JSOTSup 174; Sheffield: JSOT, 1994); Pamela Barmash, "The Narrative Quandary: Cases of Law in Literature," *VT* 54 (2004): 1–16; Asnat Bartor, "Reading Biblical Law as Narrative," *Prooftexts* 32 (2012): 292–311; Klaus-Peter Adam et al., eds., *Law and Narrative in the Bible and in Neighbouring Ancient Cultures* (FAT/2 54; Tübingen: Mohr Siebeck, 2012).

25. F. Rachel Magdalene, *On the Scales of Righteousness: Neo-Babylonian Trial Law and the Book of Job* (BJS 348; Providence: Brown University, 2007).

Figure 2. The God Shamash (right) bestows symbols of royal authority on Hammurabi, King of Babylon (eighteenth century BCE). (Wikimedia Commons, CC BY 3.0 License)

One of the great minds to combine juridical thinking with a keen awareness of the way it was frequently encoded in biblical narrative was David Daube.[26]

A unique approach to the relationship between biblical law and narrative has been advanced by Calum Carmichael, who has sought to explain the origins of the various law collections with reference to narrative contexts in the Bible. In his opinion, the collections cast no direct light on juridical practice in ancient Israel. Rather, they are derived from and act as commentary on the narrative traditions of the Bible.[27] Although Carmichael has been rightly criticized for the degree to which he has pressed this exegetical agenda,[28] his approach may not completely miss the mark. For example, it is difficult to read the rule in Lev 18:18 against marrying a woman and her sister, or the inheritance rights of the hated wife in Deut 21:15–17, and not think of the stories of Jacob in the book of Genesis. The sources of biblical law are varied, and narrative traditions may well be implicated in the generation of some of them.

This discussion gives rise to important observations about the overlap of legal discourse and narrative, which in turn raise questions of interpretation. Law always has a narrative function, in that it "tells a story" about what a particular society values, about who is an insider and who is an outsider, how the society is organized, and what it does when faced with certain forms of social disruption. By the same token, stories can be "law" in that they have a prescriptive function: they can inculcate values and norms of behavior that are as binding as any set of rules. Both functions come together in the first five books of Moses.

While a consideration of larger questions concerning the relationship between the collections of biblical law and their narrative contexts falls outside the purview of this book, a description of the literary dimensions of the Bible's legal collections is important. The ways in which literary structure interfaces with the contents of law carry important information about the overarching values that have organized a particular legal text. For that reason, the following chapters often contain analyses of the literary framework of a section of biblical law.

26. *Collected Works of David Daube*, vol. 3: *Biblical Law and Literature*, edited by Calum Carmichael (Berkeley: University of California, 2003).

27. E.g., Calum Carmichael, *Law and Narrative in the Bible: The Evidence of the Deuteronomic Laws and the Decalogue* (Ithaca: Cornell University Press, 1985), 16–17.

28. Bernard M. Levinson, "Calum M. Carmichael's Approach to the Laws of Deuteronomy," *HTR* 83 (1990): 227–57.

PART TWO

Israel at the Holy Mountain

CHAPTER 5

The Ten Commandments: Introduction

Read: Exodus 19:1–20:21; Deuteronomy 5

The introduction to this textbook made an important theological claim. In biblical thought, an experience of divine grace confers an identity on those who receive it, and this identity is often articulated by law. The connection between grace and law is powerfully illustrated in the Exodus story. The experience of Israel's liberation from slavery in Egypt is followed by the revelation of divine law on the holy mountain. Gifted with freedom and hope, Israel discovers its full vocation as the people of God at Mount Sinai.

In Exodus 19–20, the revelation of the divine will is accompanied by the natural phenomena that biblical tradition recognized as signs of a theophany, of the manifestation of YHWH in the created order.[1] Storm and earthquake, thunder and lightning underscore the significance of Israel's encounter with God on the holy mountain and emphasize the importance of the divine law that Moses and the people receive. But who is this deity that Israel encounters?

An answer to this question reveals yet another inflection in the relationship between law and grace. Law becomes not only the articulation of Israel's vocation as "a priestly kingdom and a holy nation" (Exod 19:6) but also a vehicle for knowing the nature of God. This chapter and the next will explore ways in which the Ten Commandments disclose the identity of YHWH, as well as reveal the character of his people.

1. Moshe Greenberg, "The Decalogue Tradition Critically Examined," in *The Ten Commandments in History and Tradition*, edited by Ben-Zion Segal and Gershon Levi (Jerusalem: Magnes, 1990), 87.

The Ten Commandments

The Hebrew phrase meaning "the Ten Commandments" is *ʿaśeret haddĕbarîm*. It can also be translated as "the ten words" or "the ten utterances." Its application to the instructions in Exod 20:2–17 and Deut 5:6–21 relies on Deut 4:13 and 10:4 (the same phrase also appears in Exod 34:28). Rabbinic Judaism changed the biblical phrase to *ʿaśeret haddibbĕrôt*, "the ten revealed words," to underscore the biblical tradition that they were spoken directly by God. This usage remains common in Judaism. The term "Decalogue" is often used as a synonym for the Ten Commandments. It comes from the Septuagint, which used the Greek phrase *deka logoi* to translate the Hebrew, meaning "the ten words."

This chapter starts with a brief discussion of the organization of the Decalogue. It then turns to describing relationships between the Ten Commandments and the self-presentation of ancient Near Eastern monarchs, demonstrating that YHWH is presented as Israel's ideal king. After a survey of questions connected to the origins of the Decalogue, it ends with observations about how some of its thought patterns appear in the New Testament.

Organization

Exegetical traditions differ about how to divide up verses to get to the number ten, as this chart based on Exod 20:2–17 shows:[2]

Traditions for Dividing the Ten Commandments in Exodus

Numbers in 2nd, 3rd, and 4th columns indicate the verse(s) in Exodus 20.

Commandment	*Jewish*	*Roman Catholic/Lutheran*	*Orthodox/Reformed*
I	2	3–6	(2–)3
II	3–6	7	4–6
III	7	8–11	7

2. Walter Harrelson, *The Ten Commandments and Human Rights* (OBT 8; Philadelphia: Fortress, 1980), 47. In the Middle Ages rabbinic authorities found thirteen commandments; see Nahum M. Sarna, *Exodus* (JPS Torah Commentary; Philadelphia: Jewish Publication Society, 1991), 107.

Commandment	*Jewish*	*Roman Catholic/Lutheran*	*Orthodox/Reformed*
IV	8–11	12	8–11
V	12	13	12
VI	13	14	13
VII	14	15	14
VIII	15	16	15
IX	16	17a	16
X	17	17b	17

Key problems include:

- Should Exod 20:2 be counted as a separate commandment (the rabbinic consensus) or as introductory to an initial prohibition in v. 3? Traditional Jewish commentary understood v. 2 as a self-contained statement that demanded belief in God as the exclusive sovereign of Israel.[3] Scholarly consensus regards the opening verse of the Decalogue as a "motive clause" for the commandment in Exod 20:3 (= Deut 5:7).[4] The Exodus memory contained in Exod 20:2 (= Deut 5:6) reinforces the demand for exclusive worship of YHWH, as it does in Judg 6:8–10 and Ps 81:9–10.[5]

Motive Clauses

In biblical and ancient Near Eastern law, reasons or explanations for performing certain commandments and observing certain prohibitions can be attached to the instructions themselves. These explanatory and motivational statements are called motive clauses.

In both Exodus and Deuteronomy, motive clauses are attached to the first five commandments of the Decalogue (verse references are to the Exodus text).

I motive clause (v. 2) + prohibition (v. 3)

3. Mek. 6; see Roger Brooks, *The Spirit of the Ten Commandments: Shattering the Myth of Rabbinic Legalism* (San Francisco: Harper & Row, 1990), 63–65.

4. See, e.g., Harrelson, *Ten Commandments*, 45–48; Dale Patrick, *Old Testament Law* (Atlanta: John Knox, 1985), 39; Greenberg, "Decalogue Tradition," 96–109; William H. C. Propp, *Exodus 19–40* (AB 2A; New York: Doubleday, 2006), 146; Thomas B. Dozeman, *Commentary on Exodus* (ECC; Grand Rapids: Eerdmans, 2009), 477–79.

5. Greenberg, "Decalogue Tradition," 98–99.

II	3 prohibitions (vv. 4–5a) + motive clause (vv. 5b–6)
III	prohibition (v. 7a) + motive clause (v. 7b)
IV	5 prescriptions (vv. 8–10a) + prohibition (v. 10b) + motive clause (v. 11)
V	prescription (v. 12a) + motive clause (v. 12b)

- Should the prohibition against having other gods in v. 3 be read as a separate commandment from the commandment not to make representations of YHWH in vv. 4–6?
- Is the prohibition against coveting in v. 17 one instruction or two? Deuteronomy's decision to use the prohibition *lōʾ taḥmōd* ("you shall not covet") with respect to "your neighbor's wife" (5:21a), but *lōʾ titʾawwê* ("you shall not desire") to refer to a neighbor's household (5:21b) suggests that it found two instructions at this point in the text.

Some of the differences in the chart reflecting exegetical traditions can be accounted for by assuming that later traditions tried to systematize the Decalogues of Exodus and Deuteronomy into a single sequence. However, there are reasons for thinking that Exodus and Deuteronomy do not count the Ten Commandments the same way. For example, Exod 20:5 seems to refer the command "you shall not bow down to *them* or serve *them*" to the prohibition against making "a statue or an image" (v. 4).[6] On the other hand, the lack of a conjunction in Deut 5:8 makes this phrase singular, suggesting that it regards the phrase "other gods" in v. 7 as the reference for the prohibitions against idol worship in v. 9.[7] As for the command "not to covet," the use of two different verbs in Deut 5:21 makes the decision to collapse this prohibition into a single statement debatable.

The Organization of the Decalogue in Exodus and Deuteronomy

	Verses in Exodus 20		Verses in Deuteronomy 5	
No other gods	I	2–3	I	6–10
Images	II	4–6		

6. The translation for Exod 20:4 in the NRSV is misleading. The Hebrew says "you shall not make a sculptured image, or any likeness" (cf. JPSV).

7. Cornelis Houtman (*Exodus*, vol. 3 [HCOT; Leuven: Peeters, 2000], 19) finds only nine commandments in the Decalogue of Exodus because he reads Exod 20:3–6 as a single law.

False swearing	III	7	II	11
Sabbath	IV	8–11	III	12–15
Parents	V	12	IV	16
Murder	VI	13	V	17
Adultery	VII	14	VI	18
Theft	VIII	15	VII	19
False witness	IX	16	VIII	20
Coveting	X	17	IX	21a
			X	21b

The rest of this chapter follows the numbering of Exodus, because it likely represents the older text (see below). In fact, there are a number of variations in wording between the texts of the Decalogue in Exodus and Deuteronomy.[8]

The laws of the Decalogue fall into two groups. The first section contains norms regarding Israel's relationship to God (I–IV). The second deals with human relationships in the community (VI–X). The instruction to honor parents (V) occupies a transitional place. On the one hand, it addresses relationships between members of the community. On the other hand, it lends a divine aura to parental authority: the command to honor parents finds a verbal parallel in instructions to honor God in Prov 3:9.

Purpose

Exodus 20:2/Deuteronomy 5:6 has the character of self-disclosure:[9] "I am the Lord your God, who brought you out of the land of Egypt, out of the house of slavery." The opening sentence of the Decalogue has parallels in contexts of divine revelation (cf. Gen 15:7; 17:1; 28:13; Exod 6:2; Judg 6:10). As in the case of Gen 15:7 and Exod 6:2, God's self-disclosure at the beginning of the Ten Commandments is accompanied by historical memory.

The rhetoric of self-disclosure in Exod 20:2/Deut 5:6 recalls the opening lines of inscriptions set up by human kings in the ancient Near East.[10]

8. Se, e.g., Johann J. Stamm and Maurice E. Andrew, *The Ten Commandments in Recent Research* (SBT 2; London: SCM, 1967), 14; Greenberg. "Decalogue Tradition," 92–93.

9. Brevard S. Childs, *The Book of Exodus: A Critical, Theological Commentary* (OTL; Philadelphia: Westminster, 1974), 401.

10. Propp, *Exodus 19–40*, 167.

Compare the opening verse of the Ten Commandments with the beginnings of these royal inscriptions from kings who ruled in the ancient Levant during the Iron Age. All the examples below come from inscriptions written in the Northwest Semitic family of languages, including Aramaic, Hebrew, Moabite, and Phoenician.

Opening Formulas in Northwest Semitic Royal Inscriptions

Moabite	(9th cent.)	I am Mesha, the son of Kemosh-yatti[11]
Phoenician	(9th cent.)	I am Kulamuwa, the son of Ḥayya[12]
	(8th–7th cent.)	I am Azatiwada, the blessed of Baal . . . whom . . .[13]
	(5th–4th cent.)	I am Yeḥawmilk, king of Byblos . . . whom . . .[14]
Aramaic	(8th cent.)	I am Zakkur, king of Hamath and Luʿash[15]
	(8th cent.)	I am Panamuwa, son of Qarli, king of Y'dy, who . . .[16]
	(8th cent.)	I am Bar-Rakib, son of Panamuwa, king of Sam'al[17]

In these royal inscriptions, a king presents himself as an ideal monarch. In general, these texts emphasize the king's deeds, his building projects, his military victories, and his efforts to secure a safe and prosperous kingdom for his people. The Decalogue also contains a focus on YHWH's deeds. In fact, there are three kinds of actions that determine the nature of YHWH according to the Ten Commandments:

1. Saving action in history represents an important category of experience that communicates the character of God. According to the Decalogue, Israel experienced YHWH's saving power through deliverance from slavery into freedom (Exod 20:2; Deut 5:6, 15).
2. Another important divine activity is the creation of the world (Exod 20:11).
3. The third kind of divine activity comes through speech. It is the call

11. "The Inscription of King Mesha," trans. K. A. D. Smelik (*COS* 2.23:137).
12. "The Kulamuwa Inscription," trans. K. Lawson Younger Jr. (*COS* 2.30:147).
13. "The Azatiwada Inscription," trans. K. Lawson Younger Jr. (*COS* 2.31:149).
14. "The Inscription of King Yeḥawmilk," trans. Stanislav Segert (*COS* 2.32:151).
15. "The Inscription of Zakkur, King of Hamath," trans. Alan Millard (*COS* 2.35:155).
16. "The Hadad Inscription," trans. K. Lawson Younger Jr. (*COS* 2.36:156).
17. "The Bar-Rakib Inscription," trans. K. Lawson Younger Jr. (*COS* 2.38:161).

Figure 3. The picture above reproduces a portion of an inscription written in Phoenician that praises Kulamuwa, who reigned over ancient Sam'al (near Zinçirli in modern Turkey). Often monarchs represented themselves pictorially as well as by recounting their deeds. Kulamuwa is depicted in a gesture of reverence to his gods symbolized by, among other things, the winged sun disk. In his left hand he holds a flower. Wikimedia (https://commons.wikimedia.org/wiki/File:Samal_Text.jpg)

to an ongoing bond with YHWH by obeying his commandments. Although it may seem strange to modern ways of thinking, divine speech in the biblical religious imagination also represents an event. There is something concrete about the act of address such that, in Hebrew, the same noun can mean both a spoken word and a thing: *dābār.*

The emphasis on YHWH's deeds in the Decalogue has important theological implications. According to Martin Buber, at the heart of biblical religion is a response to an event—not a reasoned philosophical principle. It is an event that confronts the human person with a reality for which there is no other word but God.[18] Each of the three modes of event listed above represents a kind of revelatory experience.

In contrast to many self-presentations by human monarchs in the ancient Near East (cf. also the stela of Hammurabi), Israel had only a verbal disclosure of the character of its divine ruler. Nevertheless, one of the purposes

18. Martin Buber, "Myth in Judaism," *Commentary* 9 (1950): 562–66.

of the Decalogue was to present Israel's God as an ideal king. In the ancient Near East, the ideal of kingship was closely connected to justice because a monarch was regarded as the guarantor of order for his people.[19] So it is no accident that much of the Ten Commandments deal with justice issues.

- The third commandment probably refers to the practice of taking an assertory (declaratory) oath in a legal process. Where the matter could not be decided on the basis of witnesses or evidence, either party in a legal dispute might call on the deity to punish them if they were not telling the truth.[20]
- The Sabbath was to be equally enjoyed by the poor as well as the socially well off (IV).
- Parents had rights to respect and care that were not to be denied (V).
- Commandments VI–IX refer to four categories basic to the legal systems of the ancient Near East: homicide, adultery (marriage), theft, and judicial procedure (laws of evidence).[21]
- Recent commentary reinforces the perception that "coveting" is an acquisitive state of mind.[22] The tenth commandment was intended to act as a brake against acquiring by illegitimate means what legitimately belongs to another.

Origins

The origins of the Decalogue have been much debated. Among questions that must be addressed are the following:

- Given the fact that the Decalogue is found in both Exodus and Deuteronomy, is one of these texts the source for the other? Some scholars

19. H. J. Boecker, *Law and the Administration of Justice in the Old Testament and Ancient Near East* (Minneapolis: Fortress, 1980), 40–49.

20. Raymond Westbrook and Bruce Wells, *Everyday Law in Biblical Israel: An Introduction* (Louisville: Westminster John Knox, 2009), 46–47.

21. Stephen A. Kaufman, "The Second Table of the Decalogue and the Implicit Categories of Ancient Near Eastern Law," in *Love & Death in the Ancient Near East: Essays in Honor of Marvin H. Pope*, edited by John H. Marks and Robert M. Good (Guilford: Four Quarters, 1987), 111–16.

22. Houtman, *Exodus*, 3:69; Propp, *Exodus 19–40*, 180.

think that the Deuteronomic Decalogue is the earlier version.[23] In its canonical form, however, Deut 5:6–21 regards Exod 20:2–17 as the prior text. The formula "as the LORD your God commanded you" in vv. 12 and 16 assumes the earlier narrative in Exodus.[24] In fact, many of the differences between Exod 20:2–17 and Deut 5:6–21 can be explained as a result of editorial activity which has expanded or altered the Exodus version.[25]

- Do the canonical versions of the Decalogue represent developments of an older prototype?[26] In this scenario, both the Exodus and the Deuteronomic versions of the Ten Commandments are derived from an earlier text that is no longer preserved.
- The Ten Commandments do not seem particularly well integrated into the narrative of Exodus 19–20 or the book of Deuteronomy. How was this text originally transmitted, and what literary processes are implicated in its present canonical contexts?

While these questions are difficult to resolve, there is one literary datum that must be taken into consideration in any attempt to account for the origins of the Ten Commandments. Clearly a number of phrases in the Decalogue use idioms and turns of speech at home in Deuteronomy and Deuteronomic literature.[27] This means that, in its current versions, the Decalogue comes from the late monarchical period or later, as this is the time in which literature using Deuteronomic rhetoric was composed.

Parallels between the Decalogue and Deuteronomic Literature

"The house of slavery" (Exod 20:2; Deut 5:6) occurs in Deut 6:12; 7:8; 8:14; 13:10.

"Bowing down and worshipping [other gods]" (Exod 20:5; Deut 5:9) has echoes in the Deuteronomistic History (e.g., Josh 23:7; 1 Kgs 9:9; 2 Kgs 17:35; 21:3, 21).

23. See Dozeman, *Exodus,* 470–72.

24. For a different interpretation of this phrase, see Bernhard Lang, "The Number Ten and the Iniquity of the Fathers: A New Interpretation of the Decalogue," *ZAW* 118 (2006): 236–37.

25. Moshe Weinfeld, *Deuteronomy 1–11* (AB 5; New York: Doubleday, 1991), 243.

26. See A. D. H. Mayes, *Deuteronomy* (NCB; Grand Rapids: Eerdmans, 1981), 162.

27. Patrick, *Old Testament Law,* 35–36; Propp, *Exodus 19–40,* 145–46. The list is based on the catalogue of Deuteronomic phraseology in Moshe Weinfeld, *Deuteronomy and the Deuteronomic School* (Oxford: Clarendon, 1972), 320–59.

"Your gates" [NRSV 'your towns'] (Exod 20:10; Deut 5:14) is a typical expression used to refer to the cities in which the addressees of Deuteronomy live (e.g., Deut 6:9; 11:20; 12:15; 15:22; 17:5).

The motivation "that your days may be long" (Exod 20:12; Deut 5:16) appears in, e.g., Deut 6:2; 25:15; 32:47.

The phrase "the land which the Lord your God is giving you" (Exod 20:12; Deut 5:16) occurs in, e.g., Deut 4:21; 15:4; 19:10; 20:16; 21:23; 24:4; 25:19; 26:1.

The presence of Deuteronomic language in the Decalogue makes it difficult to argue that the text of the Ten Commandments comes from the period of Israel's origins. As parallels with Deuteronomic rhetoric are especially prominent in the Decalogue's motive clauses, one way of discovering an earlier text would be to remove the motive clauses, but this approach is questionable.[28] Consequently, research into the origins of the Ten Commandments indicates that this text is better seen as a reflection on the meaning of the Exodus experience rather than as a verbatim account of what transpired at Mount Sinai.

Many scholars have noted that the text of the Ten Commandments sits rather awkwardly in the narratives of Exodus and Deuteronomy. Where did it come from and why was it integrated into the canonical form of either book? Some researchers have suggested that the Decalogue arose out of a ceremony of law-giving or covenant renewal.[29] The next chapter will show that motifs of covenant-making are strong in the opening commands of the Decalogue. Unfortunately, the contents of the Decalogue do not consistently reflect a ceremonial origin.[30]

Another explanation holds that the Decalogue had its origins in a desire to epitomize biblical law in pithy syntheses.[31] On this view, the Ten Commandments originated in Deuteronomic circles in an effort to summarize the import of the law for Israel.[32] In a somewhat analogous manner,

28. Patrick, *Old Testament Law,* 40. Not all explanatory motifs are secondary; see Rifat Sonsino, *Motive Clauses in Hebrew Law* (SBLDS 45; Chico: Scholars, 1980), 225–26.

29. E.g., Raymond F. Collins, "Ten Commandments," *ABD* 6:384; Weinfeld, *Deuteronomy 1–11*, 262–63.

30. Dennis J. McCarthy, *Treaty and Covenant: A Study in Form in the Ancient Oriental Documents and in the Old Testament*, 2nd ed. (AnBib 21A; Rome: Biblical Institute, 1978), 251–53.

31. This tendency was recognized in rabbinic tradition; see b. Mak. 23b.

32. E.g., Houtman, *Exodus,* 3:7–10.

later faith communities synthesized key doctrinal commitments into short statements such as the Nicene Creed or the *Yigdal* chanted in the synagogue. This theory also has its challenges, as it must explain why the epitome of law found in the Decalogue was given such a special place in the Torah.

Developments

The most sustained discussion of the Ten Commandments in the New Testament occurs in the story of the young ruler who comes to Jesus seeking the way to eternal life. Jesus refers him to the Decalogue,[33] listing the commandments against murder, adultery, theft, bearing false witness, and the requirement to honor parents (e.g., Matt 19:16–22). What stands out in this narrative and other citations of the Ten Commandments in the New Testament are two features. First, when the Decalogue is mentioned, it is the second table of the Ten Commandments that is usually given attention. Second, commandments I–III are never cited explicitly in the New Testament.

Readers are probably to understand that the dual commitments demanded by Jesus, to love God with the totality of one's being and to love one's neighbor as oneself, summarize the two tables of the Decalogue (e.g., Mark 12:28–34).[34] Nevertheless, allusions to concerns in the first table of the Ten Commandments can be found. These include warnings against idolatry (e.g., Gal 5:20; Col. 3:5) and false swearing (Matt 5:33–37). Sabbath observance and the command to have no other gods, however, raised complex issues.

Difficulties for the early church posed by the first and second commandments will be discussed in the next chapter. In the case of Sabbath worship, controversy involved not only how the Sabbath should be kept but even whether it should be kept. This is reflected in Paul's discussion about special days in Rom 14:5. In general, Christians moved Sabbath observance from the seventh day of the week to the first day of the week; but the nature of that "day of rest" and its requirements remain debated in church circles.

Apart from thinking about the meaning of some of its instructions, however, this chapter has described the Decalogue as a text of divine self-disclosure. Is there any indication that law was used in the early church as a vehicle to describe the God revealed to it in Jesus Christ? Among New

33. David Flusser, "The Decalogue in the New Testament," in Segal and Levi, *The Ten Commandments in History and Tradition*, 221–22.

34. Lidija Novakovic, "The Decalogue in the New Testament," *PRSt* 4 (2008): 377–78.

Testament texts, the Sermon on the Mount seems to correspond to this interest. The instructional language used in Matthew 5–7 not only provides behavioral norms, it also reveals the nature of the one who proclaims it.

Programmatically, the theme of the Sermon on the Mount is righteousness, an attribute of God revealed by Jesus that is to be lived out by his disciples.[35] Therefore, like the Ten Commandments, the Sermon on the Mount can be read both as a description of the vocation of God's people and as a divine revelation. This is an indicator of continuity between the method of the Torah and early Christian interpreters.

35. François P. Viljeon, "Righteousness and Identity Formation in the Sermon on the Mount," *HvTSt* 69.1 (2013): 9.

CHAPTER 6

The Second Commandment: Revealing the Nature of God

Read: Exodus 20:2–17; Deuteronomy 5:6–21

The last chapter established a case for reading the Ten Commandments not only as a revelation of the identity of God's people but also as a revelation of the divine nature. The interest in revealing the nature of God is especially prominent in the second commandment (following the organization of Exodus). However, the second commandment seems contradictory. On the one hand, it forbids Israel from making any concrete image of God. On the other hand, it reinforces the prohibition with a verbal description of God. Why is it acceptable to have verbal representations of YHWH but not visible ones?

The following discussion explores this question. After reviewing the organization of the second commandment, it will identify connections with ancient Near Eastern treaty rhetoric. This will afford insights into the imagery of intergenerational punishment and the demand for imageless worship. The chapter concludes with thoughts about the validity of prohibition against making idols in light of the fact that large parts of the Christian world seem to have no problem with statues and pictures of the deified Jesus.

Organization

The command against constructing images of YHWH consists of three prohibitions:

1. You shall not make for yourself a carved image or any picture of what

is in the sky above, or what is on the earth beneath, or what is in the water under the earth. (Exod 20:4; my translation)

2. You shall not bow down to them (Exod 20:5a)
3. or worship them. (Exod 20:5a)

These commands are followed by a motive clause:

> for I the LORD your God am a jealous God, punishing children for the iniquity of parents, to the third and the fourth generation of those who reject me, but showing steadfast love to the thousandth generation of those who love me and keep my commandments. (Exod 20:5b–6)

Treaty Rhetoric and the Second Commandment

Chapter 5 noted a difference in the organization of the Decalogue between Exodus and Deuteronomy. Exodus divides the command not to worship other gods (v. 2–3) from the ban against making visible representations of a deity (vv. 4–6). Deuteronomy, however, considers these prohibitions to belong together in a single commandment (5:6–10). Although this chapter does not follow Deuteronomy's organization, its arrangement reinforces an impression that can also be defended on other grounds: thematically, the first and second commandment are connected. Both contain language connected to the political rhetoric of the treaty genre.

Four motifs link the first and second commandments to ancient Near Eastern treaty or covenant language (references are to Exodus 20):

1. insistence on exclusive loyalty (v. 3)
2. threat of intergenerational punishment (v. 5b)
3. use of "love" as a motif of covenant loyalty (v. 6)
4. alternation of curses and blessings (v. 5b–6)

These motifs also show a connection between the theological imagination of the Ten Commandments and the concept of kingship in the ancient Near East. In fact, biblical literature often appeals to kingship motifs when it imagines how God acts in the world and towards Israel.[1]

1. For a comprehensive discussion, see Marc Zvi Brettler, *God as King: Understanding an Israelite Metaphor* (JSOTSup 76; Sheffield: JSOT, 1989).

Before exploring the relationship of each of these four motifs to covenantal thinking, it is important to make some general observations about treaties and covenants in the ancient Near East. The relationship of biblical law to the ancient Near Eastern treaty genre was discussed briefly in Chapter 3 and will also be highlighted when dealing with aspects of the book of Deuteronomy in Chapters 18 and 19. As literature on treaties and loyalty oaths in the ancient Near East and biblical texts is extensive,[2] the following will only touch on a few important points.

As Chapter 3 noted, the act of taking an oath in the presence of the gods had legal and religious significance in the ancient Near East. It was used to create or strengthen a variety of political relationships. Conceptually, modern legal science distinguishes instruments of international law from those used in domestic law. International relationships require treaties, while attempts to use oaths to secure loyalties within a particular state are called loyalty oaths. However, ancient Near Eastern cultures did not use different terms to distinguish international treaties and domestic loyalty oaths, For example, the Biblical Hebrew word *bərît,* commonly translated as "covenant," can be used in both contexts.[3] Biblical texts allude to formal political relationships between states (e.g., 1 Sam 11:1–4; 2 Sam 10:19; 1 Kgs 5:12; 2 Kgs 16:7; 17:3–4) and loyalty oaths between Israel and its monarchs (e.g., 2 Sam 5:3 and 2 Kgs 11:12).

Generally speaking, treaties are divided into two broad classes. Parity treaties establish relationships between sovereign powers of equal status. Vassal treaties establish relationships between international powers of unequal social and political status.[4] Loyalty oaths are related to the vassal treaty concept, except that they typically secure the obedience of a ruler's military, political, and temple personnel to the king. Like vassal treaties and loyalty oaths, Israel's covenants with YHWH reflect agreements taken under oath by

2. For overviews of the relationship of biblical covenants to ancient Near Eastern treaty texts, see Dennis J. McCarthy, *Treaty and Covenant: A Study in Form in the Ancient Oriental Documents and in the Old Testament,* 2nd ed. (AnBib 21A; Rome: Pontifical Biblical Institute, 1978); Noel Weeks, *Admonition and Curse: The Ancient Near Eastern Treaty/Covenant Form as a Problem in Inter-cultural Relationships* (JSOTSup 407; London: T. & T. Clark, 2004); Kenneth A. Kitchen and Paul J. N. Lawrence, *Treaty, Law and Covenant* (3 vols.; Wiesbaden: Harrassowitz, 2012).

3. George E. Mendenhall and Gary A. Herion, "Covenant," *ABD* 1:1179.

4. Raymond Westbrook, "International Law in the Amarna Age," in *Amarna Diplomacy: The Beginnings of International Relations,* edited by Raymond Cohen and Raymond Westbrook (Baltimore: Johns Hopkins University, 2000), 39. An alternative designation for international agreements that create relationships of servitude is suzerainty treaties.

a subject people to a powerful sovereign. Within this conceptual universe, all four motifs of covenant obedience listed above have a place:

1. Exodus 20:3 calls for exclusive loyalty to Israel's divine monarch because it forbids the worship of other gods.[5] This prohibition is similar to treaty demands that subjects have no other overlord except the king to whom they swear absolute obedience.[6]
2. Exodus 20:5b–6 calls for intergenerational punishment if Israel worships plastic or visual representations of YHWH. Treaties often obligated not only the subject king, but also his descendants to obey their terms. In fact, the whole family could be threatened if a disobedient subject broke the treaty stipulations.
3. The demand for exclusive loyalty is underscored by the use of the terms "love" and "hate" (NRSV "reject") to describe the worshipper's relationship to YHWH in the motive clause of Exod 20:5b–6. In this context, a subject's "love" is expressed by keeping the terms of the agreement that have been sworn under oath.[7]
4. The alternation between YHWH's threat of punishment to those who "hate" (disobey) him and the promise of covenant faithfulness (*ḥesed*) to those who "love" him reflects the conclusions of a number of ancient Near Eastern treaties, which promise that the gods will bless those who keep the treaty stipulations and curse those who break the sworn agreement.[8]

Collective Retribution

The motive clause for the second commandment sets out a doctrine of sin with intergenerational consequences.[9] That is, it sets up the possibility of

5. Dale Patrick, *The Rhetoric of Revelation in the Hebrew Bible* (OBT; Minneapolis: Fortress, 1999), 91–92.

6. Mendenhall and Herion, "Covenant," 1:1180.

7. William J. Moran, "The Ancient Near Eastern Background of the Love of God in Deuteronomy," *CBQ* 25 (1963): 77–87.

8. Alternating curses and blessings are common in Hittite treaties from the Late Bronze Age; see McCarthy, *Treaty and Covenant*, 66–67. The same phenomenon appears in Iron Age documents related to the treaty genre, although it is less common. Alternating blessings and curses are found in Deut 28:1–19 and Sefire I C.

9. Bernard M. Levinson, *Legal Revision and Renewal in Ancient Israel* (New York: Cambridge University Press, 2008), 58.

collective retribution, which refers to the idea that not only the perpetrator but the group he leads (e.g., family or nation) suffers for his crimes.

Threats of collective retribution are fairly common in treaty rhetoric. Not only the oath-breaker, but also his family and his descendants could be threatened with extermination. The death of the malefactor's family was tantamount to complete annihilation of the guilty party, who was the primary focus of the punitive action. The text-box below contains two examples from ancient Near Eastern loyalty oaths.

Threats of Collective Punishment in Loyalty Oaths

Instructions to palace personnel to insure the king's purity (ca. 1500? BCE)

On a day when (my) temper gets the best of (me), the king, and I call all of you kitchen personnel, and I put you through the river (ordeal), then he who is (thereby shown to be) innocent, he is the servant of the king, while he who is (shown to be) guilty, I, the king, will have no need of him. They (i.e., the gods) will allot him an evil fate, together with his wife (and) his sons.[10]

The Esarhaddon Succession Treaty (672 BCE)

As long as we live, our sons (and) our grandsons are alive, Assurbanipal, the great crown prince designate, shall be our king and our lord. . . . May the gods mentioned by name (in this treaty) hold us, our seed, and our seed's seed accountable (for this vow).[11]

The doctrine of collective retribution was evoked in connection with an expectation of absolute loyalty of the subject to the monarch. It should not be surprising, given the importance of the kingship metaphor in the Decalogue, to find the doctrine of intergenerational punishment expressed in connection with an expectation of undivided loyalty to YHWH. This idea is worked out in the history of Israel and Judah recounted in 1–2 Kings. The fate of both nations is closely tied to the covenant fidelity of their kings.

10. Concerning the Purity of the King, §7, translated and dated following Jared L. Miller, *Royal Hittite Instructions and Related Administrative Texts* (WAW 31; Atlanta: SBL, 2013), 81.

11. Esarhaddon's Succession Treaty, §57, translated following Simo Parpola and Kazuko Watanabe, *Neo-Assyrian Treaties and Loyalty Oaths* (SAA 2; Helsinki: Helsinki University Press, 1988), 50.

According to prophetic thinking, the disasters that overcame both the northern and the southern kingdoms were due to the lack of moral and spiritual leadership by their rulers. Passages such as 2 Kgs 21:10–15, which assigns the responsibility for Judah's destruction and exile to the sins of Manasseh, assume the doctrine of collective retribution.[12]

The motive clause in Exod 20:5–6 offers a balance to the possibility of collective punishment by holding out the promise that YHWH will show "steadfast love to the thousandth generation of those who love me and keep my commandments." While the meaning of the word "thousand" has been debated, most likely, the idea is of a limitless number of descendants.[13]

Imageless Worship

While the idea of intergenerational punishment has parallels in ancient Near Eastern treaties, the absolute insistence on imageless worship is unprecedented. Ancient Near Eastern kings had no problems erecting monuments in which they were depicted. Why can there be no pictures of the divine king, YHWH?

The idea that YHWH had no visible form seems to be very old in Israelite religion.[14] Some scholars suggest that there was a time when YHWH could also be represented in visible form; but others think that Israel's deity was never given material representation.[15] The nature of the debate can be described using the idea of the icon, a term for a religiously venerated work of art.

Not all worship practices require an icon or visible representation of a deity. Some forms of worship are aniconic, literally "without an image." The related term "aniconism" refers to religious practices directed towards

12. For a detailed and nuanced discussion of divinely caused collective punishment in the Tanakh, see Jože Krašovec, "Is There a Doctrine of 'Collective Retribution' in the Hebrew Bible?" *HUCA* 65 (1994): 35–89.

13. William H. C. Propp, *Exodus 19–40* (AB 2A; New York: Doubleday, 2006), 173.

14. Cornelis Houtman, *Exodus*, vol. 3 (HCOT; Leuven: Peeters, 2000), 23.

15. See the discussions of archaeological evidence in Herbert Niehr, "In Search of YHWH's Cult Statue in the First Temple," in *The Image and the Book: Iconic Cults, Aniconism, and the Rise of Book Religion in Israel and the Ancient Near East*, edited by Karel van der Toorn (CBET 21; Leuven: Peeters, 1997), 79–81; and Ephraim Stern, "From Many Gods to the One God: Archaeological Evidence," in *One God—One Cult—One Nation*, edited by Reinhard G. Kratz and Hermann Spieckermann (BZAW 405; Berlin: de Gruyter, 2010), 395–403.

a deity who has no concrete image. In terms of the religions of the ancient Northwest Semitic world, one can distinguish de facto aniconism from programmatic aniconism.

While the religions of Northwest Semitic peoples typically honored deities depicted in concrete forms ("idols"), there is evidence that certain worship practices were directed towards an invisible god. This kind of imageless worship can be called de facto aniconism because it existed alongside worship of gods using images. For example, evidence for the worship of an imageless god has been found in ancient Hamath and Phoenicia, both Northwest Semitic-speaking cultures in contact with Israel and Judah. The city-states on the coast of the Mediterranean Sea near present-day Lebanon spoke Phoenician. Hamath was an ancient city-state located in what is now southern Syria. In the later part of the Iron Age, the ruling class of Hamath spoke Aramaic. During the Iron Age, both cultures commonly used material representations of the gods they worshipped, but the motif of an empty throne found on cult objects at both ancient Hamath and Phoenicia suggests that their religions occasionally venerated an invisible god.[16]

By contrast, programmatic aniconism was dogmatically driven. It represented a commitment on the part of ancient Israel's intellectuals to the worship of a deity beyond the ability of human beings to represent in any concrete form.[17] In fact, according to biblical thinkers worship directed towards the material depiction of YHWH was tantamount to worshipping another god. This is the religious perspective that came to expression in prophetic literature and also in biblical law.

Nevertheless, it is certainly not the case that ancient Jews were opposed to imagining God. In fact, biblical literature is full of verbal images of YHWH, for example as king, as parent, and as shepherd. Why were these verbal tactics permissible, while pictures and statues were not? This is a difficult question to answer, but three possibilities can be grounded in the text of the Decalogue:

1. The need to emphasize the preeminence of the "word of God" as divine revelation.
2. The need to decouple YHWH's kingship from conceptions of earthly kingship.

16. Tryggve N. D. Mettinger, "Israelite Aniconism: Developments and Origins," in van der Toorn, *The Image and the Book*, 184–89.

17. Mettinger "Israelite Aniconism," 183–84.

3. The need to preserve the freedom of God

1) The previous chapter made the point that the Decalogue was intended to be a sort of verbal revelation—a written image—of the character of God. The idea of representing the divine reality through speech and writing is connected to the ways in which biblical writers conceived of God's presence in the world. Although the ancient religions of Egypt and Mesopotamia thought of divine statues as (temporary) loci for the presence of their gods, they believed these images represented a presence able to convey the effectiveness of the god to its worshippers in terms of guidance (through oracles or omens) and blessing. In biblical religion, this effectiveness is reserved for God's word.[18]

In other words, part of the problem with physical representations of God is that they rival the word of God/Torah as a medium for divine revelation. This is unacceptable in biblical religion. A primary reason for the rejection of physical images is that the Old Testament thinks that God normally interacts with the world through acts of speech.[19]

2) Images and statues of human kings were erected in order to cement a connection between the gods and earthly rulers. The inscription of Kulamuwa mentioned in the last chapter is a good example. One of the aims of this kind of politically motivated art was to sacralize human kingship. In other words, pictures and statues of a ruler indicated that the human monarch ruled by divine approval. In this regard, the refusal to represent YHWH in a concrete image had a political point to it. The imageless cult of Israel's God decoupled an equation between the political kingship of earthly monarchs and the kingdom of God. The refusal to depict their deity in concrete form enabled Israel's thinkers to call into question the legitimacy of earthly rulers who did not conform to the divine will and made it possible to imagine a society with no king but YHWH.[20]

3) In comparison with the other commandments, the prohibition against coveting (commandment X) is unusual. It does not prohibit an action, but the desire to possess something or someone in an illegitimate way. Does this

18. Jan Assmann, "What's Wrong with Images?" in *Idol Anxiety*, edited by Josh Ellenbogen and Aaron Tugendhaft (Stanford: Stanford University Press, 2011), 25.

19. B. W. Anderson, "God, OT View of," *IDB* 2:422; Patrick, *Rhetoric of Revelation*, 16.

20. See Ronald Hendel, "Aniconism and Anthropomorphism in Ancient Israel," in van der Toorn, *The Image and the Book*, 224–28.

prohibition have anything to say to the beginning of the Decalogue? Idols are objects; they can be moved and manipulated by their makers. Therefore, manufacturing images of God can also be viewed as a tactic of possession. However, YHWH's dominion over Israel demands that he not be reduced to an object possessed by the people. Divine sovereignty entails freedom.

Developments

Early Christians found themselves in a dilemma. On the one hand, they echoed the critique of idolatry found in their Jewish matrix. This is apparent in Paul's indictment of Gentile culture in Rom 1:23–25 and his denial that idols represent reality in 1 Cor 8:4. On the other hand, according to 2 Cor 4:4 Jesus is the image (literally, icon) of God. To conclude, as the author of the Fourth Gospel does, that he who has seen Jesus has seen the Father (John 14:9) was blasphemous to many first-century Jews. Nevertheless, early Christians found ways to affirm their belief in the oneness of God while claiming Jesus as their incarnate Lord.[21]

The ambiguity inherent in the claim that Jesus Christ is "the word made flesh" erupted into a strenuous debate about the validity of making images of Jesus and the saints called the "iconoclastic controversy" in the eighth and ninth centuries CE. While the side that favored icons and statues of Christ prevailed in the Middle Ages, the issue was revisited during the Protestant Reformation. At that time, Reformed Christianity reiterated its opposition to pictures of Jesus and God, a position still held by some today.[22]

The polemic against idolatry was developed metaphorically as well as literally. New Testament writers agreed with other early Jewish thinkers in making a compelling case for equating idolatry with greed (Eph 5:5; Col 3:5).[23] Their reasoning has been explained by New Testament scholar Brian Rosner: if "a god is that which one loves, trusts and serves above all else," then the pursuit of wealth, power, or pleasure can become tantamount to idolatry.[24]

21. Lidija Novakovic, "The Decalogue in the New Testament," *PRSt* 4 (2008): 378–80.

22. E.g., Harry Boonstra, "Of Images and Image Breakers," *CTJ* 32 (1997): 423–31; David Vandrunen, "Iconoclasm, Incarnation and Eschatology: Toward a Catholic Understanding of the Reformed Doctrine of the 'Second' Commandment," *International Journal of Systematic Theology* 6 (2004): 130–47.

23. Brian Rosner, "Soul Idolatry: Greed as Idolatry in the Bible," *ExAud* 15 (1999): 74. For evidence outside the New Testament see, e.g., Philo, *Special Laws* 1:21–22.

24. Rosner, "Soul Idolatry," 84.

A distinctive development of the twentieth century has taken the metaphor for idolatry in another way. A great deal of work has been done on the connection between ideology and idolatry—especially if we understand a particular ideology as a system of false ideas or false consciousness.[25] In other words, an idea or concept can be just as much an idol as a statue.

The equation between idolatry and ideology has relevance for the history of the interpretation of the prohibition against idols in the Decalogue. Dale Patrick has observed that the polemic against idolatry in the Ten Commandments has the potential to criticize ideas about God that are untrue, even if they were held to be true in some form of ancient Israelite religion.[26]

A case in point is the idea of collective retribution, which was rejected by later thinkers in Israel. Bernard Levinson has illustrated such theological reflection at work in his study of how the description of God found in Exod 20:5b–6 and its parallels (Exod 34:6–7; Num 14:18; Jer 32:18) was interpreted by later exegetes. In fact, prophetic theology came to reject the idea of collective retribution (cf. Jer 31:29–30; Ezek 18:2–4), even though it was clearly expressed in the second commandment. This exegetical agenda was carried through into rabbinic literature, which claimed that God only brought punishment on individuals who deserved it.[27]

The history of the exegesis of the ideology of collective retribution is a good example of the dynamism of biblical thinking. The motive clause in Exod 20:5–6 is capable of being interpreted as a prediction about how God will deal not only with individuals but also with Israel as a whole. Since the doctrine of collective retribution is associated with a promise of collective blessing, Jewish thinkers came to understand that individual generations may come under judgment for disobedience, but YHWH will remain faithful to his people. God's steadfast love for Israel means that the covenant people will never be completely abandoned. The Jewish thinkers who formed the early church thought in similar terms (e.g., Romans 9–11).

25. See, e.g., Walter Brueggemann, *Israel's Praise: Doxology against Idolatry and Ideology* (Philadelphia: Fortress, 1988); Bruce Ellis Benson, *Graven Ideologies: Nietzsche, Derrida and Marion on Modern Idolatry* (Downers Grove: InterVarsity, 2002).

26. Patrick, *Rhetoric of Revelation*, 117.

27. Levinson, *Legal Revision*, 84–88.

Further Reading: The Decalogue

Aaron, David H. *Etched in Stone: The Emergence of the Decalogue.* New York: T. & T. Clark, 2006.

Brooks, Roger. *The Spirit of the Ten Commandments: Shattering the Myth of Rabbinic Legalism*. San Francisco: Harper & Row, 1990.

Harrelson, Walter. *The Ten Commandments and Human Rights*. OBT. Philadelphia: Fortress, 1980.

Lang, Bernhard. "The Number Ten and the Iniquity of the Fathers: A New Interpretation of the Decalogue." *ZAW* 118 (2006): 218–38.

Segal, Ben Zion, and Gershom Levi, eds. *The Ten Commandments in History and Tradition*. Jerusalem: Magnes, 1990.

Stamm, Johann Jakob, and Maurice Edward Andrew. *The Ten Commandments in Recent Research*. SBT 2. London: SCM, 1967.

Toorn, Karel van der, ed. *The Image and the Book: Iconic Cults, Aniconism, and the Rise of Book Religion in Israel and the Ancient Near East*. CBET 21. Leuven: Peeters, 1997.

PART 3

Israel in the Village Assembly

CHAPTER 7

The Covenant Code: Introduction

Read: Exodus 20:18–24:8

Exodus 20:22–23:33 is often called the Covenant Code on the basis of the reference to the "book of the covenant" in Exodus 24:

> And Moses wrote down all the words of the Lord. . . . Then he took the book of the covenant, and read it in the hearing of the people. (Exod 24:4a, 7a)

The ideal community of the Covenant Code seems to be a self-sustaining village in the land of Israel.[1] There is no explicit mention of a professional judiciary (although some commentators have tried to find such an institution behind the provisions of Exod 21:6 and 21:22) or priesthood. While certain actions are to be performed in the presence of God, it is not stated where (cf. Exod 21:6; 22:8, 9, 11). In contrast to the legal culture that prevailed elsewhere in the ancient Near East, the society portrayed in the Covenant Code operates with no clear reference to a king.[2]

1. Douglas A. Knight, *Law, Power, and Justice in Ancient Israel* (LAI; Louisville: Westminster John Knox, 2011), 127.

2. In general, there is no mention of a human ruler who governs the community in the Covenant Code. The only exception is the reference to the *nāśîʾ* ("leader") in Exod 22:28b. One cannot rule out the possibility that the *nāśîʾ* may be a king (cf. 1 Kgs 11:34), but this title was also given to tribal chieftains (e.g., Numbers 2). Much depends on how one dates this section of the Covenant Code for interpreting the reference to the leader in 22:28; see Cornelis Houtman, *Exodus,* vol. 3 (HCOT; Leuven: Peeters, 2000), 231.

The only legal decision-making body which the Covenant Code mentions is an assembly of peers. Some rules of conduct for this legal body are set out in Exod 23:1–8.

The following chapters seek to explore how the laws of the Covenant Code act to inculcate the identity of the people of God within a particular setting: the (quasi-)autonomous village. To begin, it will be necessary to explain a few technical terms used in analyzing biblical law.[3] The chapter then turns to a description of the arrangement of the Covenant Code. The next section touches on certain questions regarding its origins. Some observations about the theological significance of its literary organization conclude the chapter.

Terminology

Conditional/Casuistic Law

Casuistic law (also called "case law") is law written in a conditional form. Usually it uses the "if-then" pattern. The "if-clause" sets out the case to be addressed. The "then-clause" typically sets out consequences for that case. Studies of conditionally formulated law may refer to the "if-clause" as the "protasis" and the "then-clause" as the "apodosis."

Casuistic law can be formulated in the third person or the second person, e.g.,

> If someone's ox hurts the ox of another, so that it dies, then they shall sell the live ox and divide the price of it; and the dead animal they shall also divide. (Exod 21:35)

(The principle of equal payments on which this law is based is discussed in Chapter 8.)

> If you take your neighbor's cloak in pawn, you shall restore it before the sun goes down. (Exod 22:26)

(This law undermines the ability of a creditor to recover his loan from a very poor person. See Chapter 9.)

3. For more information, see Rifat Sonsino, "Forms of Biblical Law," *ABD* 4:252–54.

Apodictic Law

It is common in biblical scholarship to refer to rules formulated unconditionally as "apodictic law." These laws are usually expressed in the second person ("you"). Positive apodictic commands can be called "prescriptions," e.g.,

> Six days you shall do your work, but on the seventh day you shall rest. (Exod 23:12)

Negative apodictic commands can be called "prohibitions." Prohibitions use the negative particle *lōʾ* followed by the verb form Biblical Hebrew grammarians traditionally have called the "imperfect," e.g.,

> You shall not oppress a resident alien. (Exod 23:9)

The prohibition is often considered to have more general or emphatic force than the negative imperative, which uses the particle *ʾal* followed by the (short) imperfect. Some biblical scholars call the negated imperative the "vetitive" to distinguish it from an apodictic prohibition. While the vetitive is less common than the prohibition in biblical law, it is used occasionally, e.g.,

> and do not kill the innocent or those in the right. (Exod 23:7)

Participial Law

A third form of law uses a participle to portray the action addressed by the law, e.g.,

> Whoever strikes a person mortally shall be put to death. (Exod 21:12)
>
> Literally, "someone striking a person mortally . . ."

Scholars debate whether participial laws are better considered as subsets of apodictic or casuistic constructions.[4] In favor of the apodictic relationship,

4. E.g., Hans J. Boecker, *Law and the Administration of Justice in the Old Testament and Ancient Near East* (Minneapolis: Fortress, 1980), 194–201.

participial laws do not begin with a conditional particle ("if"). In favor of the casuistic relationship, these laws contain an explicit statement of the penalty for the crime. Apodictic laws generally do not state the consequences for violating their demands.

Chiasmus and Envelope Structure

Ancient writers had a fondness for repetition. They often used recurrences of similar grammatical forms or content to arrange a text. A common form of structured repetition is called "chiasmus."[5] In this literary device, two elements are repeated in reverse order. The result can be mapped by the x-shaped letter called *chi* in Greek: χ. This arrangement has the following scheme:

A B

B′ A′

In this arrangement, A is repeated in A′ and B in B′, but the order is reversed. The order begins A + B; but it recurs as B′ + A′.

Larger spans of text can be arranged using similar principles. In these instances, reference can be made to "envelope structure" or "ring composition" as ways of organizing the text. Envelope structure may be used to organize an original composition and by a subsequent author/editor who wanted to revise it. A text can show complex as well as simple patterns of ring composition.

Repetitions point to key emphases in the text. A ring composition can orient the reader to identify those items that a writer wants to highlight in two ways. First, repetition itself is a clue to emphasis. However, ring composition can also highlight material that is not repeated and give it a central focus. Both techniques are visible in the arrangement of the Covenant Code. Key commitments are signaled by the repetition of materials in Frames A and B; highlighting is also present. The organization of the Covenant Code marks the lengthy span of case law in Exod 21:18–22:17 as a center of the text.

5. John Welch, ed., *Chiasmus in Antiquity: Structures, Analyses, Exegesis* (Hildesheim: Gerstenberg, 1981); David P. Wright, "The Fallacies of Chiasmus," *ZABR* 10 (2004): 143–68; William S. Morrow, "Legal Interactions: The *Mišpāṭîm* and the Laws of Hammurabi," *BO* 70 (2013): 309–31.

Structure

The following chart does not account for three elements in the Covenant Code.[6]

- Its laws are introduced by a narrative statement in Exod 20:22.
- Exodus 21:1 interrupts the legal discourse with a title or superscription. This probably indicates that an author/editor was aware that different legal traditions were being combined in the text.[7]
- The Covenant Code ends with a speech in Exod 23:20–33 which anticipates Israel's occupation of the land of Canaan. This lengthy span of rhetoric belongs to a different genre of law-making than the rules that precede it. The origin of Exod 23:20–33 is discussed in Chapter 19.

The Organization of Exodus 20:23–23:19

A 20:23–26			
	B 21:2–11		
		C 21:12–17	
			D 21:18–22:17
		C′ 22:18–20	
		E 22:21–24	
			F1 22:25–27
			F2 22:28–31
			F3 23:1–8
		E′ 23:9	
	B′ 23:10–12		
A′ 23:13–19			

6. My description of the structure of the Covenant Code is based on and adapted from Jörn Halbe, *Das Privilegrecht Jahwes: Ex 34, 10–26: Gestalt und Wesen, Herkuft und Wirken in vordeuteronomischer Zeit* (FRLANT 114; Göttingen: Vandenhoeck & Ruprecht, 1975), 421; and Eckart Otto, "Aspects of Legal Reforms and Reformulations in Ancient Cuneiform and Israelite Law," in *Theory and Method in Biblical and Cuneiform Law: Revision, Interpolation and Development*, edited by Bernard M. Levinson (JSOTSup 181; Sheffield: Sheffield Academic, 1994), 188.

7. Morrow, "Legal Interactions," 315–16.

A. The Outer Frame

		Topic	Dominant Syntax	Addressee
A	20:23	Against idolatry	Unconditional	2nd Person
	20:24–26	Rules for building altars	Unconditional	2nd Person
A′	23:13	Against idolatry	Unconditional	2nd Person
	23:14–19	Festivals and sacrifices	Unconditional	2nd Person

Both sections of text are organized similarly: rules against wrong worship are followed with rules to ensure right worship. Most of these rules are written in the second person singular;[8] and most of these instructions are formulated unconditionally.

B. The Sabbatical Frame (6/7 Motif)

Directly inside the outer frame appear laws that use a 6/7 motif that recalls the rhythm of sabbatical observance:[9]

		Topic	Dominant Syntax	Main Addressee
B	21:2–11	Rules about slaves (6/7 motif)	Conditional	3rd Person
B′	23:10–12	Sabbatical rules (6/7 motif)	Unconditional	2nd Person

Unlike the outer frame, this structure is defined by similarities in content, not form. After a period of six years, a seventh year of release is called for in 21:2 and 23:10–11. Exodus 23:12 continues the theme with rules for observing the weekly Sabbath. All the rules for Frame B are concerned with economically distressed persons. The slave laws of 21:2–11 are discussed in Chapter 9.

8. Exceptions: 20:23 and most of 23:13, which are in the 2nd person plural.

9. I reject the suggestion that a redactional feature such as the 6/7 motif that connects the slave law in Exod 21:2 and the sabbatical rules in 23:10–12 is a "fortuity" (cf. Wright, "Fallacies of Chiasmus," 168).

C. Capital Crimes

Directly after laws about slavery, the Covenant Code changes its form again.

		Topic	Dominant Syntax	Main Addressee
C	21:12–17	Capital crimes	Participial	3rd Person
C′	22:18–20	Capital crimes	Participial	3rd Person

Each rule in 21:12–17 begins with a participle that describes the perpetrator and ends with the formula *môt yûmāt,* "he shall be put to death."[10] The crimes include:

homicide (v. 12)
physical harm to a parent (v. 15)
kidnapping (v. 16)
cursing a parent (v. 17)

All these injuries were considered crimes against the family, and it was presumed that a family member would undertake the role of avenging them. In the case of murder, a concession was made in the case of unintentional homicide: the perpetrator could obtain asylum at one of YHWH's cult places (v. 13) until a process of adjudication took place. However, divinely sanctioned asylum would not avail someone convicted of intentional homicide (v. 14). The story about the execution of Joab illustrates the fact that the altar was not considered automatic protection in such a case (1 Kgs 2:28–31).

The three laws in 22:18–20 are less unified in their formulations. Most similar to the group in 21:12–17 is 22:19, which also uses the formula *môt yûmāt.* The death penalty formulas in vv. 18 and 20 are quite different. Commentators do not agree about what is meant when it is said that someone doing sorcery should not be kept alive (22:18).[11] The statement that anyone who sacrifices to a god other than YHWH "shall be devoted to destruction" (22:20) has a parallel in laws regarding the elimination of apostate Israelites in Deuteronomy 13.

10. Martin Buss ("Logic and Israelite Law," *Semeia* 45 [1989]: 56) interprets this phrase as "he is liable to the death penalty." That is, the law indicates a right that can be exercised by the offended party, but it was not necessarily always implemented.

11. See the surveys in Houtman, *Exodus,* 3:212; William H. C. Propp, *Exodus 19–40* (AB 2A; New York: Doubleday, 2006), 255–57.

D. The Case Law Collection

		Topic	*Dominant Syntax*	*Main Addressee*
D	21:18–22:17	Injury and property crimes	Conditional	3rd Person

The rules about capital crimes in 21:12–17 and 22:18–20 frame a large collection of laws written in conditional ("if-then") form. Block D will be described in Chapter 8.

E. Laws against Oppression

		Topic	*Dominant Syntax*	*Addressee*
E	22:21–24	Oppression	Unconditional	2nd Person
E′	23:9	Oppression	Unconditional	2nd Person

The repetition of the command not to oppress the alien (22:21 and 23:9) makes a bracket around rules for social relationships. The laws in section E share a concern for the landless person (*gēr*), the vocabulary of oppression, and the motif of Exodus memory.

F. Laws of Rights and Duties

		Topic	*Dominant Syntax*	*Addressee*
F1	22:25–27	Lending	Conditional	2nd Person
F2	22:28–31	Obligations	Unconditional	2nd Person
F3	23:1–8	Parties-at-law	Unconditional	2nd Person

The laws against oppressing the socially marginal frame a series of instructions that focus on rights and duties (Section F). Groups of rules relate to relationships with economic inferiors (22:25–27), social superiors (22:28–31), and peers in the village assembly (23:1–8). Exodus 23:1–8 shows signs of a chiastic arrangement.[12] Framed by unconditional formulations in the second person, 23:4–5 contain a pair of conditionally formulated instructions enjoining care for the property of an opponent-at-law.

12. Wright ("Fallacy of Chiasmus," 157) finds a genuine chiastic arrangement in Exod 23:1–7.

Origins

The Covenant Code is an amalgam of smaller collections of law combined over a significant period of time. Preexilic, exilic, and postexilic interventions may all have contributed to its canonical shape. An important problem concerns the Covenant Code's combination of third person case laws, which are not primarily concerned with religious practices, and the second person unconditional laws that are. Ancient Near Eastern parallels show that third person case laws circulated in collections independent of second person apodictic law.[13] Or, to take the reverse situation: the rules regulating cultic practices in Exod 23:14–19 have close parallels in Exod 34:18–26.[14] These laws for right worship are contained in the legal collection of Exod 34:10–26, which is composed solely of apodictic law. This parallel shows that cultic law could circulate independently of criminal law in ancient Israel. What was the reason, therefore, that Israel's thinkers brought differing legal traditions into a single collection? The next section will attempt to answer this question.

Broadly speaking, there are three eras in which the Covenant Code has been dated:

1. The Covenant Code's laws substantially reflect Israel's legal and religious culture during the time of the judges (the Iron I period).[15]

Attribution to the time of the judges is attractive because the rather simple political, economic, and religious structures reflected in the Covenant Code seem to fit that time period. However, there are problems with a theory that connects all of the Covenant Code to the Iron I era. One of the most important is the way the text is now organized. There is a profound discrepancy between the society described in the laws of the Covenant Code and the culture implicated in their collection and organization. It is possible that many of its case laws represent a selection of legal decisions originally

13. William S. Morrow, "A Generic Discrepancy in the Covenant Code," in Levinson, *Theory and Method in Biblical and Cuneiform Law,* 138.

14. Scholarly literature on the significance of the parallels between Exod 23:14–19 and 34:18–26 is extensive. For a recent summary and indications of the dependency of 34:18–26 on 23:14–19 see Shimon Gesundheit, *Three Times a Year: Studies on Festival Legislation in the Pentateuch* (FAT 82; Tübingen: Mohr Siebeck, 2012), 36–43.

15. E.g., Boecker, *Law and the Administration of Justice,* 143–44; Raymond Westbrook, "Cuneiform Law Codes and the Origins of Legislation," in *Law from the Tigris to the Tiber: The Writings of Raymond Westbrook,* vol. 1: *The Shared Tradition,* edited by Bruce Wells and F. Rachel Magdalene (Winona Lake: Eisenbrauns, 2009), 92.

made in village settings.[16] Still, the village setting cannot explain the origin of scribal techniques implicated in their organization. The methods used to arrange and transmit the laws in the Covenant Code show the signs of highly trained scribes. One must assume the scribes who compiled and organized the Covenant Code were trained in urban settings under the patronage of palace or temple (perhaps both; but they have chosen not to allude to these institutions). What the laws in Exod 20:23–23:19 depict is a culture that acts without reference to bureaucratic institutions—whether they were in place or not.[17]

2. The Covenant Code was composed during the monarchical period. Since several of its laws are pre-Deuteronomic, it may have been codified during the eighth century—possibly in the time of King Hezekiah.[18]

Exod 20:24–26 must be pre-Deuteronomic in origin. These instructions permit the sacrifice of animals at a multiplicity of cult sites, a rule which was modified in favor of a single legitimate place of sacrifice in Deuteronomy 12.[19] If one assumes that Deuteronomy was composed in the late monarchical period or later, that dates key portions of the Covenant Code to an earlier time period. While the era of the judges is theoretically possible for the composition of the Covenant Code's altar law, there are indications that it deals with issues relevant to the monarchical period:

- Verse 24 seeks to limit worship sites to ones in which a divine revelation was attested. This is reminiscent of the critique against the proliferation of cult places made by the prophets (e.g., Jer 3:6; Hos 4:13).
- Verse 25 prohibits the construction of an altar using hewn stones. The medieval Jewish commentators Rashi and Nachmanides associated this command with the biblical tradition that David was not permitted to build the First Temple because he was a man of war. As iron implements were often used in warfare, their use was forbidden in

16. Eckart Otto, "Town and Rural Countryside in Ancient Israelite Law: Reception and Redaction in Cuneiform and Israelite Law," *JSOT* 57 (1993): 20–21.

17. Morrow, "Legal Interactions," 322–26.

18. Rainer Albertz, *A History of Israelite Religion in the Old Testament Period* (Louisville: Westminister John Knox, 1994), 1:183–84; Frank Crüsemann *The Torah: Theology and Social History of Old Testament Law* (Minneapolis: Augsburg Fortress, 1996), 166.

19. Bernard M. Levinson, *Deuteronomy and the Hermeneutics of Legal Innovation* (New York: Oxford University Press, 1997), 28–36.

Figure 4. Stones from this altar were discovered in the walls of the last building phase of the fortress at Tel Beersheba. The altar was not built of field stones, but of carefully dressed stones, the building material forbidden in Exod 20:25. This altar was dismantled and desacralized at the end of the eighth century BCE.

the construction of the First Temple.[20] In other words, there may be within v. 25 an implied criticism of the monarchical sponsorship of Israel's shrines.

3. Much of the Covenant Code is postmonarchical. This theory may best explain the fact that it shows influences from cuneiform law, while also clarifying the lack of reference to a human king.[21]

There are indications that knowledge of Mesopotamian legal traditions influenced the composition of the case laws in Exod 21:18–22:17. This idea will

20. Michael Dobkowski, "'A Time for War and a Time for Peace': Teaching Religion and Violence in the Jewish Tradition," in *Teaching Religion and Violence*, edited by Brian K. Pennington (New York: Oxford University Press, 2012), 57.

21. E.g., John Van Seters, *A Law Book for the Diaspora: Revision in the Study of the Covenant Code* (New York: Oxford University Press, 2003), 45.

be discussed further in Chapter 8. The exilic period is a time when Israel's intellectuals could have encountered Mesopotamian legal traditions directly.[22] Moreover, there would have been an incentive in the exilic community to articulate a vision of Israel without a king, as the Davidic monarchy was no more.

Theology

To what extent does the Covenant Code reflect real social conditions in ancient times? One ought to expect some connection between what the Covenant Code describes and actual social conditions found in ancient Israel,[23] although its lack of references to the palace or related bureaucratic structures seems somewhat utopian. Probably, an ancient Israelite village would not have enjoyed the social and political autonomy this law collection seems to imply.[24]

Compositions such as the Covenant Code, however, are works of theory as well as practice. Ancient Jewish intellectuals used law to convey a vision of what it meant to live as the people of God. In other words, the Covenant Code can be read as a work of theology as well as a body of instructions. The Covenant Code means to describe an ideal community, one that regulates itself without the apparatus of an ancient state and whose only king is God.

As Israel's true king, YHWH is concerned with the totality of human life. This belief is conveyed strongly in prophetic literature, which typically indicts the kingdoms of Israel and Judah for social injustices as well as unacceptable religious practices. It is not surprising, therefore, that the religious imagination of ancient Israel might use law to convey the same insight. The result was the kind of synthesis of civil, social, and religious instructions that one finds in the Covenant Code. As noted in Chapter 4, the extent of this synthesis is unique in ancient Near Eastern instructional literature. One reason for this singularity in Israelite legal composition can be found in the monotheistic confession. The organization of the Covenant Code in its canonical form illustrates this need to incorporate the plurality of life's experiences in a monotheizing matrix.[25]

22. Morrow, "Legal Interactions," 328.

23. Bruce Wells, "What Is Biblical Law? A Look at Pentateuchal Rules and Near Eastern Practice," *CBQ* 70 (2008): 242.

24. Knight, *Law, Power, and Justice*, 125–26.

25. James A. Sanders, *From Sacred Story to Sacred Text: Canon as Paradigm* (Philadelphia: Fortress, 1987), 21.

Within its synthesis there is a prioritization of commitments. The outer frame (A) of the Covenant Code defines the community in terms of its obligations to YHWH. Rules governing right relations between the members of the community are set out within it. What does it mean that regulations for Israel's common life are embraced by commands related to right worship? The implication is that getting right with God is essential to building good community. This impression is reinforced by the sermonlike address with which the Covenant Code ends. As Israel anticipates its entry into the land of promise, it is commanded to eliminate the material manifestations of an idolatrous culture (Exod 23:20–33).

Developments

Later Jewish groups would continue to work out the significance of creating a viable community whose common life was embraced by its commitments to the God of Israel. In the New Testament, this is expressed by Jesus when he identified the first and greatest commandment with the traditional affirmation of the oneness of God in Deut 6:4. It is the second greatest commandment, to love one's neighbor as oneself, that addresses the common social life (Matt 22:34–40 and parallels). Rabbinic teachings were similar.[26] Ancient Jewish thinkers believed strongly that building a solid community began with establishing a viable relationship with God. This basic commitment is indicated by the arrangement of the Covenant Code.

26. David Flusser and R. Steven Notley, *Jesus* (Jerusalem: Magnes, 1997), 88–90.

CHAPTER 8

Restoration or Revenge? The Case of the Goring Ox

Read: Exodus 21:18–22:17

In the idealized village society assumed in the Covenant Code, the normative ethical actor is a land-owning, freeborn male. He is the one who participates in the village assembly (Exod 23:1–8). He is the one who must appear at the pilgrim festivals (23:17), and it his family that is threatened in the case he mistreats the poor (22:24). Other members of the community are dependent on his largess, including widows, orphans, and the landless resident or immigrant (22:21–22). Preservation of the integrity of his family (21:12–17), his body (21:18–32), and his possessions (21:33–22:17) is, therefore, of great importance.

One of the legal remedies used to protect the rights and interests of the freeborn adult Israelite is the principle of "eye for an eye." The technical term for this legal concept is *lex talionis* (defined below). Contrary to popular belief, the application of the principle of "eye for an eye" does not permit excess or egregious punishment. On the contrary, it was meant to act as a brake against overreactions to criminal and civil damages.[1]

This chapter begins by describing the system of case laws found in the center of the Covenant Code (Exod 21:18–22:17), which are often identified in biblical scholarship as *mišpāṭîm* ("judgments").[2] The concept of *lex talionis*

1. Shalom M. Paul, *Studies in the Book of the Covenant in the Light of Cuneiform and Biblical Law* (Eugene: Wipf & Stock, 2006), 40.

2. William Morrow, "Legal Interactions: The *Mišpāṭîm* and the Laws of Hammurabi," *BO* 70 (2013): 310.

that they assume will be illustrated with regard to the laws of the goring ox in Exod 21:28–32, 35–36. After these biblical instructions are described in their own context, they will be compared to similar laws in Mesopotamian legal collections. This discussion will provide an opportunity to consider the distinctiveness of the social vision of the *mišpāṭîm*. The chapter ends by indicating some related developments in postbiblical times.

Structure

Inside the envelope created by the Covenant Code's laws on capital crimes is an extensive collection of laws written in the casuistic style: Exodus 21:18–22:17 (section D according the structural scheme set out in Chapter 7). Biblical scholars vary in the ways that they divide the *mišpāṭîm* into sections. The organizational analysis set out here, however, does not depend on ideas regarding their original form or history.[3]

The Organization of the Case Laws in Exodus 21:18–22:17

I. Fatal and nonfatal injuries to human beings

21:18–19	Injuries from a brawl
21:20–21	Fatal assault on one's own slave
21:22–25	Brawl affecting a pregnant woman
21:26–27	Liberation of male or female slave
21:28–32	The goring ox (a)

II. Damage to animals and property

21:33–34	Agricultural damages (a) Animals
21:35–36	The goring ox (b)
22:1–4	Theft
22:5–6	Agricultural damages (b) Crops
22:7–9	Deposits

3. The schema which follows is based on a synthesis of analyses by, among others, John Van Seters, *A Law Book for the Diaspora: Revision in the Study of the Covenant Code* (New York: Oxford University Press, 2003); Bernard S. Jackson, *Wisdom-Laws: A Study of the Mišpāṭîm of Exodus 21:1–22:16* (Oxford: Oxford University Press, 2006); David P. Wright, *Inventing God's Law: How the Covenant Code of the Bible Used and Revised the Laws of Hammurabi* (New York: Oxford University Press, 2009).

22:10–13	Use of animals 1: profit-sharing models[4]
22:14–15	Use of animals 2: rental models
22:16–17	Seduction

Note that two sections address problems involved with goring oxen (21:28–32 and 35–36). They differ because the first deals with the death of human beings, while the second addresses problems when one ox has killed another. Their separation suggests a distinction between cases in which human beings are injured and/or killed (I) and those which involve damages to livestock and other kinds of property (II).

Lex Talionis in Biblical Law

The term *lex talionis* is taken from ancient Roman law in order to classify a number of regulations found in biblical and ancient Near Eastern sources. As a legal principle, it can be defined following Lev 24:19–20:

> Anyone who maims another shall suffer the same injury in return: fracture for fracture, eye for eye, tooth for tooth; the injury inflicted is the injury to be suffered.

A similar statement occurs in Exod 21:23–25:[5]

> If any harm follows, then you shall give life for life, eye for eye, tooth for tooth, hand for hand, foot for foot, burn for burn, wound for wound, stripe for stripe.

But was it always applied literally?

The statement of the talionic principle in Exod 21:23–25 is followed by the law on eye and tooth loss to a male or female slave in vv. 26–27. Notice, however, that restitution is not applied literally. The master does not lose his eye or tooth in an act of revenge. Rather, the slave secures his or her release as compensation for the injury. Their injuries are not addressed by a strict application of retributive justice.

4. Following Jackson, *Wisdom-Laws*, 344–66.

5. See also Deut 19:21.

In fact, throughout the *mišpāṭîm* the major concern is not revenge. The goal of the legal system in the Covenant Code is the regulation of social conflict. This is accomplished by attempts to rule out violent extralegal reactions ("lynch law") and to heal disturbed social relationships.[6] In other words, the concerns of the *mišpāṭîm* are more aligned with modern concepts of civil damages (tort) than crime.[7] This principle can be illustrated by the laws about the goring ox.

Exodus 21:35–36 attempts to address two concerns: first, a need to compensate for the dead animal and second, a need to ensure that neither party in the dispute obtains an advantage over the other. This second concern explains the logic of remediation in the case of an unpredictable attack (v. 35). The law carefully ensures that both sides are treated equally: both get a share of the live ox and the dead ox. What is paramount is that an imbalance in economic and social relations between the two parties is redressed.

Treatment is different, of course, in the case where the ox should have been restrained by its owner (v. 36). The negligent owner is responsible for replacing the dead ox with an equivalent animal—although the law does not say how such equivalence is to be determined. Even so, the advantage does not go entirely to the injured party as the dead animal belongs to the culpable farmer.

The emphasis is on restoring broken social relationships, not punishing the guilty party. In a strict "eye for an eye" system, one would expect the injured farmer to have the right to kill an ox belonging to the negligent owner. Inflicting losses of this kind, however, makes no sense in a society composed (at least ideally) of interdependent farmers.

One circumstance where biblical law clearly applies the talionic principle is murder: "life for life." Yet, as noted in Chapter 7, there are provisions for unintentional homicide (Exod 21:13–14) that diverge from the application of a strictly retributive form of justice. Exodus 21:28–32 also deals with the death of human beings in cases that fall short of premeditated murder.

Exodus 21:28 treats the case of an unpredictable death of a person when gored by an ox. A law that recognized the unimpeded right to revenge would demand the death or replacement of a family member as compensation.[8] Although the ox is killed by stoning (a detail discussed below), the owner is free from revenge or compensation because he was not negligent.

6. Eckart Otto, *Theologische Ethik des Alten Testaments* (Theologische Wissenschaft 3.2; Stuttgart: Kohlhammer, 1994), 25–29.

7. Douglas A. Knight, *Law, Power, and Justice in Ancient Israel* (LAI; Louisville: Westminster John Knox, 2011), 143.

8. Jackson, *Wisdom-Laws,* 231–33.

Exodus 21:29–32 addresses fatal situations in which the owner of the ox was negligent. In general, biblical law does not allow for monetary ransom (the technical term is "composition") in the case where a slaying has been intentional (see Num 35:31).[9] Yet, the principle set out in Numbers does not necessarily apply in the case of the goring ox, because the owner was indirectly involved. Consequently, there is provision for monetary compensation when the ox has caused the death of a free person or his family member, although it must be negotiated on a case-by-case basis (v. 30). Exodus 21:32, however, limits the talionic principle with respect to the death of a slave. In contrast to the legal remedies imposed for the death of a free person, a fixed fine is appropriate because the slave occupies a shadowy status between full humanity and property.[10]

Comparisons with Ancient Near Eastern Law

The laws of the goring ox in Exod 21:28–32 and 35–36 show that Israel's thinkers were capable of exploring complex problems in ancient jurisprudence as well as setting down principles for real life. Similar concerns likely generated a number of the laws in ancient Near Eastern legal collections.[11] A difficult legal situation that involved the confluence of more than one juridical principle can be called a "border case." A border case allowed ancient scribes and would-be jurists opportunities to puzzle out how conflicting legal principles might work themselves out. The laws of the goring ox in 21:28–32 fit this description: issues involving homicide and negligence converge, and their relative importance needs to be decided.

A number of such legal issues regularly preoccupied ancient Near Eastern scribes. Raymond Westbrook groups these concerns in terms of the abuse of power, revenge and the application of the talionic principle, maltreatment of slaves, and theft.[12] As a work of ancient jurisprudence, therefore, the case of the goring ox is a classical locus for comparing biblical law with legal reasoning in the ancient Near East. Prominent in

9. Moshe Greenberg, "More Reflections on Biblical Criminal Law," in *Studies in Bible, 1986*, edited by Sara Japhet (ScrHier 31; Jerusalem: Magnes, 1986), 10.

10. Greenberg, "More Reflections," 14.

11. Martha T. Roth, *Law Collections from Mesopotamia and Asia Minor*, 2nd ed. (WAW 6; Atlanta: Scholars, 1997), 4.

12. Raymond Westbrook, *Studies in Biblical and Cuneiform Law* (CahRB 26; Paris: Gabalda, 1988).

this discussion are provisions in the Laws of Eshnunna and the Laws of Hammurabi.

Mesopotamian Laws about Goring Oxen

Laws of Eshnunna (LE)

§53 If an ox gores another ox and thus causes its death, the two ox-owners shall divide the value of the living ox and the carcass of the dead ox.[13]

Laws of Hammurabi (LH)

§250 If an ox gores to death a man while it is passing through the streets, that case has no basis for a claim.

§251 If a man's ox is a known gorer, and the authorities of his city quarter notify him that it is a known gorer, but he does not blunt (?) its horns or control his ox, and that ox gores to death a son of a member of the *awīlum*-class, he (the owner) shall give 30 shekels of silver.

§252 If it is a man's slave (who is fatally gored), he shall give 20 shekels of silver.[14]

The rule in LE §53 is so close to Exod 21:35 that a number of biblical scholars have suggested that it was translated from the Akkadian source. Unfortunately, there is no known vector by which the Laws of Eshnunna could have been transmitted, either in Mesopotamia itself or across the fertile crescent. So, the nature of the relationship between the biblical law and its Mesopotamian equivalent remains undetermined.[15]

Exodus 21:28–32 and LH §§250–52 also show an extraordinary level of agreement; in fact, their correspondence has often been considered one of the convergences between biblical and ancient Near Eastern legal traditions *par excellence*. Nevertheless, while it shows important similarities with comparable rules in the Laws of Hammurabi, the biblical system also manifests some significant differences. For example, LH §251 assesses a penalty for the

13. "The Laws of Eshnunna," trans. Martha Roth (*COS* 2.130:335).

14. Adapted from "The Laws of Hammurabi," trans. Martha Roth (*COS* 2.131:350), following Roth, "On *mār awīlum* in the Old Babylonian Law Collections," *JNES* 72 (2013): 267–72.

15. Morrow, "Legal Interactions," 324–25.

death of a free person in fixed monetary terms. Biblical law diverges from this pattern. While it also allows for monetary ransom, the amount is not fixed but has to be determined in negotiation with the aggrieved family. The difference between the two legal systems suggests that human life has a value in biblical law that cannot be strictly fixed economically.[16]

Another divergence between the biblical law and the Laws of Hammurabi is found in the treatment of the habitual goring ox when it has killed a person. Biblical law requires the ox be destroyed because it has taken a human life. The gravity of the offense is indicated by the manner in which the ox is killed: by stoning. If it were simply a matter of getting rid of a dangerous animal while denying the owner any material benefit of the corpse,[17] various measures can be imagined. But stoning is a rather awkward and very public way of inflicting death. Other biblical laws that use this term (Hebrew root *s-q-l*) deal with important violations to sacred space and human relationships (e.g., Deut 13:10; 22:21, 24).

The ox is stoned to death because it has violated a chain of being that is assumed in biblical law. At the top of this hierarchy is God, whose rights are not to be violated by human beings. Human beings stand in the middle, below God but above animals. Animals are not to kill people (see Gen 9:5). Human life has a value in biblical law that goes beyond financial and social utility.[18]

Another area of difference between biblical and cuneiform law can be found in the realm of property crimes. Unlike cuneiform law, biblical law never demands the death penalty for theft.[19] But caution is required before putting too much distance between biblical and ancient Near Eastern legal thought. For example, the Covenant Code does not allow physical mutilation for the commission of a crime. Tongues (cf. LH §192), eyes (cf. LH §193), breasts (cf. LH §194), and hands (cf. LH §§195; 218) are not forfeit for various wrongs in biblical law. These penalties in the Laws of Hammurabi seem to constitute literal applications of the talionic principle. However, careful study of the vocabulary used in the talionic laws found in ancient Near Eastern le-

16. J. J. Finkelstein, *The Ox That Gored* (TAPS 71; Philadelphia: American Philosophical Society, 1981), 38–39; Otto, *Theologische Ethik*, 31.

17. So, e.g., Bernard S. Jackson, "The Goring Ox," in *Essays in Jewish and Comparative Legal History* (SJLA 10; Leiden: Brill, 1975), 114; Westbrook, *Studies in Biblical and Cuneiform Law*, 83–88.

18. Moshe Greenberg, "Some Postulates of Biblical Criminal Law," in *Yehezkel Kaufmann Jubilee Volume*, edited by Menachem Haran (Jerusalem: Magnes, 1960), 19–20.

19. Greenberg, "Some Postulates of Biblical Criminal Law," 17–19.

gal collections suggests that these penalties were not necessarily literally applied. Their value was to emphasize the need for comparable compensation when damages were incurred.[20] In this respect, biblical law and cuneiform law share similar viewpoints.

Connections between the *mišpāṭîm* and cuneiform law exist both on the level of form and content. Consequently, there has been a long history of attempts to explain their connections, especially with the Laws of Hammurabi. This collection was widely known and copied throughout the Mesopotamian world for more than 1,000 years. Correspondences on the level of content are difficult to interpret, however. Biblical scholars have noted that, even when the *mišpāṭîm* and the Laws of Hammurabi address the same issue, they may solve the problem in distinct ways.[21] Nevertheless, it is difficult to dismiss the impression that the organization of the *mišpāṭîm* owes something to the influence of cuneiform law in general[22] and the Laws of Hammurabi specifically.

In particular, agreements between the organization of LH §§196–214 and Exod 21:18–27 are complex and impressive. In both cases bodily injuries are principally treated under the aspects of liability for consequences. Punishments follow the principles of talion in the case of free persons but material compensation for slaves, while bodily injuries are separated according to extenuating circumstances. It is difficult to escape the impression, therefore, that at some point Israelite scribes came into contact with the Laws of Hammurabi.[23]

It is not at all clear, however, when the legal thinkers of Israel could have encountered this Mesopotamian classic. There is a case for imagining that the legal traditions embodied in the Laws of Hammurabi could have been encountered directly (perhaps during the exile) or indirectly (perhaps through the mediation of Aramaean scribes during the Iron Age).[24] In either circumstance, evidence for dependency and similar sophistication of organization in the Covenant Code's *mišpāṭîm* raises the question that was also posed in the last chapter. Why have the Israelite scribes who compiled

20. Jan Rothkamm, *Talio esto: Recherches sur les origines de la formule <œil pour œil, dent pour dent> dans les droits du Proche-Orient ancien, et sur son devenir dans le monde gréco-romain* (BZAW 426; Berlin: de Gruyter, 2011), 83–88.

21. E.g., Paul, *Studies in the Book of the Covenant,* 81.

22. E.g., Eckart Otto, "Town and Rural Countryside in Ancient Israelite Law: Reception and Redaction in Cuneiform and Israelite Law," *JSOT* 57 (1993): 19–22.

23. Morrow, "Legal Interactions," 323–24.

24. Morrow, "Legal Interactions," 326–31.

these laws chosen not to allude to the institutions to which they belonged and where they were trained—palace and/or temple?

The *mišpāṭîm* presuppose a level of community organization in which the social institutions that sponsored and trained scribes in the ancient Near East were not involved. In this respect, there is something to be said for the attempt to locate the basic logic of the *mišpāṭîm* in a cultural milieu of "self-help." The rules in Exod 21:18–22:17 can be read as a compilation of "wisdom law," intended to guide litigants in the application of legal principles to resolve their disputes prior to consultation with formally constituted juridical institutions.[25] But the picture on the surface is belied by the many convergences between cuneiform law and the Covenant Code at deeper levels of form and content.[26]

So why did Israel's scribes choose to hide their own social attachments when compiling the materials that would culminate in the collection of *mišpāṭîm* found in the Covenant Code? They may have done so partly out of commitment to a social vision that wanted to flatten distinctions between members of the society in terms of economic and political power.[27] This strategy represents a repudiation of the social vision of cuneiform law which presupposes a system of social hierarchies overseen by a human monarch.

The social vision expressed in the *mišpāṭîm* is that Israel is, more or less, a community of equals whose only king is YHWH, their God. A sign of this egalitarian tendency can be found in the covenantal framework that now surrounds the Covenant Code in Exodus 19 and 24. YHWH does not make his covenant with a king. Instead, all of Israel is addressed by the divine lawgiver. The people answer as a whole, "All that the LORD has spoken we will do" (Exod 24:7). Each land-owning Israelite becomes, in a certain sense, the covenant partner of God. Each and every person addressed is directly responsible to YHWH, who is the ultimate source of the law. God, in turn, has invested the responsibility for maintaining the law directly in the people themselves—not a human monarch.[28]

25. Jackson, *Wisdom-Laws*, 32–35.

26. See Roger Tomes, "Home Grown or Imported? An Examination of Bernard Jackson's *Wisdom-Laws*," *ZABR* 14 (2008): 443–62.

27. Simeon Chavel ("A Kingdom of Priests and Its Earthen Altars in Exodus 19–24," *VT* 65 [2015]: 169–222) thinks that the Covenant Code was set up as an intentional foil to royal ideology.

28. Joshua Berman, *Created Equal: How the Bible Broke with Ancient Political Thought* (New York: Oxford University Press, 2008), 40–44.

Developments

Commitments to an ethos of egalitarianism such as that displayed in the Covenant Code have a long history in Judaism. A number of examples can be found among groups in first-century CE Judea. In the case of the proto-rabbinic movement, for example, interpreters of the oral law contended for power with a hereditary priesthood. Although they developed their own elites, status was based on learning, not on inherited privilege. The opportunity of mastering the discipline of Torah study was technically open to anyone.

The New Testament contains memories that also point to the dynamics of egalitarian social structures. John the Baptist called for a revised social order in which distinctions based on wealth were to be challenged (Luke 3:11). Peter proclaimed an outpouring of the Holy Spirit that would fall on all members of society (Acts 2:14–21). And Jesus said, "call no one your father on earth, for you have one Father—the one in heaven" (Matt 23:9).

From this social perspective, it is worth revisiting questions about the relationship of the Sermon on the Mount to the ethics of Old Testament law. Although Jesus refutes a literal application of "an eye for an eye and a tooth for a tooth" (Matt 5:38–42), this teaching is not necessarily opposed to the values embodied in the *mišpāṭîm*. Throughout Matt 5:21–48, the emphasis is on preserving good relationships in the community, even at the expense of standing on one's legal rights.[29] This overarching value of community solidarity is also presupposed in the casuistic laws of the Covenant Code.

29. Herbert W. Basser, *The Mind Behind the Gospels: A Commentary to Matthew 1–14* (Boston: Academic Studies, 2009), 145–50.

CHAPTER 9

The Bible and Slavery: Humanitarian Concerns

Read: Exodus 21:2–11; 22:21–23:12; Deuteronomy 15:12–18

The last chapter made a case for finding an egalitarian ethic in the *mišpāṭîm* of Exod 21:18–22:17. The Covenant Code uses law in an attempt to describe the values and commitments that characterize the ideal Israelite community by taking its point of reference from the land-owning male. Nevertheless, it assumes the possibility that a freeborn Israelite might be reduced to slavery and forced to work for another member of the community. How could the society that told the Exodus story also countenance the ownership of slaves? This question was keenly felt in the abolitionist controversies of the nineteenth century. In this debate, advocates for slavery actually had the easier case, because they could point to passages in the Bible that regulated slavery.[1]

This chapter begins with a description of the slave laws in Exod 21:2–11. Then it turns to a discussion of their humanitarian concerns. Comparison with laws in the well-known Mesopotamian classic, the Laws of Hammurabi, follows. The last section addresses responses to slavery in the first century CE.

Structure

This discussion follows the description of the organization of the Covenant Code in Chapter 7. Properly speaking, the rules for slaves in Exod 21:2–11

1. Mark Noll, "Battle for the Bible: The Impasse over Slavery," *ChrCent* 123 (2 May 2006): 20–25.

most resemble the laws in section D, the *mišpāṭîm* ("judgments") that make up Exod 21:18–22:17. They are largely written in conditional (casuistic) form in the third person. Nevertheless, three features set the slave laws apart from the casuistic laws, despite the fact that the *mišpāṭîm* also talk about slaves (cf. Exod 21:26–27, 32). The laws in Exod 21:2–11

- are set outside the lengthy collection of case laws in 21:18–22:17;
- though mainly written in the third person, begin in the second person;
- contain a 6/7 motif similar to the sabbatical laws in 23:10–12: a male slave can serve for no longer than six years; in the seventh year he must be set free.

Other ancient Near Eastern law collections show no interest in highlighting the interests of slaves by providing them such a prominent place in the organization of their texts. Why are the laws in 21:2–11 given this kind of attention?

Background

The Case of the Male Slave in Exodus 21:2–6

While much has been written about the identity of the "Hebrew slave," it is best to consider this law as regulating the circumstances in which a freeborn Israelite becomes a slave.[2] Free persons could be enslaved for a number of reasons.[3] Sometimes the slavery was temporary; other times it was permanent. Both situations are considered in vv. 2–6.

The most common reason for temporary slavery was related to economic distress; but slavery could also be a penalty for committing a crime (cf. Exod 22:1). Permanent slavery was also possible, especially through capture in a war. The Bible says little about the treatment of males who were permanently enslaved, although the possibility is mentioned in passages

2. Bernard M. Levinson, "The 'Effected Object' in Contractual Legal Language: The Semantics of 'If You Purchase a Hebrew Slave' (Exod. XXI 2)," *VT* 56 (2006): 502–3; Bernard S. Jackson, *Wisdom-Laws: A Study of the Mišpāṭîm of Exodus 21:1–22:16* (Oxford: Oxford University Press, 2006), 83–84.

3. See Raymond Westbrook, "Slave and Master in Ancient Near Eastern Law," in *Law from the Tigris to the Tiber,* vol. 1: *The Shared Tradition*, edited by Bruce F. Wells and F. Rachel Magdalene (Winona Lake: Eisenbrauns, 2009), 172–81.

such as Gen 17:12; Lev 25:45–46; and the reference to forced labor in Deut 20:10–11.

The Case of the Female Slave in Exodus 21:7–11

The situation of the female slave is opposite to that of the male slave. While ordinarily a male slave was to be given his freedom, ordinarily a female slave was not. This is due to the circumstances for which she was acquired: as a sexual partner. The law does not state whether the young woman is being taken as a wife or as a concubine. The difference is that the children of a wife are heirs to the husband's estate, while the children of a concubine are not. Perhaps both possibilities are covered by the text. What is clear is that the girl comes from a freeborn Israelite family, and this gives her legal rights. She cannot simply be sold to a third party. Even if she possesses the status of a slave-wife, her owner has responsibilities to her of a contractual nature.

Women bought for sexual purposes (Hebrew *ʾāmâ*) became permanent members of the household. However, the Covenant Code has very little to say about the children of an *ʾāmâ*. Would they be given their freedom some time in the future if their mother was a native born Israelite? Their servile status is assumed in the Sabbath law of 23:12; but there is no indication about what their ultimate fate would be. Unlike the *ʾāmâ,* a man must decide to become a permanent slave (21:5–6).

The Humanitarian Context

The biblical writers were caught between a rock and a hard place. They faced the reality that slavery was a well-known practice of the ancient world. Rather then try to abolish the practice, they chose a different strategy—one calculated to make readers uneasy about the ethics of slave-owning. These laws represent an early strategy for raising readers' conscience about the institution of slavery and (implicitly) calling it into question. Overall, their tactics reflect an ethic of concern for the vulnerable, a major theme in the Torah.[4]

The writers of the Covenant Code integrated laws about slaves into

4. Johanna W. H. van Wijk-Bos, *Making Wise the Simple: The Torah in Christian Faith and Practice* (Grand Rapids: Eerdmans, 2005), 185–91.

patterns of instructions that connect fair treatment of socially disadvantaged persons with the worship of YHWH:

1. As with 21:2, the Sabbath laws in 23:10–12 contain the 6/7 motif.[5]
2. Exod 21:2 begins with a formula used for setting out primary rights and duties.
3. There are rules for lending to the poor designed to prevent indebtedness in Exod 22:25–27.
4. The esteem of freedom is reinforced by Exodus memory and expectations for the participation of free males in Israel's pilgrim festivals.

1) The 6/7 motif in the Sabbath laws

The origins of the Sabbath idea in biblical religion are unclear. (It is safe to conclude, however, that attempts to derive the custom from the Mesopotamian world have not been successful). References to the Sabbath in 2 Kgs 4:23; Isa 1:13; Hos 2:11; and Amos 8:5 suggest that the custom of observing a day of work stoppage was kept before the exile,[6] although it is debatable if there was a weekly Sabbath in the preexilic period. Weekly Sabbath-day observance became a prominent mark of Jewish life in the Second Temple period.

A number of sabbatical institutions contain provisions for the relief of the poor and the enslaved. This concern is manifest in the Ten Commandments (Exod 20:8–11; Deut 5:12–15), in the rules for the Jubilee Year (Leviticus 25), and in Deuteronomy's demand to cancel debts every seven years (15:1–11). The 6/7 motif of the slave law in Exod 21:2 alludes, therefore, to a set of concerns connected to care for the disadvantaged in Israelite law.

Exodus 23 mentions two sabbatical institutions. Every seven years, farmers are supposed to leave their fields fallow (unploughed and unseeded) and not harvest their vineyards and their olive orchards (vv. 10–11). The effect is to enact a kind of welfare system meant to benefit the socially disadvantaged: "so that the poor of your people may eat." It has no reference to agricultural reality, since fields would have been left fallow much more

5. Eckart Otto, *Theologische Ethik des Alten Testaments* (Theologische Wissenschaft 3.2; Stuttgart: Kohlhammer, 1994), 83.

6. Gerhard F. Hasel, "Sabbath," *ABD* 5:852–53.

frequently in antiquity (probably every two or three years). Every seven days, there is to be a day of rest (v. 12). While everyone is to observe a work stoppage, the named beneficiaries are domestic animals and disadvantaged persons: the child of the slave wife (the *ʾāmâ* named in 21:7) and the resident alien (*gēr*).

2) Exodus 21:2 and laws of primary rights and duties

Exodus 21:2 is a casuistic law: it sets out a situation in the "if"-clause and proceeds to suggest some solution in the "then"-clause. However, this law differs from many casuistic laws in the Covenant Code. Most casuistic laws are remedial; they aim to set out some kind of compensation or penalty when personal or community interests have been harmed. But another kind of casuistic law is more interested in setting out primary rights and duties than stating particular penalties if they are violated.[7] These instructions often begin with the formula "If you . . ." For this reason, they are sometimes called "if-you" laws. A number of if-you laws address humanitarian concerns (e.g., Exod 22:25, 26–27; 23:4, 5). The opening of Exod 21:2 recalls this formula.[8] This is evidence for associating 21:2–11 with humanitarian concerns found elsewhere in the Covenant Code.

In fact, biblical literature allows for the possibility that slaves had rights which could be the subject of a lawsuit against their master. Note, for example, that Job defends his innocence before God by rhetorically asking, "If I have rejected the cause of my male or female slaves, when they brought a complaint against me . . ." (Job 31:13). The word meaning "complaint" is a term for a lawsuit in Biblical Hebrew (*rîb*).

3) Instructions favoring the poor in cases of debt

Exodus 22:25–27 addresses issues related to making loans to poor persons: v. 25 prohibits loans for interest (the prohibition against being a creditor [*nōšê*] forbids making a loan for profit), while vv. 26–27 discuss taking a

7. Dale Patrick, "Casuistic Law Governing Primary Rights and Duties," *JBL* 92 (1973): 180–84.

8. Harry W. Gilmer, *The If-You Form in Israelite Law* (SBLDS 15; Missoula: Scholars, 1975), 49; Jackson, *Wisdom-Laws*, 106–7.

piece of clothing as the guarantee for a loan. Similar rules appear in Lev 25:36–37 and Deut 23:19–20.[9] These instructions have the effect of turning the institution of lending into a voluntary action. Only loans given in charity to help a needy neighbor are permitted. Such loans might prevent a poor person from falling into the situation described in Exod 21:2–6.

Exodus 22:26–27 deals with the custom of taking a piece of property in order to secure a loan ("distrainment"). The thought was that if the debtor defaulted, the creditor would still have some compensation by virtue of holding the pledged property. In addition, the confiscation of a piece of the debtor's property might act as an incentive to pay an outstanding loan. The demand in 22:26–27 that the creditor return the debtor's coat to him at night is decidedly one-sided. It effectively limits the creditor's rights to force the recovery of his loan in cases where the debtor is in extreme economic distress.

Other biblical laws have a similar tenor. Some items cannot be taken as pledges in compensation for nonpayment of a loan: a millstone (Deut 24:6) or a widow's garment (Deut 24:17). The effect of such laws is to deprive the creditor of the means of enforcing his loan. Similarly, how can the creditor make good on his loan if he is not allowed to enter the house of the borrower to take his pledge (Deut 24:10–11)? In the Bible, the laws against taking pledges exist to protect the debtor. No attention is given to the rights of the creditor as to how he might recover his loan when an extremely poor debtor defaults.[10] These provisions may be seen as efforts to protect a poor borrower from falling into a situation where he (or she) has no choice but to sell himself into slavery for nonpayment of a loan.

4) Motifs of exodus and freedom

The Sabbath regulations are followed by rules for pilgrim festivals (Exod 23:14–17) as they are elsewhere in the Torah (e.g., Exod 34:17–23; Leviticus 23). Worship and freedom are connected in the festival laws in 23:14–17. Those able to choose to make the pilgrim feast must be (by implication) free persons who have control over their property (because they can offer it as sacrifices) and over their own bodies (because they have the freedom

9. For a comparison of biblical laws on borrowing and lending, see Miroslav Varšo, "Interest (Usury) and Its Variations in the Biblical Law Codices," *CV* 50 (2008): 223–38.

10. Avi Shevka, "Biblical Laws of Loans: A Comparative Perspective" [Hebrew] (PhD diss., Hebrew University of Jerusalem, 2010), 269.

to travel). The value placed on freedom is also implicit in the slave law of 21:2–6, which presupposes that the Israelite community normally consists of free persons.[11]

Note that the command to observe the seven-day Festival of Unleavened Bread (Exod 23:15) makes an association with the time of the Exodus: "at the appointed time in the month of Abib, for in it you came out of Egypt." In the Covenant Code, Exodus memories motivate care for the disadvantaged (22:21 and 23:9). They may also be implicit in 21:2–11. The verb chosen to describe the slave's movement to freedom in 21:2, 3, 4, 5, 7, 11 means "to go/come out" (*yāṣāʾ*). The same verb is used in the Exodus memory of 23:15. David Daube claims that the motif of "going out" in the Exodus narratives has been borrowed from legal language such as that used in 21:2.[12] Be that as it may, it would be difficult for ancient readers familiar with the Exodus story not to hear echoes of it in the vocabulary of the Covenant Code's slave laws.[13]

The humanitarian impulse found in the Exodus motif is implicated in the derivation of Deut 15:12–18 from Exod 21:2–6.[14] Whereas it remains implicit in the context of Exod 21:2–6, Exodus memory is explicit in Deut 15:15. Deuteronomy makes three major modifications to the law in Exodus:

1. Deuteronomy 15:12 begins, "If a member of your community, whether a Hebrew man or a Hebrew woman, is sold to you and works for you six years, in the seventh year you shall set that person free." These words only make sense if not all women sold into debt slavery were intended for sexual purposes. Evidently, women could be forced into other forms of indentured service in the case of severe poverty or nonpayment of the loan. This possibility is also implied by the rules in Exod 21:26–27.
2. Where Exod 21:2 states that the freed slave is to go out with nothing

11. Cornelius Houtman, *Exodus*, vol. 3 (Leuven: Peeters, 2000), 112.

12. M. David Daube, "The Exodus Pattern in the Bible," in *Collected Works of David Daube*, vol. 3: *Biblical Law and Literature*, edited by Calum Carmichael (Berkeley: University of California, 2003), 116.

13. Thomas B. Dozeman, *Commentary on Exodus* (ECC; Grand Rapids: Eerdmans, 2009), 527–28.

14. A majority of biblical critics regard the slave law in Deut 15:12–18 as derived from and responding to details in Exod 21:2–6; e.g., Bernard M. Levinson, "The Manumission of Hermeneutics: The Slave Laws of the Pentateuch as a Challenge to Contemporary Pentateuchal Theory," in *Congress Volume: Leiden 2004*, edited by André Lemaire (VTSup 109; Leiden: Brill, 2006), 281–324. A few scholars think Exod 21:2–11 is later than the Deuteronomic law; e.g., John Van Seters, "Law of the Hebrew Slave: A Continuing Debate," *ZAW* 119 (2007): 169–83.

owing (*ḥinnām*), Deut 15:13–14, 18 urge the creditor to make financial provision for the Hebrew slave, presumably to address the poverty that led to debt slavery in the first place. The argument is that the indentured slave's labors have been the equivalent of those of a hired servant and they should be rewarded accordingly.[15]

3. A further modification is found in the administration of the slave mark,[16] in the case that the debt slave prefers permanent indenture to his freedom. Exod 21:6 requires the marking to be done "before God." Modern commentaries offer different interpretations of this requirement, while generally rejecting an older view that taking the slave before God referred to a procedure conducted before judges. It is unclear whether the action of entering into permanent slavery was to be done in the presence of the owner's household gods (once a legitimate part of Israel's religion; cf. 1 Sam 19:13) or at a local shrine. The phrase "before God" is missing from Deuteronomy, presumably because of its demand to centralize all acts of sacrificial worship at a single place (see Chapter 20).

Comparison with the Laws of Hammurabi

Comparison with Mesopotamian law frequently contrasts the provisions of Exod 21:2–6 with some of the Laws of Hammurabi:

Laws of Hammurabi §117

If an obligation is outstanding against a man and he sells or gives into debt service his wife, his son, or his daughter, they shall perform service in the house of their buyer or of the one who holds them in debt service for three years; their release shall be secured in the fourth year.[17]

15. See Mattiahu Tsevat, "The Hebrew Slave according to Deuteronomy 15:12–18: His Lot and the Value of His Work, with Special Attention to the Meaning of משנה," *JBL* 113 (1994): 587–95.

16. The slave mark involved some kind of distinctive ear piercing; see Sandra Jacobs, *The Body as Property: Physical Disfigurement in Biblical Law* (LHBOTS 582; London: T. & T. Clark, 2015), 193–200.

17. "The Laws of Hammurabi," trans. Martha Roth (*COS* 2.131:343).

Why does the biblical law allow for six years, while the Babylonian law seems more lenient? LH §117 deals with a sale to repay the loan. But Exod 21:2–6 may be written in terms that allow for the possibility of distrainment as well as debt repayment.[18] As noted above, distrainment means taking persons or property in order to force the payment of the loan. Notice that the slave is to be released at the end of the six-year period "without debt" in 21:2 (*ḥinnām*). This implies that the loan may still be outstanding. There is a case, therefore, for suggesting that a point of comparison can be found in the Laws of Hammurabi §115:

Laws of Hammurabi §115

If a man has a claim of grain or silver against another man, distrains a member of his household, and the distrainee dies a natural death while in the house of her or his distrainer, that case has no basis for a claim.[19]

According to the Mesopotamian law, the person has been distrained because of the nonpayment of the loan. Distrainment remains in force as long as the loan is not paid—regardless of the amount of time that has gone by. The time spent as a distrainee may pay off the interest accruing on the loan, while leaving the principle unpaid. In contrast, the Israelite law fixes a six-year period regardless of the amount of the loan or the conditions under which it was made. At the end of six years, the loan is fully discharged and the enslaved person becomes free. As in the case of Exod 22:25–27, biblical law takes the side of the borrower—unlike Mesopotamian law, which usually mediates between the rights of the creditor and the debtor.

Developments

One of the weaknesses of biblical slave laws is that they have little to say about the treatment of chattel slaves, particularly in the case of non-Israelites. While rabbinic teachings address legal situations in which Jewish men and women became slaves to other Jews, the issue seems to be disputed in Sec-

18. Jackson, *Wisdom-Laws,* 82.

19. Roth (*COS* 2.131:343).

ond Temple times. In fact, the rather utopian adaptation of Exod 21:2–6 in Leviticus 25 did away with the category of slave for relations between Jews altogether (see Chapter 17).

The slave trade was well entrenched in the economy and society of the Hellenistic world. Several sources existed for obtaining slaves, but exploitation of peoples defeated in war was the most primary. Slaves were regarded as permanent possessions in Greco-Roman culture; but slave owners had the right to free their slaves if they chose. Thinkers in the ancient world held contradictory opinions about slavery. They regarded the practice both as a necessity and as "contrary to nature."[20] Yet, this contradiction never led the ancient world to seriously question the evils of slavery.

In this regard, there is no large difference to be found in the attitudes of the early church.[21] New Testament writers pursued the same tactics they found in their Scriptures. They tried to promote a sympathy for the humanity of slaves among their owners (e.g., the book of Philemon). Nevertheless, as with the legal precedents in the Torah, they stopped short of demanding an end to slavery.

20. M. I. Finley, "The Old World's Peculiar Institution," in *The Light of the Past,* edited by G. Highet (New York: American Heritage, 1965), 58.

21. Keith Bradley, "Engaging with Slavery," *BibInt* 21 (2013): 540.

Further Reading: The Covenant Code

Chavel, Simeon. "A Kingdom of Priests and Its Earthen Altars in Exodus 19–24." *VT* 65 (2015): 169–222.

Finkelstein, J. J. *The Ox That Gored*. TAPS 71. Philadelphia: American Philosophical Society, 1981.

Jackson, Bernard S. *Wisdom-Laws: A Study of the Mishpatim of Exodus 21:1–22:16*. New York: Oxford University, 2006.

Marshall, J. W. *Israel and the Book of the Covenant: An Anthropological Approach to Biblical Laws*. SBLDS 140. Atlanta: Scholars, 1993.

Morrow, William S. "Legal Interactions: The Mišpāṭîm and the Laws of Hammurabi." *BO* 70, no. 3–4 (2013): 309–31.

Otto, Eckart. "Town and Rural Countryside in Ancient Israelite Law: Reception and Redaction in Cuneiform and Israelite Law." *JSOT* 57 (1993): 3–22.

Paul, Shalom M. *Studies in the Book of the Covenant in the Light of Cuneiform and Biblical Law*. Eugene: Wipf & Stock, 2006.

Sprinkle, Joe M. *The Book of the Covenant: A Narrative Approach*. JSOTSup 174. Sheffield: JSOT, 1994.

Van Seters, John. *A Law Book for the Diaspora: Revision in the Study of the Covenant Code*. New York: Oxford University Press, 2003.

Westbrook, Raymond. "Slaves and Master in Ancient Near Eastern Law." In *Law from the Tigris to the Tiber: The Writings of Raymond Westbrook*, vol. 1: *The Shared Tradition*, edited by Bruce Wells and F. Rachel Magdalene, 161–216. Winona Lake: Eisenbrauns, 2009.

Wright, David P. *Inventing God's Law: How the Covenant Code of the Bible Used and Revised the Laws of Hammurabi*. New York: Oxford University Press, 2009.

PART FOUR

Israel in the Courts of the Lord

CHAPTER 10

Priestly and Holiness Law: Introduction

Many people resolve to read the Bible from cover to cover, only to find themselves bogged down somewhere in the middle of Leviticus. More than one writer has referred to this material as "scriptural Sominex™"! While the narratives of Genesis and Exodus are gripping, it is hard to see the point of the many different rituals and instructions that make up Leviticus and Numbers. A key problem is that holiness is not a feature of the divine nature that speaks to many modern readers. It is difficult to imagine just how important this concept was in antiquity, including the religion of Israel; but any attempt to study biblical law must reckon with the fact that a large amount of instructional space is given over to examining the experience of the sacred—both as gift and vocation.

This section of the book is called "Israel in the Courts of the Lord" because it proposes to describe a system of law that takes as its central point of reference the tabernacle and the requirements for entering and living in proximity to its various categories of sacred space. The need to nurture healthy relationships with the sacred required sustained reflection on the nature of divine holiness and how to interact with it in life-giving ways.

Israel's religious thinkers believed that their nation had been set apart from others to be YHWH's holy people (e.g., Exod 19:6; 22:31; Deut 7:6; 14:21). In fact, as these passages suggest, the motif of holiness is ubiquitous in biblical law. However, it is the subject of sustained reflection in laws associated with Priestly writers (P) and the related Holiness school (H). Their writings are concentrated in (but not limited to) laws and narratives found in Exodus 25–Numbers 36.

This chapter will describe some basic features of Priestly and Holiness law in Exodus, Leviticus, and Numbers. Subsequent chapters will draw out various aspects of the thought of P and H. This will include the religious imagination symbolized in the tabernacle (Chapter 11) and the sacrificial system (Chapters 12–15). Chapters 16–17 will show how H extends the concern for holiness to matters of everyday morality beyond those found in P. Some of these chapters may seem fairly technical. To a certain extent, this is unavoidable because P and H can be quite detailed in setting out ritual requirements. Although sacrificial practices are often given fairly brief attention in introductions to the Old Testament, they deserve careful study for two reasons. First, animal sacrifice was an important component of ancient Israelite religion. Second, the use of sacrificial imagery and metaphors in the New Testament makes it advisable to understand the religious system from which they were derived.

This chapter begins with a short discussion of the idea of holiness. It proceeds to discuss why distinctions can be made between P and H and to give a brief account for the origins of these categories of law. Finally, some remarks will address the continuity of Holiness thinking in communities that read the Torah in the first century CE.

Holiness in Priestly Thought

As this introduction is interested in broad descriptions of theology and worldview, some of its discussions do not make rigid distinctions between the outlooks of P and H. In fact, P and H share a characteristic vocabulary and worldview which distinguishes their work from other styles in the Pentateuch.[1] For this reason, the book will use expressions such as "Priestly thought" to refer to ideas commonly shared between Priestly and Holiness law. This can be justified because Holiness law was developed from and dependent on Priestly materials. Where it is necessary to distinguish the two sources, discussion will revert to the abbreviations P and H to refer to these bodies of literature.

The motivations for observing the various rules and rituals that appear in Priestly thinking arise out of the raw data of religious experience: Israel's encounter with the holy. Unfortunately, the Torah provides its readers with no definition of what it means by the idea of the holy. One has to read be-

1. A classic list of stylistic traits in Priestly literature is found in Samuel R. Driver, *An Introduction to the Literature of the Old Testament* (Cleveland: Meridian, 1967), 131–35. Driver recognizes that this list does not distinguish between P's and H's rhetoric.

tween the lines of both biblical narrative and law to discover how the sacred was conceived by ancient Israel's intellectuals.[2]

One important concept wrapped up in the idea of holiness is separateness: YHWH manifests a kind of moral perfection and power that distinguishes him from the created order because he is not subject to the contingencies of death, disease, or sin. Holiness is also a desirable condition; for it is associated with justice, health, and peace—all characteristics of the divine. When people live in harmony with the holy, life prospers and flourishes. Priestly thinking is confident that the Creator wants to live in harmony with the community that divine revelation has called into being, although it is also aware that boundaries between what is of God and what is human need to be carefully negotiated.

According to Priestly thought, conformity to the conditions of holy living is a matter of life and death! This concern merits a considerable amount of attention in P and H. Two problems have to be addressed: one is the ontological difference between the Creator and the creation; the other is the effects of bringing what is unclean, impure, or immoral into contact with the realm of the sacred. As the holy Creator, YHWH was regarded as the source of blessing; but approached in the wrong way his presence could become a curse.

An important contrast can be drawn between P and H in terms of how they approach problems in maintaining good relations with the holy. P is concerned almost exclusively with what goes on in the sanctuary. Therefore, much of P sets out proper rituals for sacrifice or addresses problems connected to maintaining ritual purity. By contrast, H extends the concern for holiness and purity to everyday life. This means that many laws in H have a moral focus, as this form of Holiness thinking is concerned with the proper treatment of the land of Israel and the people of Israel. These differing values are apparent in their conception of holy persons. According to P, only the sanctuary and its priests are holy; but H regards holiness as a vocation for all of the people of Israel.[3]

Origins

The legal material in Exodus–Numbers reached its canonical form through a lengthy history of composition and editing, so an introductory chapter

2. Holiness is a complex concept. For a survey of Holiness thinking in the Old Testament, see David P. Wright, "Holiness (OT)," *ABD* 3:237–49.

3. Jacob Milgrom, *Leviticus 1–16* (AB 3; New York: Doubleday, 1991), 457.

can only indicate some broad lines of agreement. As noted above, the rules in Exodus 25–Numbers 36 are generally assigned to one of two styles of instruction: P and H. Since scholars debate how to distinguish P from H,[4] it is most straightforward to account for their differences by focusing on materials where their perspectives predominate. The book of Numbers contains some laws from P sources, but large parts of Numbers belong to H.[5] Given its admixture of both styles, Numbers will not figure prominently in the discussions that follow. Laws from P dominate in Exodus 25–31 and Leviticus 1–16. Laws from H dominate in Leviticus 17–26.

Older critical scholarship tended to view texts coming from H as prior to P. Since Ezekiel shows a number of influences from H, it was thought that relative dating of both styles could be undertaken on this basis. P materials were regarded as later than H and were largely consigned to the late exilic or postexilic eras. This opinion has now been turned on its head by an extensive amount of scholarship demonstrating that H revises and assumes texts and concepts from P.[6]

The question of relative dating continues to assert itself, however. Many researchers think that the book of Ezekiel represents a good benchmark for discovering the emergence of a distinct school of Holiness thinking.[7] However, there is also an argument for dating its emergence earlier (see below).[8] Part of the significance of this debate is that it raises questions about the relationship between the scribal activity that generated laws in the Holiness style and the origins of the book of Deuteronomy. In any event, it now seems clear that H writers had at their disposal P materials. From that perspective, it is plausible that some P materials originated in the preexilic era.

Does that mean that we can be confident that H writers and editors were the ones who brought the materials in Exodus–Numbers into their canonical form? Not so fast! There are indications that writers using the P style played a substantial role in editing the Pentateuch in the postexilic

4. Compare, e.g., the arguments in Milgrom, *Leviticus 1–16,* 13–35, and Israel Knohl, *The Sanctuary of Silence: The Priestly Torah and the Holiness School* (Minneapolis: Fortress, 1995), 59–110.

5. Knohl, *Sanctuary of Silence,* 105–6.

6. E.g., Knohl, *Sanctuary of Silence,* 111–23; Jacob Milgrom, *Leviticus 17–22* (AB 3A; New York: Doubleday, 2000), 1439–43; Jeffrey Stackert, *Rewriting the Torah: Literary Revision in Deuteronomy and the Holiness Legislation* (FAT 52; Tübingen: Mohr Siebeck, 2007), 14–15.

7. Henry T. C. Sun, "Holiness Code," *ABD* 3:256.

8. Milgrom (*Leviticus 17–22,* 1361–64) would date almost all of H to the preexilic period.

period.[9] For example, the laws in Leviticus 27 are written in the P style, but they now stand as a supplement to the H materials ending in Leviticus 26.[10] Evidently, there are late P compositions as well as early ones.[11] In fact, H materials also have a history of internal revision.[12] So, any attempt to explain the emergence of Exodus–Numbers must account for a number of variables.

While there is certainly room for debate, the development of laws in the P and H styles may have occurred something like this:

A Model for Development of P and H in Exodus–Numbers

Preexilic era:

Small collections of P laws

Late preexilic era:

Scribes write laws in the H style; they also compile and edit P laws.

Exilic and postexilic eras:

Scribes capable of writing in the P and the H styles continue to supplement and edit Exodus–Numbers.

Laws in the P Style

P is characterized by a particular literary style as well as by content. In terms of content, instructional materials in the P style form the basic and predominant layers of rules for building the tabernacle (Exodus 25–31) and for the sacrificial system (Leviticus 1–16). In the preexilic period, laws in the P style probably circulated in small collections that were later compiled into

9. David M. Carr, *The Formation of the Hebrew Bible: A New Reconstruction* (New York: Oxford University Press, 2011), 214–21; Konrad Schmid, *The Old Testament: A Literary History* (Minneapolis: Fortress, 2012), 147–52.

10. See Jacob Milgrom, *Leviticus 23–27* (AB 3B; New York: Doubleday, 2000), 2407.

11. Alexander Rofé, *Introduction to the Literature of the Hebrew Bible* (JBS 9; Jerusalem: Simor, 2009), 243.

12. Eckart Otto, *Theologische Ethik des Alten Testaments* (Theologische Wissenschaft 3.2; Stuttgart: Kohlhammer, 1994), 236.

large literary units. Illustrations of this process can be seen in P's rules for sacrifices in Leviticus 1–7.

Leviticus 1–7 probably circulated independently of its present context as a compilation of sacrificial regulations.[13] Section markers such as those in Lev 4:1; 5:14; 6:1, 8, 19, 24; 7:22, 28 point to a process in which smaller units of ritual instruction were gathered together to produce Leviticus 1–7 as a whole. It is often supposed that the rituals regarding sin and guilt offerings in Lev 4:2–6:7 were products of the crisis in conscience and theology that arose in the exilic period. However, there are suggestive parallels between the concern for purification in Israel and the world of Hittite ritual.[14] These similarities focus the scholarly gaze away from the Mesopotamian world and towards Asia Minor. Such cultural influences would be better accounted for before the exile, not after.

Nevertheless, there are grounds for assuming the sacrificial system continued to develop in the postexilic period. Some of these innovations appear in the Pentateuch. An example of historical development is found in the calendar of sacrifices in Numbers 28–29 (a P text).[15] Numbers 28:3–4 requires that the daily lamb offering (Hebrew *tāmîd*) be sacrificed morning and evening. But 2 Kgs 16:15 indicates that in preexilic times there was only a morning burnt offering in the Jerusalem temple. Also, Ezek 46:13–15, an exilic text which anticipates the inauguration of a new, perfected form of worship in Jerusalem, only knows of a morning *tāmîd*. It appears that the institution of a morning and evening *tāmîd* was not in force during preexilic times.[16]

Laws in the H Style

Laws in the style of H use vocabulary and rhetoric that can be distinguished from P.[17] Overall, Leviticus 17–26 has a structure that resembles the covenantal form of Deuteronomy; for that reason, previous scholarship often referred to

13. Claus Westermann, *Handbook to the Old Testament* (Minneapolis: Augsburg, 1967), 67.

14. Moshe Weinfeld, *The Place of the Law in the Religion of Ancient Israel* (VTSup 100; Leiden: Brill, 2004), 42–47; Yitzhaq Feder, "A Levantine Tradition: The Kizzuwatnean Blood Rite and the Biblical Sin Offering," in *Pax Hethitica: Studies on the Hittites and Their Neighbours in Honour of Itamar Singer*, edited by Yoram Cohen, Amir Gilan, and Jared L. Miller (Wiesbaden: Harrassowitz, 2010), 101–14.

15. Knohl, *Sanctuary of Silence*, 9.

16. Baruch A. Levine, *Numbers 21–36* (AB 4A; New York: Doubleday, 2000), 397–98.

17. Driver, *Literature of the Old Testament*, 49–50; Knohl, *Sanctuary of Silence*, 106–10; Rofé, *Literature of the Hebrew Bible*, 233–34.

Leviticus 17–26 as the "Holiness Code."[18] Both sets of instructions begin with a form of centralization law and end with a row of blessings and curses. But it may be better to refer to sets of laws in the style of H as opposed to thinking of a single composition, as it is not clear that H was ever compiled as a legal collection by itself.[19] This book, therefore, sometimes refers to the "Holiness school" as the group of scribes responsible for the various legal materials in the H style.

A continuing issue of debate concerns the relationship of H to the laws of Deuteronomy (D). There are three possibilities:

1. H precedes D;
2. H follows D;
3. H and D developed simultaneously, but in different scribal circles.

The lines of this debate are most strongly drawn around the origins of Leviticus 17. From the perspective of many scholars, Leviticus 17 no less than Deuteronomy 12 assumes the presence of only one legitimate altar where sacrifice may take place. This is certainly true of Leviticus 17 in its canonical form, although Jacob Milgrom has argued that its rules were originally meant to regulate worship for a class of regional sanctuaries serviced by Levitical priests.[20] Some exegetes hold that Deuteronomy 12 reacts to the instructions of Leviticus 17, while others assume that Leviticus 17 is a reaction against Deuteronomy 12.[21] This is a difficult argument to solve because of the reference points in each chapter. For its part, Deuteronomy 12 does not refer to the wording of Leviticus 17, nor vice versa. But one need not take a rigid view of the priority of all of H to D or the reverse. The legal collections of Deuteronomy and H may have developed in dialogue with each other. There is a good case that H, no less than D (see Chapter 18), originated in the late monarchical era.[22] Both modes of thought could have continued during the exile, albeit in separate social circles. H would have been cultivated among the priests of whom Ezekiel is a representative.[23] D's

18. See Dale Patrick, *Old Testament Law* (Atlanta: John Knox, 1985), 151; Stackert, *Rewriting the Torah,* 12–14.

19. Sun, "Holiness Code," 255–56; Frank Crüsemann, *The Torah: Theology and Social History of Old Testament Law* (Minneapolis: Augsburg Fortress, 1996), 277–79.

20. Milgrom, *Leviticus 7–22,* 1503–14.

21. See the review of scholarship in Stackert, *Rewriting the Torah,* 7–10.

22. Rofé, *Literature of the Hebrew Bible,* 235.

23. Ezekiel shows dependency on the rhetoric of H. See Rofé, *Literature of the Hebrew Bible,* 235–36.

thought, however, was carried on by scribes and priests once associated with the royal court.[24]

Developments

Priestly thought offers an excellent illustration of the dynamic relationship between stability and adaptability in biblical law. Evidently, Israel's theologians were preoccupied with the nature of holiness and its demands on Israel over a long period of time. But the endeavor to define what holiness meant for Israel did not stop with the editing of the Torah into its canonical form. Ongoing attempts were made to resolve various divergences between the laws, fill in gaps, and develop their implications. In fact, this exegetical trajectory is visible in the books of Ezra and Nehemiah. These books report developments beyond those found in the laws of P and H. Among them:

- Leviticus 23:39–43 commands the building of the *sukkâ* (the booth for the harvest festival), but it does not say how. This is determined in Neh 8:13–18 based on the list of agricultural products found in Lev 23:40.
- New provisions are introduced to guarantee the steady provision of wood for the altar (Neh 10:34).

These are small examples of exegetical work that in time would create a body of oral law that would stand alongside the written Torah.

By the beginning of the rabbinic era, the oral law was considered to be authoritative as the written law.[25] Such a claim has merit when considered in the light of the Mosaic tradition described in Chapter 3. Priestly thought involves a commitment to the exegesis and development of preexisting religious tradition. For example, the laws in Lev 19:5–8 (an H text) presuppose material in P (cf. Lev 7:16–18), but they also adjust P's wording and add an explanation for the prohibition.[26] There is no reason to assume that this process of reflection and commentary was confined to the Old Testament canon.

24. For the association of Deuteronomic thought with exiles connected to the royal court, see Rainer Albertz, *Israel in Exile: The History and Literature of the Sixth Century B.C.E.* (SBLStBL 3; Atlanta: Society of Biblical Literature, 2003), 284.

25. George F. Moore, *Judaism: In the First Centuries of the Christian Era* (New York: Schocken Books, 1971), 1:251–62.

26. Milgrom, *Leviticus 17–22*, 1349.

The exegetical activity reflected in the development of P and H, therefore, is evidence of great intellectual and cultural vitality. Concern for authentic connection with the Holy One of Israel appears as a theme of many extrabiblical works from the Second Temple period, e.g., Jubilees, Maccabees, the works of Philo, and the Dead Sea Scrolls. These writings come from Jewish groups intensely concerned with matters of ritual and moral purity, the same issues that preoccupy P and H.

The same preoccupations constitute an important backdrop for the emergence of both the rabbinic movement and the early church. In many ways, the various models for relating to the biblical God proposed by groups of Jewish thinkers in the first century CE were grounded on assumptions about the nature of holiness and what it demanded of human beings by way of authentic response.[27] The importance of these questions is underscored by the first petition in the prayer Jesus taught his disciples, "hallowed be your name."[28] The opening of the Lord's Prayer makes common cause with the underlying concerns of P and H: holiness is a matter of ultimate concern for all who wish to worship the God of Israel.

In this regard, it is worth reflecting on the realism that Priestly thinkers had towards the Holy One. They regarded YHWH as a being who has to be approached with care. Has the God of the Christian church ceased to be dangerous? As church history has witnessed a great deal of violence perpetrated in the name of Christ, this question merits careful consideration. Of the many examples that can be given, the persistence of Christian anti-Semitism bears special mention. Whatever may be the value in identifying the Christian communion as (a) successor to biblical Israel, using this claim as an agenda for persecution and disenfranchisement of Judaism is contrary to all that is holy. It remains imperative to approach the idea of God with due caution, as it can unleash curse as well as blessing. Bad theology can be lethal!

27. J. Stanley Glen, *The Parables of Conflict in Luke* (Philadelphia: Westminster, 1962), 134–39.

28. This petition finds parallels in the openings of other traditional Jewish prayers that acknowledge the holiness of God. See Herbert W. Basser, *The Mind Behind the Gospels: A Commentary to Matthew 1–14* (Boston: Academic Studies, 2009), 165–67.

CHAPTER 11

The Tabernacle: A Palace in the Wilderness

Read: Exodus 25–40

At Sinai, Moses received the plans for a portable shrine. This moveable temple is called the "tabernacle" or the "tent of meeting." It stretches the imagination that such an elaborate building could have been built by oppressed slaves within a year or so of fleeing Egypt. What is the point of reporting that this splendid holy place was erected in the wilderness? This can be addressed by underscoring the fact that the tabernacle and its complex of rituals mean to reflect the kingdom of God.

At the heart of Israel's life in the wilderness stands not simply a temple, but a palace. In fact, the center of the tabernacle, the holy of holies, is conceived as a throne room. Moreover, Israel's Priestly thinkers believed that the real presence of the heavenly king had located itself in the tabernacle. Following a brief discussion of the structure and origins of the laws for building the tabernacle is a focus on aspects of its symbolism. The chapter ends with some remarks about how the symbol of the tabernacle developed in postbiblical times.

Origins of the Tabernacle Laws

Two sets of instructions for building the tabernacle bracket the story about Israel's worship of the "golden calf":

The Structure of the Tabernacle Laws in Exodus

Exodus 25–31 Construction of the tabernacle I
Exodus 32–34 Israel worships the golden calf
Exodus 35–40 Construction of the tabernacle II

The design of the tabernacle is set out twice. Exodus 25–31 can be described as a "prescriptive ritual text" because it gives instructions for the building of the tabernacle (I). The same details are re-presented in Exodus 35–40 (II), which can be described as a "descriptive ritual text." Descriptive ritual texts resemble temple archives that record the disbursement of goods and material for religious purposes.[1] The description of the furnishings for the tabernacle seems to be more systematic in Exodus 35–40.[2] Nevertheless, both texts reflect the same theological viewpoint. The following discussion will focus primarily on the prescriptions in Exodus 25–31.

Why has the canonical form of the Torah created a span of text by having the construction of the tabernacle bracket the golden calf incident? First, the golden calf story acts as a foundation narrative for the selection of the tribe of Levi as priestly functionaries at the tabernacle. Second, this narrative of judgment, forgiveness, and covenant renewal finds its context literally *inside* the tabernacle texts. Literary arrangement, therefore, serves to place an emphasis on prayer (32:11–14) and writing (34:1) by putting these activities inside the tabernacle texts. As explained below, this emphasis was important for readers during the postexilic period.

In its present form Exodus 25–31, therefore, contains features that reflect concerns of the postexilic era. For this reason, some scholars think this text should be regarded as a fiction.[3] Nevertheless, its origins are not easily dated. In ancient Near Eastern literature, various texts recount receiving instructions for building temples from the gods. Examples include the cyl-

1. Baruch A. Levine and William W. Hallo, "Offerings to the Temple Gates at Ur," *HUCA* 38 (1967): 17–18.

2. For example, the incense altar seems out of place in Exodus 30. See Carol Meyers, "Realms of Sanctity: The Case of the 'Misplaced' Incense Altar in the Tabernacle Texts of Exodus," in *Texts, Temples, and Traditions: A Tribute to Menahem Haran*, edited by Michael V. Fox et al. (Winona Lake: Eisenbrauns, 1996), 33–46.

3. E.g., Hanna Liss, "The Imaginary Sanctuary: The Priestly Code as an Example of Fictional Literature in the Hebrew Bible," in *Judah and the Judeans in the Persian Period*, edited by Oded Lipschitz and Manfred Oeming (Winona Lake: Eisenbrauns, 2006), 663–89.

inders of Gudea (late third millennium BCE)[4] and the Sippar Cylinder of the Neo-Babylonian king Nabonidus (ca. 553).[5] These texts stand on their own and are not integrated into larger narratives. They provide extrabiblical evidence for thinking that the instructions to build the tabernacle could have been transmitted independently of their present narrative context.[6]

Below, it will be shown that the tabernacle design recalls (or anticipates) the temple of Solomon. Although the canonical form of Exodus 25–31 must be dated to the postexilic period, it is not outside the realm of possibility that its core was set down in the monarchical era. Perhaps the ascription of the tabernacle's design to Moses was originally intended to deflect criticism from the fact that Solomon's temple was constructed on a Phoenician (i.e., Canaanite) model. The attribution to Moses might also reflect a conflict for control of the temple between the Jerusalem priesthood and the monarchy (cf. 2 Chr 26:16–21; Ezek 43:6–9).[7]

The Symbolism of the Tabernacle

The Organization of Exodus 25–31

Sections		Speech Headings
I Tabernacle	25:1–27:19	YHWH said to Moses (25:1)
II Tent of Meeting	27:20–31:11	YHWH said to Moses (30:11)
		YHWH said to Moses (30:17)
		YHWH said to Moses (30:22)
		YHWH said to Moses (30:34)
		YHWH said to Moses (31:1)
III Sabbath observance	31:12–17	YHWH said to Moses (31:12)
IV Tablets	31:18	

4. "The Cylinders of Gudea," trans. Richard Averbeck (*COS* 2.155:417–29).

5. "The Sippar Cylinder of Nabonidus," trans. Paul-Alain Beaulieu (*COS* 2.123:310–13).

6. For a comparison of temple-building accounts in the ancient Near East and the Bible, see Victor A. Hurowitz, *"I Have Built You an Exalted House": Temple Building in the Bible in Light of Mesopotamian and North-West Semitic Writings* (JSOTSup 115; Sheffield: JSOT, 1992).

7. See Cornelis Houtman, *Exodus,* vol. 3 (HCOT; Leuven: Peeters, 2000), 332.

Exodus 25–31 can be divided into four sections. The instructions here describe a cult-place referred to as both "tabernacle" (I) and "tent of meeting" (II). While these titles may have source critical value in certain sections of the Pentateuch, that is not their significance here. Rather, a distinction is drawn between the physical structure of this cult-place ("tabernacle") and its purpose ("tent of meeting").[8]

Section III contains instructions regarding Sabbath observance.[9] Similar instructions also begin the descriptive ritual text in Exod 35:2–3. Why emphasize the practice by this kind of repetition? The combination of Sabbath observance with tabernacle construction points to the exilic era and its aftermath.[10] During that time, honoring the Sabbath became a marker of Jewish identity, especially when many Jews had no access to the Second Temple. There was a message here for readers who lived in the Jewish diaspora: Sabbath observance was a sacred task that put them in harmony with the goals of tabernacle worship.

Section IV is a narrative notice that ties the revelation of the tabernacle's plans with the golden calf incident in Exodus 32–34. Readers are to understand that the tables of the law given to Moses were to be placed in the tabernacle. Chapter 5 noted that one of the functions of the tablets of the law was to represent the nature of God to the community. Tellingly, the culmination of the tabernacle dedication service is a realization of the presence of God in the holy of holies (Exod 40:34). The two endings of the tabernacle instructions inform each other. Their implication is that divine presence is found in the written law as well as in the holy of holies, a belief that became extremely important as the scriptural concept developed in the Second Temple period.

8. Thomas B. Dozeman, *Commentary on Exodus* (ECC; Grand Rapids: Eerdmans, 2009), 602–3.

9. Exod 31:12–17 and its parallel in 35:2–3 show signs of the rhetoric of H. See Israel Knohl, *The Sanctuary of Silence: The Priestly Torah and the Holiness School* (Minneapolis: Fortress, 1995), 16. This shows that the tabernacle laws underwent revision from an earlier form.

10. Moshe Weinfeld, *The Place of the Law in the Religion of Ancient Israel* (VTSup 100; Leiden: Brill, 2004), 18.

Design of the Tabernacle

Attempting to use the instructions to imagine exactly how the tabernacle could have been built is challenging.[11] For example, various details about the construction of its frame and the coverings have to be reconciled and put into a coherent picture. Nevertheless, the overall dimensions of the tabernacle and the placement of its furnishings are not in dispute:

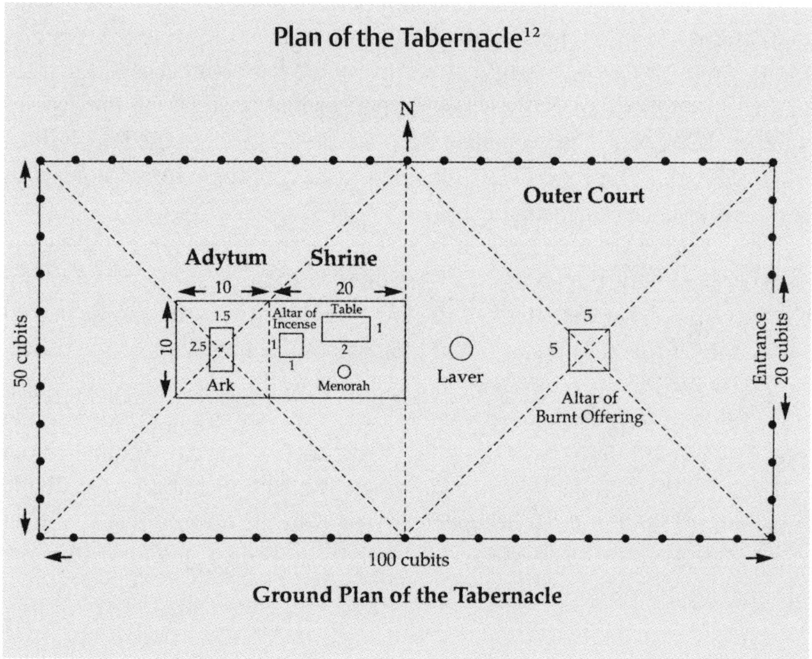

A prominent characteristic of the tabernacle plan is its symmetry.[13] The total enclosure represents a rectangle that can be divided into two perfect squares. The holy of holies occupies the center of the square opposite the courtyard.

11. E.g., Richard E. Friedman, "The Tabernacle in the Temple," *BA* 43 (1980): 241–48; William H. C. Propp, *Exodus 19–40* (AB 2A; New York: Doubleday, 2006), 495–528.

12. From Jacob Milgrom, *Leviticus 1–16* (AB 3; New York: Doubleday, 1991), 135. Copyright Yale University Press. Used by permission.

13. The motif of symmetry extends into the way in which the various tribes of Israel were to camp around the tabernacle (Numbers 2). Their distribution is illustrated in Dale Patrick, *Old Testament Law* (Atlanta: John Knox, 1985), 149.

Exactly in the center of the holy of holies is the ark of the covenant. Corresponding to it in the courtyard square is the altar of sacrifice.

The design of the tabernacle has a parallel in the description of Solomon's temple (1 Kings 6–7). Both buildings have a tripartite structure that includes a cubelike adytum (the holy of holies), a rectangular room called the holy place (shrine) through which it was accessed, and an outer courtyard in which sacrificial offerings were burnt on an altar. The connection between the descriptions of the tabernacle and Solomon's temple reinforces the idea that the tabernacle recalls the First Temple.[14] Originally, the Solomonic temple was surrounded by a single courtyard, as was the tabernacle. There was no division between an area for lay men and lay women; that was a development made in the Second Temple period.[15]

Worldview

The tabernacle represents an important space for the articulation of the Priestly worldview. Six perspectives can be emphasized:

1. Graded holiness
2. The tabernacle and creation
3. The tabernacle as a dwelling place for God
4. The tabernacle as an expression of ancient psychology
5. The tabernacle as portable palace
6. The tabernacle as center and periphery

1) "Graded holiness" is an important value in Priestly thinking, which is reflected in the design of the tabernacle.[16] As one moves through the instructions for building the tabernacle from inside to outside, there is a progression from what is more valuable (made of gold and silver) to what is less valuable (made of bronze), from what is most holy (the shrine with the ark of the covenant) to what is less holy (the courtyard of the tabernacle).[17]

14. Menahem Haran, *Temples and Temple-Service in Ancient Israel* (Winona Lake: Eisenbrauns, 1985), 198–92.

15. Haran, *Temples and Temple-Service*, 192–93.

16. Discussed at length in Philip Peter Jenson, *Graded Holiness: A Key to the Priestly Conception of the World* (JSOTSup 106; Sheffield: JSOT, 1992).

17. Haran, *Temples and Temple-Service*, 158–65.

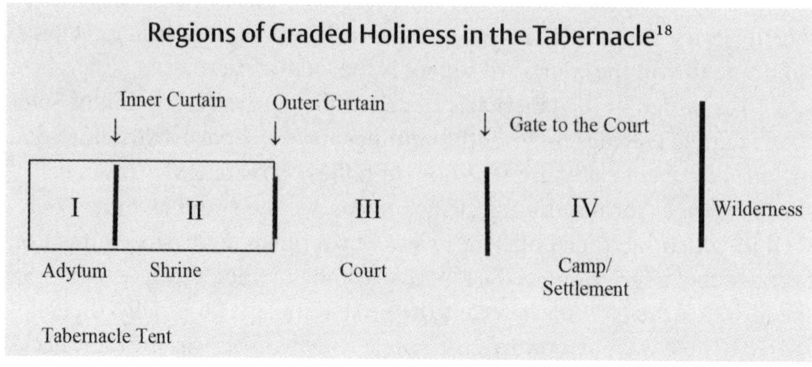

As a sacred space, the holy of holies sits innermost in a series of defined spaces. Each has its own boundaries and conditions for entry. Movement towards the most holy place becomes restricted to fewer and fewer people. Only members of the priestly tribe of Levi can enter the "holy place" (shrine II), and only the person who represents Aaron can enter the "holy of holies" (adytum I); see Lev 16:2–3. It is possible that the courtyard of the tabernacle (III) was divided into spaces in which lay persons and priestly functionaries could mingle and spaces restricted to priestly activities, but this is difficult to determine.[19] As we will see in Chapter 15, persons living in the camp (IV) had to keep themselves in a state of ritual cleanness in order to enter the courtyard of the tabernacle. Outside the camp was the wilderness, a place that could have clean and unclean spaces. Certain kinds of ritually impure people (e.g., lepers) were required to live outside the camp until they were declared to be ritually clean.

2) The seven speeches of Moses in Exodus 25–31 recall the Priestly account of the creation of the world in seven days (Gen 1:1–2:3). In fact, there are indications that the tabernacle not only recalls, but actually fulfills, God's intentions in the creation of the world. For example, prominent in the holy place is the menorah, most likely a symbol of the tree of life. Just as the spirit of God (*rûaḥ ʾĕlohîm*) was present at the creation of the universe (Gen 1:2), the *rûaḥ ʾĕlohîm* is bestowed on Bezalel so he can build the tabernacle (Exod 31:3). In addition, the tabernacle is dedicated on New Year's day (Exod 40:17), which parallels the first day of creation.[20] The presence of the tabernacle in

18. Based on Jenson, *Graded Holiness*, 89–93.

19. Jenson, *Graded Holiness*, 91.

20. Ralph W. Klein, "Back to the Future: The Tabernacle in the Book of Exodus," *Int* 50 (1996): 266.

the midst of Israel, therefore, offers the possibility of restoring the relationship between humanity and God that was broken by the first generations of people who had been created (cf. Genesis 3; 4; 6). According to P's worldview, the divine initiative at repairing this broken relationship realized its fulfillment in the indwelling of YHWH in the tabernacle (Exod 40:34–35).[21]

3) In paradise, God was present to humanity (Gen 3:8). A major function of the tabernacle is to symbolize the presence of God among the people. The adytum, or holy of holies, contains two objects that are separate yet physically associated with each other: the "mercy seat" (*kippōret*) and the "ark" (*'ārôn*). While the *kippōret* sits upon the ark, it is not the cover for the ark. Rather, the ark acts as a base on which the *kippōret* sits.[22] Each object conveys something about the presence of God.

Cherubim face each other with their wings extending across the *kippōret* (Exod 25:18–20). Most scholars believe that the cherubim were similar to the composite creatures found in ancient Near Eastern art associated with guarding palaces and thrones. The cherub motif makes the holy of holies a sort of throne-room for the divine presence.[23] YHWH may have been imagined as seated on the wings of the cherubim, with the *kippōret* representing his throne while the ark served as his footstool.

The other symbol of the divine presence is the ark. The ark in the tabernacle synthesizes various ark traditions in the Bible, and scholars have different views about what an ark might have originally contained.[24] But according to Exod 31:18, "When [God] finished speaking with Moses on Mount Sinai, he gave him the two tablets of the testimony (*'ēdūt*), tablets of stone, written with the finger of God." Exod 25:16 indicates that these tablets were deposited in the ark. Exodus 34:28 and Deut 10:4 identify these tablets with the Ten Commandments. Noted in Chapters 5–6 is evidence that one of the purposes of the Ten Commandments is to represent God to the community. The idea that God is present through the reading of authoritative texts has a powerful resonance in Judaism.

4) What might the tabernacle tell us about how ancient Israel understood the human psyche? According to contemporary depth psychology, God can be understood as an archetype or symbol of the Self.[25] If the sacred spaces

21. Eckart Otto, *Das Gesetz des Mose* (Darmstadt: WBG, 2007), 179–80.

22. Haran, *Temples and Temple-Service*, 246–51.

23. Haran, *Temples and Temple-Service*, 252–53.

24. Houtman, *Exodus*, 3:373.

25. E.g., Viktor E. Frankl, *The Unconscious God: Psychotherapy and Theology* (New York:

Figure 5. A prince is seated on a cherub throne during a victory celebration. Note the composite nature of the supernatural guardian, whose other wing probably extends across the throne as a seat for the ruler: human head, leonine body, eagle's wings. From James B. Pritchard, ed., *The Ancient Near East in Pictures Relating to the Old Testament* (Princeton: Princeton University Press, 1954), p. 111 #332. © The Oriental Institute of the University of Chicago. Used with permission.

constructed by ancient Israel and its neighbors were designed to evoke a sense of the presence of a deity,[26] they might also say something about ancient concepts of human nature. The fact that there is a document containing YHWH's covenant commands in the very heart of the holy of holies suggests something about how early Jewish thinkers thought about human psychology. They assumed that, like YHWH, human nature is essentially relational, moral, and good. It is not intrinsically marred by sin; it is capable of hearing God and responding well.[27]

5) Tent shrines are well attested in ancient Near Eastern sources.[28] It may be significant that a prominent feature of Persian monarchy was the tent-palace.[29] The lengthy description of the tabernacle would convey a subtle

---

Simon and Schuster, 1975), 148–58; Ithamar Gruenwald, "Jewish and Christian Messianism: The Psychoanalytic Approach of Heinz Kohut," in *Psychology and the Bible: A New Way to Read Scripture*, edited by J. Harold Ellens and Wayne G. Rollins (Westport: Praeger, 2004), 1:253–54.

26. Mark S. Smith, "Like Deities, Like Temples (Like People)," in *Temple and Worship in Biblical Israel*, edited by John Day (LHBOTS 422; London: T. & T. Clark, 2007), 3–27.

27. For a connection between depth psychology and covenantal thinking, see James Olthuis, "The Covenanting Metaphor of the Christian Faith and the Self Psychology of Heinz Kohut," *SR* 18 (1989): 313–24.

28. Weinfeld, *Place of the Law*, 41.

29. Pierre Briant, *From Cyrus to Alexander: A History of the Persian Empire* (Winona Lake: Eisenbrauns, 2002), 256–58.

message in this regard. While Judah had been reduced to a province in the vast Persian Empire, biblical ideology contended that the God who reigned in the portable palace in the wilderness was the true king of Israel.

6) While the tabernacle is depicted as standing in the center of Israel's camp in the wilderness, it also represents a divinely ordained dwelling erected in the very periphery of civilization: in the desert. Paradoxically, God is most present in an environment where humanity is most absent. Benjamin Sommer has suggested that the Priestly tabernacle anticipated a doctrine of creation found in Jewish mysticism (Kabbalah) in which the creator of the world remains in exile from his creation.[30]

Developments

Later Jewish thinkers developed the tabernacle idea in a number of ways.[31] What follows concentrates on the idea that the tabernacle symbolizes divine presence even when access to it or its corresponding structures (i.e., the temple) was no longer possible. For that reason, it could be realized metaphorically as well as literally. At least three different aspects of the tabernacle contributed to its symbolic appropriation by groups in early Judaism:

1. the lengthy repetitions between Exodus 25–31 and 35–40;
2. the role of Sabbath observance;
3. the tabernacle as the center of a community.

1) Nowadays, it is common to think about the virtual reality that is accessible through computer games. Still, a form of virtual reality has been accessible to human beings through imaginative acts of reading long before the advent of modern technology. As Mark George points out, the tabernacle narratives and laws create a mental space as well as a physical space.[32] This was very important in the postexilic period, when large numbers of Jews had no access to

30. Benjamin D. Sommer, "Conflicting Constructions of Divine Presence in the Priestly Tabernacle," *BibInt* 9 (2001): 58–63.

31. See Craig R. Koester, *The Dwelling of God: The Tabernacle in the Old Testament, Intertestamental Jewish Literature, and the New Testament* (CBQMS 22; Washington: Catholic Biblical Association of America, 1989).

32. Mark K. George, *Israel's Tabernacle as Social Space* (AIL 2: Atlanta: Society of Biblical Literature, 2009), 18–19.

the temple in Jerusalem. They were spread across the Mediterranean world and the Near East, with significant populations in Egypt and Babylonia.

In the absence of access to the temple, a strategy of virtual access was available through reading the Torah. This is one of the reasons for the repetition of the description of the tabernacle in Exodus 35–40 and the lengthy and detailed instructions for the sacrificial cult in Leviticus 1–16. The same strategy would play an important role in preserving Jewish identity after the destruction of the Second Temple; for according to rabbinical teaching Torah study became the equivalent of temple service.[33] As the rabbis say, after the end of the temple "we pray and read."[34]

2) As noted above, Sabbath laws come at the end of the prescriptive ritual text in Exod 31:12–17 and they also begin the descriptive ritual text in Exod 35:2–3. This detail seems out of place in its immediate context; after all, no other sacred observances are listed in the same breath as instructions to build the tabernacle. Yet, this repetition of the Sabbath laws constitutes a form of ring composition. The structure is deliberate; it underscores the idea that Sabbath observance can work to create identity when the tabernacle/temple is not accessible.

Abraham Joshua Heschel observes that while orthodox Judaism continues to look for the day when the temple is restored, in many ways Judaism has become a religion of sacred time rather than sacred space.[35] This development is anticipated by the prominence given to the Sabbath rules in the tabernacle texts. Beginning in the exilic period a key mark of Jewish identity was Sabbath observance. Coupled with study of the Scripture, Jews who observed the Sabbath in the diaspora could claim an identity with the generation that once camped around the palace in the wilderness and had access to its spiritual benefits.

3) A third development appears in attempts to identify community groupings with the congregation gathered around the tabernacle. For example, while it seems that early Christians worshipped in the Jerusalem temple, the New Testament symbol system transformed tabernacle/temple imagery in order to signify the body of Christ. Texts such as John 1:14 and 1 Cor

33. Max Kadushin, *The Rabbinic Mind*, 3rd ed. (New York: Bloch, 1972), 213–14.

34. Sandor Goodhart, *The Prophetic Law: Essays in Judaism, Girardianism, Literary Studies, and the Ethical* (East Lansing: Michigan State University Press, 2014), xxiv.

35. Abraham Joshua Heschel, *God in Search of Man: A Philosophy of Judaism* (New York: Farrar, Straus and Giroux, 1983), 200.

3:16 represent Christian claims that saw in the advent of Jesus a new reality that superseded temple worship.[36] This is plainly stated with respect to the tabernacle in Heb 9:11–12.

The theologies of Christian supersessionism have become, quite properly, the subject of intense scrutiny in recent decades, coupled as they are with the rhetoric of anti-Judaism. Nevertheless, adaptation of temple/tabernacle imagery to the Jesus movement rests on a Jewish foundation. According to early Judaism, the earthly temple/tabernacle was a physical manifestation of a heavenly prototype (Exod 25:9). Even when the physical tabernacle or temple disappeared, the spiritual reality these sacred spaces symbolized remained. For that reason, it could be realized in metaphorical as well as literal ways. Just as God was present in the midst of the tabernacle, so the divine presence was thought to manifest itself in the virtual sacred space that was the spirit-filled body of Christ.

36. Koester, *The Dwelling of God*, 186.

CHAPTER 12

Sacrifice: Communication and Community-Making

Read: Leviticus 1–10

One of the persistent caricatures of Old Testament religion is that it is centered on an angry deity whose rage is unappeased except by the frequent offering of bloody sacrifices. The goal of this chapter and those that immediately follow (13–15) is to oppose this reductionist and unfair description of the purpose of sacrificial rituals in Priestly Torah. Admittedly, the enthusiasm with which biblical writers view the sacrificial cult (e.g., 1 Kgs 8:62–64; 2 Chr 35:7–9; Pss 66:13–15; 116:17–19) is hard for many contemporary readers to share. Consequently, it is difficult to put oneself into the mindset of ancient readers, most of whom would not question the utility of animal sacrifice as a way of coming near to God.

A brief survey such as this can only indicate some likely paths through the large and dense literature on the nature of sacrifice in biblical culture and in comparable societies around the world. The survey begins by trying to identify the features that characterize sacrifices in Priestly literature. This will lead to a discussion of sacrifice as means of ritual communication. The chapter concludes with a brief reflection on the social vision communicated by sacrificial rituals in Leviticus.

What Biblical Rituals Are Best Called Sacrifices?

In order to understand the nature of biblical sacrifice, it is important to observe that cultic acts of sacrifice belong to the larger category of ritual.

Rituals

Scholars generally acknowledge that the concept of "ritual" is hard to define. However, it would not go too far wrong to claim that a ritual is a set of formalized actions, done repeatedly, that communicate important social values to the people who participate in it.[1] Just what these social values are and how a particular ritual communicates them varies tremendously; but, in general, participation in ritual activities helps to strengthen relationships between group members. By the same logic, engaging in effective ritual actions in sacred space serves to establish and maintain authentic community with the deity. It follows, therefore, that sacrifices (like other rituals) are important forms of social communication.

Sacrifices

What criteria distinguish a sacrifice from other kinds of rituals in biblical law? Problems involved in classifying the cereal offering described in Leviticus 2 throw some light on this question. Despite the fact that it appears in a list of animal offerings in Leviticus 1–3, the cereal offering is generally ignored by theorists of biblical sacrifice.[2] If one comes to the text with the idea that sacrifice *must* involve killing an animal in sacred space, then not much consideration will be given to offerings of grain or other vegetable products as forms of sacrifice. Recent scholarship has suggested, however, that the element common to all priestly forms of sacrifice is burning.[3] From this perspective, the cereal offering of Leviticus 2 qualifies as a sacrifice, for a portion is burned on the altar.

However, is burning sufficient to mark sacrifice in Priestly literature? Another important component is blood offering. This is apparent in the ritual of the red heifer. The red heifer is killed outside the camp. After it has been bled (by having its throat cut, the usual way of killing a domestic animal), some of its blood is ritually sprinkled in the direction of the tabernacle; but most of its blood is burned with the rest of the animal and collected as

1. David Janzen, *The Social Meanings of Sacrifice in the Hebrew Bible* (BZAW 344; Berlin: de Gruyter, 2004), 34–35.

2. Christian A. Eberhart, *The Sacrifice of Jesus: Understanding Atonement Biblically* (Minneapolis: Fortress, 2011), 76–77.

3. Gary Anderson, "Sacrifice and Sacrificial Offerings (OT)," *ABD* 5:873; Eberhart, *Sacrifice of Jesus*, 78–79.

ashes (Num 19:3–5). If the requirement is that burning has to take place on the altar, then the slaughter and burning of the red heifer cannot count as a sacrifice. Yet, the red heifer is explicitly called a "purification offering" (*ḥaṭṭā't*) in Num 19:9. It seems to possess this status because some of its blood is offered in the direction of the sanctuary.[4]

Therefore, it seems that there were (at least) two markers of sacrifice in ancient Israelite religion. One is burning all or parts of the offering on the altar. The other is blood offering. More will be said about their meaning in the next few chapters below. Still, the significance of blood offering is emphasized even in ritual instructions for sacrifices that involve burning, such as the purification rituals described in Leviticus 4. This an important observation for thinking about the appropriation of sacrificial imagery in the New Testament. Jesus's death is connected to the sacrificial system through the metaphor of blood offering (e.g., Rom 3:25; Eph 1:7; Heb 9:12)—not through burning.

The Communication Value of Biblical Sacrifices

Above, the word "sacrifice" has been used as if its meaning was clear and undisputed. In fact, there is a great deal of debate about what a sacrifice is and how to identify an action as a sacrifice in any given culture.[5] Even the definition of sacrifice offered above may seem rather arbitrary. Who is to say that other forms of offering rituals should not be considered sacrificial? Nevertheless, despite a lack of scholarly consensus about what constitutes a sacrifice in the various religions of the world, some commonalities in their communication functions can be discerned. There are three that concern this discussion:

1. social solidarity
2. social indexing
3. conflict resolution

Not every sacrificial action corresponds equally to all three of these categories.

4. Jacob Milgrom, *Leviticus 1–16* (AB 3; New York: Doubleday, 1991), 171–73.

5. Milgrom, *Leviticus 1–16*, 442–43; James W. Watts, "The Rhetoric of Sacrifice," in *Ritual and Metaphor: Sacrifice in the Bible*, edited by Christian A. Eberhart (RBS 68; Atlanta: Society of Biblical Literature, 2011), 5–8.

1) Social solidarity

Various parallels can be drawn between the sacrificial practices of ancient Israel and societies in the Levant, Anatolia, Greece, and Mesopotamia.[6] These parallels, however, cannot fully explain how the various sacrificial practices found in Priestly literature operated. Each system has its own particularities and structure. Nevertheless, some consensus exists among theorists about the social effects of sacrificial actions across cultures. There is general agreement that the effect of sacrificial rituals is the construction of some kind of viable community.[7]

Sacrifices are ritually consumed in two ways. They are consumed as food by their offerers or priestly representatives. They are also consumed by fire on the altar and by blood sprinkling. Consequently, we can think of the communication functions of sacrifices in terms of the benefits of sharing a meal. Not only is hunger assuaged, but social relationships are created and reinforced by eating together.

Ancient societies such as Israel, of course, believed that their social boundaries included divine beings as well as human beings. In order to (literally and symbolically) feed the group's need for social solidarity, it made sense that the holy reality also participated in the rituals of consumption that reinforced the health and relationships of the group. Certain sacrifices, therefore, symbolize holy communion. The items consumed by the deity went up in smoke on the altar. The net effect of the shared meal was to reinforce a sense of connectedness between its divine and human participants.

6. See the extensive discussion of cultural parallels in T. H. Gaster, "Sacrifices and Offerings, OT," *IDB* 4:148–53.

7. See Walter Burkert, *Homo Necans: The Anthropology of Ancient Greek Sacrificial Ritual and Myth* (Berkeley: University of California Press, 1983), 1–12; René Girard *The Scapegoat* (Baltimore: Johns Hopkins University Press, 1986), 24–44; Maurice Bloch, *Prey into Hunter: The Politics of Religious Experience* (Cambridge: Cambridge University Press, 1992), 24–45; Nancy Jay, *Throughout Your Generations Forever: Sacrifice, Religion, and Paternity* (Chicago: University of Chicago Press, 1992), 30–40; Janzen, *Social Meanings of Sacrifice,* 36–75.

2) *Social indexing*

Another important component of meals, especially in ancient Mediterranean cultures, is that they often demonstrate who is at the center of the group and who is on the periphery.[8] We can recognize this function of meals by the fact that some modern nonsacrificial rituals (such as weddings and award dinners) have a head table. Often the people being honored at a banquet are served first and their (relative) social importance is represented spatially by where the table is placed in the banquet hall.

Sociologists sometimes refer to the ranking function of meals as a form of social indexing. Many sacrificial rituals engaged in types of social indexing.[9] The distribution of food communicates relative degrees of importance. This function of the ceremonial meal is also visible in priestly rites of sacrifice. Offering choice pieces of the animal to the deity (e.g., some of the fat) or giving the animal entirely to the altar (as in whole burnt offerings) communicates the importance of the heavenly king and the desire on the part of his people to live in healthy positive relationships with him.

3) *Conflict resolution*

Theorists of sacrifice have also noted that sacrificial rituals serve to address conflicts that threaten a sense of solidarity.[10] That is, sacrifice can also represent movement away as well as movement towards. This function can be charted by the following table.

8. Rick F. Talbott, *Jesus, Paul, and Power: Rhetoric, Ritual, and Metaphor in Ancient Mediterranean Christianity* (Eugene: Cascade, 2010), 158.

9. Jay, *Throughout Your Generations Forever*, 6–7.

10. Prominent here are the theories of René Girard about the origins and functions of sacrifice. For a summary, see Robert Hamerton-Kelly, "Religion and the Thought of René Girard," in *Curing Violence*, edited by Mark I. Wallace and Theophis H. Smith (Sonoma: Polebridge, 1994), 15–16. Other theorists also find hostile attitudes and actions represented in sacrificial actions. See Bloch's theory of "rebounding violence" *(Prey into Hunter*, 24–45) and Jay's idea that alimentary sacrifice in many traditional agrarian societies provided ritual means to rank male hierarchies (*Throughout Your Generations Forever*, 40).

A Typology of Sacrificial Actions[11]

Positive Pole		**Negative Pole**
At-one-ment		Atonement
Communion		Expiation
Conjunction	← Movement →	Disjunction
Joining		Separation
Integration		Differentiation

Sacrificial rituals were thought to have the power to arrest the movement of individuals and groups towards the negative pole and help them move towards a positive state of being. Just how sacrifice actually effected this kind of movement is a matter of continuing debate and discussion. Certainly none of its ancient practitioners thought about what they were doing in such abstract terms. Movement away from symbols of sin and death is represented in the chart by terms such as "expiation," "separation," and "disjunction." An offering ritual may also serve to strengthen the group by creating a new sense of cohesion and solidarity with the positive values of life (salvation). This motivation is represented in the chart by terms such as "communion," "joining," and "conjunction."[12]

According to Leviticus, the primary sacrifices that address movement away from a negative realm of being are purification and reparation offerings. They will be described in more detail in Chapter 14. But it is worth noting here that they involve a paradox; for they assume that the products of death could arrest the movement towards the negative sphere associated with death.

What particularly marks rituals of purification and reparation offerings is the sprinkling of blood towards some symbol of the divine presence. It is difficult to explain why these ceremonies of blood offering were thought to reduce the perception of conflict. Some of these explanatory difficulties are created by ambiguities in the semantic field of the main verb which connotes "expiation" or "atonement" in Leviticus, the Hebrew root *k-p-r*. One opinion

11. Jay, *Throughout Your Generations Forever,* 17–18. The chart is based on William S. Morrow, "Violence and Religion in the Christian Tradition," in *Teaching Religion and Violence*, edited by Brian K. Pennington (AAR Teaching Religion Series; New York: Oxford University Press, 2009), 109.

12. For the importance of polar thinking in Leviticus, see the chart in Douglas Davies, "An Interpretation of Sacrifice in Leviticus," *ZAW* 89 (1977): 394.

holds the idea that *k-p-r* connotes "cleansing"; it sees the use of the blood in rituals for sin as having a kind of cleaning property, almost as if it were a sort of cultic "detergent."[13] Others insist that the concept signified by *k-p-r* is more closely related to associations with the idea of "covering." In this case, there has been a breach or break in the integrity of the community which needs to be covered over and repaired. According to this view, the sacrificial blood repairs a breach in the covering provided by YHWH's covenant.[14] A third possibility regards *k-p-r* as connoting the idea of "ransom."[15] In this case, the divine king requires compensation for an offense against his sovereignty or glory.

It is likely incorrect to insist that only one of these opinions is correct. Several motivations were probably involved in expiatory sacrifices. Generally, however, they were directed towards defusing the potential of conflict between the holy realm and the compromised condition of the offerers. To that end, worshippers used sacrifices of purification and reparation to act out their resolve to break relationships with symbols of sin, death, and chaos. They did so in more than one way. For example, their sacrifices could cleanse the sanctuary of pollution through blood offerings (Lev 4:1–5:13). Worshippers could also compensate for unacceptable actions by offering a fine along with the sacrifice (the reparation offering of Lev 5:14–6:7) and by making confession of their sins—as the case required.[16]

Biblical Israel: A Consecrated Society

Sacrificial rituals, therefore, are ways of creating and maintaining a human society in symbolic terms. They received their religious importance in ancient Israel from the belief that a viable human community includes good

13. Paradigmatic is Milgrom (*Leviticus 1–16*, 254–58), who talks about the blood of the purification offering as a kind of "ritual detergent."

14. Mary Douglas, "Atonement in Leviticus," *JSQ* 1 (1993): 109–30; see the appreciative comments of Douglas's position in Roy E. Gane, *Cult and Character: Purification Offerings, Day of Atonement, and Theodicy* (Winona Lake: Eisenbrauns, 2005), 192–93.

15. E.g., Yitzhaq Feder (*Blood Expiation in Hittite and Biblical Ritual: Origins, Context, and Meaning* [WAWSup 2; Leiden: Brill, 2012], 194–96) suggests that the rite of sprinkling blood on the horns of the altar appears to be based on traditional ideas of compensation for murder. This ancient idea has been transformed in a cultic rite for expiating guilt conceived in more general and also less violent terms. See also Mark Boda, *A Severe Mercy: Sin and Its Remedy in the Old Testament* (Siphrut 1; Winona Lake: Eisenbrauns, 2009), 70–71.

16. Boda, *A Severe Mercy*, 62–67.

relations between God and the people. A key interest of biblical sacrifice, therefore, is to communicate Israel's commitment to its God. This is an important point to keep in mind when thinking about the motivations and reasons for sacrifice. Especially in the Christian church, there is a pervasive opinion that the chief motivation for sacrifice in the Old Testament is to deal with sin. Unfortunately, this view is one-sided at best and does not represent the richness and even the primary interests of the priestly system of sacrifices.

Of course, there are grounds for discerning a distinct uneasiness about matters related to purification and sin in Leviticus. This anxiety emerged out of Israel's precarious situation in the exilic and postexilic eras. Throughout the Babylonian captivity and into the Persian and Hellenistic periods, Israel had no control of its political boundaries. It found itself mixed up in a cosmopolitan and globalized world with multiple challenges to its religious identity. In many ways, the community centered around the Second Temple (symbolized by the tabernacle) was a minority group, seeking ways to maintain its integrity in a world indifferent to its values and sense of self.[17]

It should come as no surprise, therefore, that a significant goal in the offering system of Priestly literature is boundary maintenance. This appears, for example, in the concern for graded holiness illustrated by the plan of the tabernacle in the last chapter. Ritual means are used to keep Israel closely tied to the sacred life of sanctuary service, while keeping various threats that could compromise the integrity of the community at bay. These techniques have to be viewed within a social context in which Israel's cultural and ethnic boundaries were severely compromised. The fact that this anxiety can be discerned, however, should not be used to diminish the rich communication values that biblical sacrifice sought to impart. Sacrifice communicated social solidarity, devotion, and consecration to God as well as the need to distance oneself from threats to the body politic. These multifaceted interests of sacrificial ritual will be explored in the next three chapters.

17. Daniel Smith-Christopher, *A Biblical Theology of Exile* (OBT; Minneapolis: Fortress, 2002), 145–46.

CHAPTER 13

Gift Offerings: Commitment and Belonging

Read: Exodus 12–13; Leviticus 1–7; 17; 23; Numbers 28–29

Traditional Jewish exegesis makes a distinction between "gift offerings" and "debt offerings." Debt offerings are made to discharge a moral or ritual infraction. But gift offerings are mainly offered as symbols of praise, dedication, and worship.[1] This chapter begins by showing how the structure of Leviticus 1–7 underscores the importance of gift offerings. It will then turn to a description of major kinds of sacrifices that constituted the system of gift offerings in priestly thought, ending with some remarks on the applicability of this category to ideas about sacrifice in the New Testament.

Structure

Leviticus 1–7 can be divided into two sections.

The Structure of Leviticus 1–7

I Instructions for the people (Lev 1:1–6:7)

Gift offerings (1–3)

1 *ʿōlâ* whole burnt offering

1. Baruch J. Schwartz, "Leviticus," in *The Jewish Study Bible*, edited by Adele Berlin and Marc Zvi Brettler (New York: Oxford University Press, 2004), 206.

2 *minḥâ* cereal offering
3 *zebaḥ šělāmîm* sacrifice of well-being

Debt offerings (4:1–6:7)
4:1–5:13 *ḥaṭṭā't* purification offering (sin offering)
5:14–6:7 *'āšām* reparation offering (guilt offering)

II Administrative order
6:8–13 Rituals for whole burnt offerings (*'ōlâ*)
6:14–18 Rituals for cereal offerings (*minḥâ*)
6:19–23 The cereal offering at the ordination of a priest
6:24–30 Rituals for purification offerings (*ḥaṭṭā't*)
7:1–6 Rituals for reparation offerings (*'āšām*)
7:7–10 Priestly perquisites for guilt, sin, burnt, and cereal offerings
7:11–21 Rituals for sacrifices of well-being
 11–15 Thanksgiving offerings
 16–18 Vow and freewill offerings
 19–21 Necessity for ritual cleanness
7:22–27 Prohibitions against the consumption of hard fat (suet) and blood
7:28–36 Perquisites of the priests
7:37–38 Summary

Section I describes five major classes of sacrificial rituals. Although the actions of the priestly functionaries are described, these instructions actually address the laypeople who are required to bring sacrifices to the tabernacle. Many commentators follow the lead of rabbinic authorities and explain the organization of the text in terms of a progression from voluntary offerings to mandatory offerings.[2] That is, while whole burnt offerings, cereal offerings, and thanksgiving offerings were required on certain occasions, they could also be offered voluntarily, out of free will, by members of the community. On the other hand, purification and reparation offerings were required when various infringements on the realm of the sacred had to be managed.

Another term for voluntary offerings is the phrase "gift offerings" introduced above. The distinction between gift offerings and debt offerings corresponds to the two poles between which ritual movement took place in the priestly system (see the last chapter). Movement away from the negative

2. Jacob Milgrom, *Leviticus 1–16* (AB 3; New York: Doubleday, 1991), 282; Timothy M. Willis, *Leviticus* (AOTC; Nashville: Abingdon, 2009), 55–56.

realm of being was effected by "purification" and "reparation" offerings (the meaning of these terms will be explained in the next chapter). Movement towards the positive realm of being was effected by gift offerings. The fact that they come first in the list of sacrifices in Leviticus 1–6 is not accidental. This organization indicates that the fundamental orientation of the priestly sacrificial system was to communicate praise, thanksgiving, and dedication to the deity.

Section II deals with the same ritual requirements but shows a different way of organizing the priestly sacrifices.[3]

Classification of Priestly Sacrifices by Mode of Consumption

1. Unipolar (everything goes to God)	*ʿōlâ*	whole burnt offering
2. Bipolar	*minḥâ*	cereal offering
(shared between God and the priests)	*ḥaṭṭaʾt*	purification offering
	ʾāšām	reparation offering
3. Tripolar	*šālēm*	sacrifice of well-being
(shared between God, priests, and the laity)		

1. The whole burnt offering is a "unipolar" sacrifice because its flesh is totally consumed on the altar in the courtyard of the tabernacle.
2. Portions of the cereal offering, purification offering, and reparation offerings were normally burnt on the altar, but the remainder was consumed by priests.[4] They are classified as "bipolar" offerings, because they had two points of reference. Priests must eat their portions of the cereal, purification, and reparation offerings in a "holy place," which is defined as the court of the tabernacle (Lev 6:26).
3. Sacrifices of well-being involved three parties. While portions were burnt on the altar, priests received the breast meat (Lev 7:31). The rest was to be consumed by the lay worshippers in any ritually clean context, not necessarily the courtyard of the tabernacle. The length of text

3. In Lev 6:8–7:36 instructions about priestly perquisites frame rules about ritual constraints on the laity.

4. There are some exceptions. Purification offerings made on behalf of the high priest or the community were totally consumed by fire (some on the altar and the rest outside the camp); see Lev 4:1–21. The cereal offering made at the consecration of priests was totally consumed on the altar (Lev 6:19–23).

given over to the conditions under which the sacrifices of well-being must be eaten (7:11–36) underscores the importance of this sacrifice. As this offering was required in order to eat the meat of domestic animals, it was probably the most common type of sacrifice in preexilic Israel. Its importance and frequency are further indications that the priestly sacrificial system cannot be reduced to offerings for the expiation of sin.

Types of Gift Offerings

Burnt Offering (ʿōlâ)

English translations for Hebrew *ʿōlâ* vary, but it is typical to translate this word as "(whole) burnt offering" (e.g., NRSV, JPSV). The whole burnt offering was available to Israelites in various forms depending on their economic and social status. The most prestigious offering is mentioned first: the ox (Lev 1:3–9).[5] It was also permitted to sacrifice a sheep or goat (vv. 10–12), or a turtledove or pigeon (vv. 14–17). Except for the skin (Lev 7:8), the *ʿōlâ* was an animal offering that was completely burnt on the altar.

What are the benefits of the whole burnt offering? According to Lev 1:3 it is "acceptance" (*rāṣōn*). The motif of acceptance connotes the idea that YHWH recognizes the offerer as a loyal member of the community, one of his people. For this reason, the whole burnt offering was often offered after a person had made a purification sacrifice in order to communicate his or her complete integration into the community. For example, after her ritual purification, the new mother of Leviticus 12 would offer a whole burnt offering as a way of signifying her status as a person fully capable of entering sacred space (see Chapter 15).

But according to Lev 1:4, the whole burnt offering is also connected with the idea of "atonement" (*kappēr*). This association is difficult to explain, as Priestly law typically does not set out its underlying premises. On the basis of Lev 1:4, rabbinic authorities concluded that the whole burnt offering could act as an expiatory sacrifice for a range of sins that fell outside the scope of the purification offering.[6] However, this concern is not primary in Leviticus. Overall Leviticus 1 does not imply that the worshipper is seek-

5. Erhard S. Gerstenberger, *Leviticus* (OTL; Louisville: Westminster John Knox, 1996), 27.
6. Milgrom, *Leviticus 1–16*, 175.

ing forgiveness or expiation. Moreover, in the purity rituals of Leviticus 12–15, the whole burnt offering is presented *after* the purification offering. The whole burnt offering, therefore, has a different function than expiation for conditions of ritual impurity. These observations underscore the puzzle of the reference to expiation in Lev 1:4. A number of explanations have been advanced.[7] From a canonical perspective the reference may be to the Day of Atonement, where it is stated that, in addition to the scapegoat and sin offerings, burnt offerings will make atonement for the presiding priest and the people (Lev 16:24).

Leviticus 1 is particularly detailed in distinguishing the obligations of laypersons from the priest. The sacrificial ceremony consists of a number of steps whose responsibilities can be divided as follows:[8]

- Laying/leaning a hand on the animal (layperson)
- Slaughtering (layperson)
- Presenting the blood (priest)
- Skinning and cutting up the animal (layperson)
- Stoking the fire and arranging the wood on the altar (priest)
- Washing the entrails and shins (layperson)
- Laying and burning (parts of) the animal on the altar (priest)

The fact that lay and priest must work together communicates a form of social solidarity: the individual does what all Israel must do. This division of labor also reinforces a division in society, whereby some persons are allowed to come closer to the sanctuary than others. The principle of graded holiness, which also manifests itself in the design of the tabernacle, is in force. Priestly functionaries were subject to behavioral restrictions ("taboos") that laypersons did not have to observe (cf. Leviticus 21). Consequently, priests were able to move closer to the sacred realm.

An important component of lay participation involved laying (or pressing) a hand on the animal. Scholars debate its significance, but it is likely that the gesture of hand-pressing was meant to convey the idea of own-

7. See the survey in Willis, *Leviticus*, 6–7.

8. Both Gerstenberger (*Leviticus,* 29) and Christian A. Eberhart (*The Sacrifice of Jesus: Understanding Atonement Biblically* [Minneapolis: Fortress, 2011], 63–66) describe the process for sacrificing the whole burnt offering in seven steps; but they do not agree entirely. The seven points listed here are not intended as a definitive description of all of the ritual actions carried out for the *ʿōlâ*. In fact, depending on how fine the analysis, there could be as many as ten steps (Milgrom, *Leviticus 1–16,* 160).

ership. It was important to mark the animal as the property of the offerer.[9] But for what purpose? Are we to understand that the animal is being offered as substitute for a human being? In other words, does the claim of ownership also imply a vicarious process, in which the animal is being offered in the place of a person? Likely not. What appears to be involved is a sort of transaction in which the hand-leaning effectively signifies not only ownership, but also the transfer of ownership.[10] Thereafter, the animal belongs to God and the sanctuary.

Cereal Offering (minḥâ)

The *minḥâ* is often translated into English as "cereal offering" or "grain offering." It can be a cake baked in an oven (Lev 2:4) or made up of grains toasted (vv. 5–6), fried (v. 7), or parched (v. 14). If made of dough it must be unleavened (v. 11). Two forms of ritual consumption are typically associated with the *minḥâ*. A small portion is burnt on the altar in conjunction with incense. The major portion, however, is eaten by the priest under ritually clean conditions (Lev 2:3, 10).

The cereal offering had several different ritual contexts. It could be offered on its own; it also accompanied some animal offerings (Lev 7:11–14). Additionally, it was connected with offering firstfruits from the grain harvest (Lev 2:14). One of its functions, however, seems to have been as a substitute for the whole burnt offering for those too poor to bring an animal sacrifice.[11] This is implied by its position in Leviticus, as there is evidence that Leviticus 2 interrupts a more primary literary relationship between chapters 1 and 3.[12] Destitution and poverty, therefore, were not to be barriers to the worship of YHWH. Even the poorest of Israelites were not deprived of the means for presenting themselves as committed members of the people of God.

9. Milgrom, *Leviticus 1–16*, 150–51; Eberhart, *Sacrifice of Jesus*, 63–64.

10. Roy E. Gane, *Cult and Character: Purification Offerings, Day of Atonement, and Theodicy* (Winona Lake: Eisenbrauns, 2005), 56.

11. Milgrom, *Leviticus 1–16*, 196.

12. See Milgrom, *Leviticus 1–16*, 203–4.

*Sacrifice of Well-Being (*zebaḥ šělāmîm*)*

The technical term *zebaḥ šělāmîm* has been translated into English by several phrases, including "sacrifice of well-being," "communion sacrifice," or the "peace offering." The translation problem can be traced to the multiple meanings of the Hebrew root *š-l-m* (the Hebrew noun shalom [*šālôm*], connoting "peace, health, harmony" is derived from the same root letters). None of these translations is beyond dispute. The choice here follows the tradition in the NRSV.

There are different classes of the sacrifice of well-being.[13] This sacrifice could be offered as a freewill offering, in order to fulfill a vow, or as a thanksgiving sacrifice (*tôdâ*) in recognition of answered prayer. While P makes the thanksgiving offering (*tôdâ*) a subcategory of the sacrifice of well-being, there are distinct conditions under which the *tôdâ* was eaten. Vow and freewill offerings can be eaten over two days; but the thanksgiving offering must be eaten in one day (Lev 7:15–18). In this way, the *tôdâ* resembles two other sacrifices: Passover (Exod 12:10) and the priestly consecration offering (Exod 29:31–34). Each must be consumed along with unleavened bread; none of the meat can be left over until the next day. What is left over must be consumed by fire.

The thanksgiving offering (*tôdâ*) is connected to the Lament-Thanksgiving cycle. It shows that a significant occasion for offering a sacrifice in ancient Israel would have been an opportunity for offering praise to YHWH for answering prayer. An individual lament or complaint prayer was used to address situations of personal distress. Following a successful recovery or relief from the experience of distress, the affected person would arrange for a feast at a shrine to which family and friends would be invited. The meat would be furnished by the thanksgiving sacrifice. Many psalms of individual lament anticipate performing the thanksgiving rite.[14] One example is found in Ps 22:22–31. Not only does this part of the psalm anticipate a public celebration of God's saving power, but the meal at the sanctuary becomes an occasion for acting out social cohesion as well as thanksgiving because the grateful celebrant invites the "poor" to partake of the feast

13. For a thorough discussion of the complexities involved in understanding the meaning of the rituals subsumed under the category of the *zebaḥ šělāmîm* and their history, see Martin Modéus, *Sacrifice and Symbol: Biblical* Šělāmîm *in a Ritual Perspective* (ConBOT 52; Stockhom: Almqvist & Wiksell International, 2005).

14. William S. Morrow, *Protest against God: The Eclipse of a Biblical Tradition* (Hebrew Bible Monographs 4; Sheffield: Sheffield Phoenix, 2006), 71.

(Ps 22:26). Whether the term used for the poor (*ʿănāwîm*) denotes those who were truly socially disadvantaged or connotes pious Israelites, a similar thought is conveyed. The sacred feast affirms solidarity with one's neighbors and commitment to the God of Israel.

The ability of all of the sacrifices of well-being to make human community is tied up with the fact that they provide meat for human consumption. Meat from cattle, sheep, and goats was probably not everyday fare for the average Israelite. The religious ceremonies around meat consumption were, therefore, occasions for rejoicing. As Jacob Milgrom notes,

> Such an occasion perforce was rare, for only kings and aristocrats could afford the depletion of their flocks. For the commoner, the occasion had to be a celebration—and because the meat was probably too much for the nuclear family, it had to be a household or even a clan celebration—hence the joyous character of the sacrifice.[15]

These sacrificial rituals recall a time when the slaughter of any animal for meat was a religious act. The Holiness laws in Leviticus 17 are clear about the religious importance of the sacrifice of well-being. They insist that the blood of any domestic animal slaughtered for food has to be presented at the tabernacle. Failure to do so incurs bloodguilt (v. 4). The language alludes to the rhetoric of murder[16]—as if the nonritualized killing of a domestic animal makes the person into a criminal who must be punished. Behind these concerns, one can detect a feeling of guilt for taking the life of another living being. It is worth asking what has happened to that sympathy for the lives of animals in the modern supermarket or fast-food restaurant.

Primary occasions for the presentation of well-being sacrifices would have been the three major pilgrimage festivals. Originally, each was connected to harvest. The Festival of Unleavened Bread celebrates the beginning of the barley harvest; Weeks (or Pentecost) marks the beginning of the wheat harvest; and Sukkot recalls the harvesting of grapes, olives, and other agricultural products. All three of Israel's major festivals entailed some kind of pilgrimage to a shrine or sacred site for sacrifice. In Hebrew, these harvest festivals are designated by the term *ḥag*. To this day its Arabic cognate, *ḥajj*, is the name for the pilgrimage to Mecca that is one of the five pillars of Islam.

15. Milgrom, *Leviticus 1–16*, 221.

16. Jacob Milgrom, *Leviticus 17–22* (AB 3A; New York: Doubleday, 2000), 1456–57.

Passover Sacrifice

Exodus 12 tells the foundation legend of Passover. As in comprehensive festival texts such as Leviticus 23 and Numbers 28–29, the Passover offering is mentioned separately from the rituals for the seven-day Festival of Unleavened Bread (Lev 23:5; Num 28:16–17). Rules for the Festival of Unleavened Bread appear separately from the rules for the Passover in Exodus 13. The fact that Priestly legislation distinguishes the two is one of a number of lines of evidence that suggest that Passover and the Festival of Unleavened Bread had different origins,[17] although just how and when they were connected remains a matter of debate.

Recent study has concluded that there are strong reasons for assigning all of Exodus 12 to Priestly authors.[18] Consequently, Exodus 12 tells readers the legend of the first Passover according to P, but it does not indicate how Priestly writers thought the sacrifice should be carried out in later times. By late Second Temple times, the Passover had become a kind of *tôdâ*: a thanksgiving sacrifice offered on the altar that remembered the Exodus experience.[19] This development suggests that Priestly thinkers also regarded the Passover as a type of thanksgiving sacrifice.[20]

Subsuming the Passover sacrifice to the model of the thanksgiving offering has implications for understanding its meaning in ancient Israelite religion. No less than the other kinds of sacrifices of well-being, the Passover lamb was a type of gift offering, which communicated Israel's commitment to honor YHWH. In fact, this is already implied in the Passover legend itself. It was not offered as remedy for sin but as an act of dedication. For it was

17. Baruch M. Bokser, "Unleavened Bread and Passover, Feasts of," *ABD* 6:756.

18. Shimon Gesundheit, *Three Times a Year: Studies on Festival Legislation in the Pentateuch* (FAT 82; Tübingen: Mohr Siebeck, 2012), 61–66. This means that an older opinion that P did not regard the Passover as a sacrifice is doubtful. Note that Exod 12:27 specifically calls the Passover a *zebaḥ*, P's technical term for a sacrifice.

19. m. Pesaḥ. 6.1

20. P, therefore, agrees with non-P instructions that accord the Passover the same status as a Thanksgiving sacrifice; e.g., on Exod 34:25 see Menahem Haran, *Temples and Temple-Service in Ancient Israel* (Winona Lake: Eisenbrauns, 1985), 344–45. According to Deuteronomic law, the Passover meal must be killed and eaten at the same place where all legitimate sacrifices have to be brought (Deut 16:1–2). Moreover, Deuteronomy requires that the Passover offering be boiled (Deut 16:7)—the normal way to prepare sacrificial meat for eating—instead of being roasted whole as demanded by Exod 12:8–9 (William S. Morrow, *Scribing the Center: Organization and Redaction in Deuteronomy 14:1–17:1* [SBLMS 49; Atlanta: Scholars, 1995], 131–32).

precisely those who were marked by this ritual of devotion that the angel of death passed over (Exod 12:13).

Developments

The prominence of gift offerings in the sacrificial system of Leviticus has importance for Christian readers because there is a tendency in the church to associate sacrifice with rituals for the expiation of sin. Unfortunately, such an understanding ignores the rich meanings of sacrifice in Priestly traditions. Gift offerings were occasions for joy and praise.

This perspective is conveyed in several ways. First, the fact that the gift offerings are set out at the beginning of Leviticus illustrates an important goal of the sacrificial system. It exists not only to restore Israel's relationship with the Creator, but to enable worshippers to communicate personal commitment to YHWH and the pleasure of belonging to the people of God. Second, the primary interest of gift offerings is to express joy and delight in divine service. This emphasis continues into late Second Temple times. For example, writers such as Philo and Josephus describe Passover celebrations as occasions of great joy and high spiritual expression.[21]

Sacrificial rituals offered occasions to open oneself up in an act of self-giving to the one who had already given to Israel. For the same reason, St. Paul can adjure his readers, "I appeal to you therefore, brothers and sisters, by the mercies of God, to present your bodies as a living sacrifice, holy and acceptable to God, which is your spiritual worship" (Rom 12:1).[22] Here, Paul does not consider sacrifice as either a hardship nor simply a remedy for sin. On the contrary, it allows worshippers to achieve fulfilling relationships with their God—a spirituality of sacrifice that was extremely important to Priestly thought as well.

21. Bokser, "Unleavened Bread and Passover," 762.

22. Willis, *Leviticus*, 27.

CHAPTER 14

Hazards of the Holy Life 1: Debt Offerings

Read: Leviticus 4:1–6:7; 16; Numbers 15; 35

This is the first of two chapters on sacrificial rituals connected to the system of debt offerings in biblical law. In this chapter, the focus will be on actions that can be regarded as "sins." It begins by identifying the two forms of debt offerings described in Priestly law: the purification offering and the reparation offering. It will then turn to the different gradations of sin addressed in Priestly law; this distinction will help to clarify the interests of the purification offering and the reparation offering. What follows are brief consideration of the rituals of the Day of Atonement and some developments in late Second Temple times.

Names of the Sacrifices

Scholars debate how the terms *ḥaṭṭāʾt* (Lev 4:1–5:13) and *ʾāšām* (Lev 5:14–6:7) should be translated. At stake are rather sophisticated discussions as to how the tabernacle and the community are affected when persons act contrary to the good order of the society that has God at its center.[1] Traditionally, the term *ḥaṭṭāʾt* was translated as "sin offering" and *ʾāšām* as "guilt offering." Recent scholarship, however, has made the case that purification is a pri-

1. For an illustration of the complexities involved in analyzing relationships between biblical sacrifices, see Naphtali Meshel, "Toward a Grammar of Sacrifice: Hierarchic Patterns in the Israelite Sacrificial System," *JBL* 132 (2013): 543–67.

mary interest of the *ḥaṭṭāʾt*.[2] For this reason, the present discussion will use the term "purification offering" to refer to the *ḥaṭṭāʾt*. The term "reparation offering" will refer to a characteristic concern of the *ʾāšām*.[3]

The ritual procedures for purification and reparation offerings were fairly identical. Individuals normally brought a female sheep or goat for a purification offering (Lev 4:27–35), but a ram for the reparation offering (6:6). In each case, the priest would collect the blood of the animal in a bowl (*mizrāq*).[4] Most of the blood would be poured out at the base of the altar, but some would be daubed on the horns of the courtyard altar. The fat portions were burnt on the altar and the rest of the animal eaten by priests under ritually clean conditions in the courtyard of the tabernacle.

Both the purification offering and the reparation offering were capable of substitutions, though not in the same way. The animal normally required for a purification offering could be substituted by a meal offering if the person was very poor (Lev 5:11–13). For the reparation offering, a monetary gift could be substituted (Lev 5:15, 18; 6:6). Permissions for substitutions that did not require an actual animal offering should give pause to theories that identify a single sacrificial action (such as blood offering) as *the* effective action for atonement. It suggests that the intention behind the sacrifice was as important as the form of the sacrifice. These substitutions anticipate a development in Judaism in which repentance will emerge as the most important element in obtaining forgiveness.[5]

The Concept of Sin in Priestly Law

Why was it necessary to have purification or reparation offerings? Atonement rituals were required to address the effects of sin. According to Priestly theology, there were three classes of sin:[6]

1. "high-handed" (= defiant)	inexpiable through sacrifice
2. inadvertent	expiable through sacrifice
3. nondefiant deliberate	expiable through sacrifice

2. See John E. Hartley, *Leviticus* (WBC 4; Dallas: Word, 1992), 55–57.

3. See Hartley, *Leviticus,* 76–80.

4. Jonathan S. Greer, "An Israelite *Mizrāq* at Tel Dan?" *BASOR* 358 (2010): 33–36.

5. George F. Moore, *Judaism in the First Centuries of the Christian Era* (New York: Schocken, 1971), 1:520–34; Jacob Milgrom, *Leviticus 1–16* (AB 3; New York: Doubleday, 1991), 1:373–78.

6. Roy E. Gane, "Loyalty and Scope of Expiation in Numbers 15," *ZABR* 16 (2010): 252.

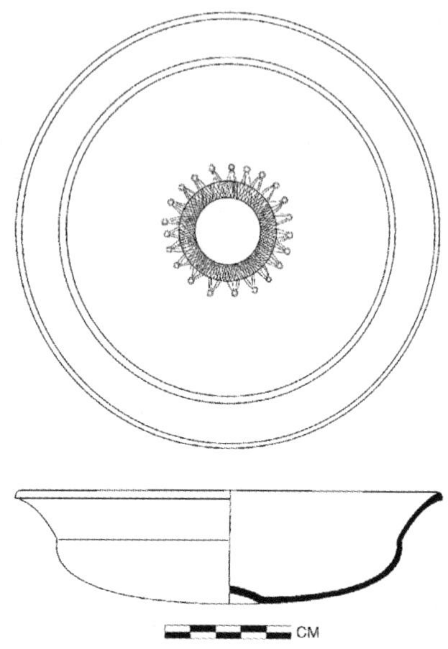

Figure 6. This bronze bowl was found along with other cultic utensils in a small chamber adjacent to the high place at Tel Dan. Dated to c. eighth century BCE, it is plausibly identified as a *mizrāq*, the ceremonial bowl used by Israelite priests to collect blood from sacrificial animals (e.g., Exod 27:3; Num 4:14). The raised boss in the center is a stylized pomegranate, a symbol attested in Israelite temple worship (e.g. Exod 28:33–34). Drawing of *mizrāq* from Tel Dan after Avraham Biran, "The Dancer from Dan, the Empty Tomb and the Altar Room," *IEJ* 36 (1986): 186. Courtesy of the Nelson Glueck Institute, Hebrew Union College/Jewish Institute of Religion. Used with permission.

1) High-handed sins

All sins can be expiated according to Priestly law, but not all could be expiated by the sacrificial system. Priestly law assumes that some sins can only be dealt with by putting the guilty party to death. It demanded that human agencies administer the death penalty for adultery, idolatry, and murder. All three sins were thought to defile the holy land, if they were not remedied by the elimination of the offending parties.[7]

The implacable position that Priestly law takes towards adultery, idolatry, and murder is representative of its general attitude to what it refers to as "high-handed sins." High-handed sins are infractions against moral and cultic regulations committed deliberately and in full knowledge (Num 15:30–31). In such cases, there is no forgiveness. The perpetrator is to be cut off from his or her people, either by judicial action or divine punishment.

The following chart lists the sins and crimes for which biblical law demands the death penalty.

7. Jonathan Klawans, *Impurity and Sin in Ancient Judaism* (New York: Oxford University Press, 2000), 26–31.

The Death Penalty in Biblical Law

Infraction	Reference	Penalty
Blood-shedding	Gen 9:6	Unspecified
Murder	Exod 21:12; Lev 24:17, 21; Num 35:16–21, 31	(*môt*) *yûmāt*[8] "be put to death"
Striking parents	Exod 21:15	
Kidnapping	Exod 21:16	
Cursing parents	Exod 21:17; Lev 20:9	
Culpable manslaughter	Exod 21:29	
Bestiality	Exod 22:19; Lev 20:15–16	
Violations of the Sabbath	Exod 31:15; 35:2	
Adultery	Lev 20:10	
Incest (father or son's wife)	Lev 20:11–12	
Sex between men	Lev 20:13	
Unauthorized priestly practice	Num 1:51; 3:10; 18:7	
Preaching apostasy	Deut 13:5	
Eating the forbidden fruit	Gen 2:17	(*môt*) *yāmût*[9] "die"
Refusing to enter the land	Num 26:65	
False prophecy	Deut 18:20	
Sabbath violation	Exod 31:14	*yûmāt*/being "cut off"
Idolatry/child sacrifice?	Lev 20:2–3	*môt yûmāt*/stoning/ being "cut off"
Violation of sacred space	Exod 19:13	stoning/killed by arrows
Cursing God	Lev 24:16	*môt yûmāt*/stoning
Working on the Sabbath	Num 15:35–36	
Worshipping other gods	Deut 17:5–6	
The goring ox	Exod 21:28, 32	stoning
Individual worship of other gods	Deut 13:10	
Chronic disobedience of parents	Deut 21:21	
Adultery	Deut 22:21, 24	
Rape	Deut 22:25 (implied)	
Worshipping other gods	Exod 22:20	the "ban" √*ḥrm*
Worshipping other gods	Deut 13:12–18	
Sex with a mother and her daughter	Lev 20:14	burning
Priest's daughter becomes a harlot	Lev 21:9	
(Female?) sorcery	Exod 22:18	not leaving alive
Holy War	Deut 20:16	
Refusing to be circumcised	Gen 17:14	being "cut off" √*krt*
Eating leavened bread during the Festival of Unleavened Bread	Exod 12:15, 19	

8. The formula has its finite verb in the Hophal.

9. The formula has its finite verb in the Qal.

Unauthorized use of sacred oil or incense	Exod 30:33, 38
Violating sacrificial food taboos	Lev 7:20, 21, 25; 19:8
Domestic animal slaughter outside the cult place	Lev 17:4, 9
Eating blood	Lev 7:27; 17:14
Breaking sexual prohibitions	Lev 18:29
Necromancy and magic	Lev 20:6
Brother and sister incest	Lev 20:17
Sex with menstruating woman	Lev 20:18
Priestly service while unclean	Lev 22:3
Refusing to fast on Yom Kippur	Lev 23:29
Doing work on Yom Kippur	Lev 23:30 (implied)
Refusing to keep Passover	Num 9:13
Intentional violation of ritual purity	Num 15:30–31
Refusal of ritual purification	Num 19:13, 20

This list shows that there were various categories of capital crimes in biblical law and that they carried different forms of the extreme penalty. The use of the phrase *môt yûmāt* was previously discussed in Chapter 7. It means that the guilty party must be put to death, although the form of execution is not indicated. Many of the crimes for which the death penalty was required would have been addressed by legal process, but not all. For the most part, the threat of "being cut off" (from the Hebrew root *k-r-t*) seems to have been a threat of divine punishment administered without human agency, although there is overlap.[10] In some cases, such as Sabbath violation and idolatry, human agencies were expected to administer punishment; but divine agency could also be involved.

Nevertheless, it is not obvious that in all cases where the extreme penalty was demanded it was literally carried out. Capital laws in the Torah also had a metaphorical aspect, and death penalty language can be used by biblical writers to point to matters of significant social and religious concern. That is, they "seek to give essentials of correct behavior under the auspices of Yahweh himself. They do so by selecting certain provisions from different fields of human life as token rules to indicate divine reign."[11] Therefore, some biblical death penalty laws had more of an ideological than a practical value. For example, there are passages in the Tanakh that indicate adultery could be punished without resort to the extreme penalty (see Chapter 22).

10. Milgrom, *Leviticus 1–16*, 457–58.

11. Erhard S. Gerstenberger, "'. . . (He/They) Shall Be Put to Death': Life-Preserving Death Threats in Old Testament Law," *ExAud* 11 (1995): 54.

In some situations, death penalty language points to banishment or exile instead of the administration of the extreme penalty. This is apparent in cases such as the violation of the divinely-ordained food rule in Eden (Gen 2:17), the death of the rebellious generation in the wilderness (Num 26:65), and the analysis of Israel's exile that appears in passages such as Lev 18:24–28 and 26:33.

With respect to murder, differences exist between the justice system according to Priestly thinkers and other legal theorists in ancient Israel. Numbers 35:30–34 is categorical in its rejection of the practice of "composition" (ransom) in the case of homicide. While the Covenant Code also demands the death penalty for premeditated murder, it allows the owner of the goring ox to pay a ransom for his life in a case of diminished responsibility (Exod 21:30). Priestly law does not permit this milder penalty, nor will it allow a ransom to be paid in order to free a person from bloodguilt in a case of nonculpable manslaughter. Those who killed another person accidentally are given a place to flee in the cities of refuge (Num 35:13–15), but they are constrained to stay there until the presiding high priest dies (vv. 22–28). They are not allowed to pay a ransom for their lives in order to leave in safety.[12]

2) Sacrifices for inadvertent sins

The polar opposite of high-ended sins are those done unintentionally or inadvertently. In this respect, the instructions that begin Leviticus 4 are rather vague: "When anyone sins unintentionally in any of the LORD's commandments about things not to be done, and does any one of them . . ." (Lev 4:2). The language of the parallel in Num 15:22–31 is also imprecise.[13] The rabbis thought that two issues were at stake:[14]

1. The offender either was unaware that an offense had been committed or did not know what the penalty was.
2. A person may have assumed that the action was permissible when it was not.

The only illustrations of inadvertent sins demanding purification sacrifices

12. Baruch A. Levine, *Numbers 21–36* (AB 4A; New York: Doubleday, 2000), 559.

13. Baruch A. Levine, *Numbers 1–20* (AB 4; New York: Doubleday, 1993), 395–96.

14. Levine, *Numbers 1–20*, 395.

are found in Lev 5:1–6. They concern not speaking up when adjured by an oath using God's name (v. 1), uttering an oath in God's name without thinking about the consequences (literally, "swearing," v. 4), or touching unclean things inadvertently (vv. 2–3). Common to these infractions is the violation of divine privilege, either by involuntarily becoming a channel for communicating uncleanness or by using the divine name irresponsibly.

Purification sacrifices focus, therefore, on violations of cultic taboos such as accidentally working on a Sabbath, eating a category of forbidden food (e.g., unintentionally ingesting blood), or neglecting to purify oneself ritually (e.g., forgetting that one has just touched a corpse). These ritual violations are examples of offenses for which divine punishment (rather than by human agency) would be called for. As the chart on references to the death penalty punishment showed, this penalty is called "cutting off." Evidently, divine punishment could be warded off by means of purification sacrifices in cases of inadvertent or unintended violations of holiness taboos.

3) Expiation for deliberate sins

The priestly system also perceives the possibility that persons in Israel could willfully violate divine commands without, however, intending to betray a basic loyalty to the God of Israel.[15] This concern seems to have been addressed by the reparation offering. While purification offerings deal mainly with the violation of cultic taboos, reparation offerings address the misappropriation of holy things for personal use, including offerings meant for the sanctuary, and the misuse of oaths.[16] For example, according to Lev 6:1–7 persons who realized that they had committed perjury by taking an oath of innocence using the divine name, even though they were guilty, could offer a reparation offering.

There may also have been ritual remedies for deliberate sins apart from the reparation offering. Traditionally, the *ʿōlâ* (whole burnt offering) described in the last chapter had expiatory functions (e.g., Job 1:5; 42:8).[17] Morover, they were sacrificed on the Day of Atonement to make atonement for the high priest and the people (Lev 16:24). The expiatory force of the

15. Gane, "Loyalty and Scope of Expiation," 261–62.

16. Milgrom, *Leviticus 1–16*, 347.

17. Milgrom, *Leviticus 1–16*, 174–75; Timothy M. Willis, *Leviticus* (AOTC; Nashville: Abingdon, 2009), 33–34.

whole burnt offering is also attested in postbiblical times. For example, rabbinic authorities regarded the daily lamb offerings (the *tāmîd*) as capable of effecting atonement when the temple was extant: the evening *tāmîd* atoned for the transgressions residents of Jerusalem had committed during the day, while the morning *tāmîd* cleansed the transgressions of the night.[18]

Unfortunately, Priestly literature makes no concerted attempt to organize its various sacrifices into a coherent system. This is not an accident, but reflects a different way of thinking and arranging information than the discursive approach common in modern cultures. This way of constructing a religious worldview will be discussed further in Chapter 16. In general, however, one can conclude that Priestly theology had means for expiating intentional as well as unintentional sins. A key component for forgiveness in both categories was knowledge, recognition, and confession of guilt.[19] Once an infraction becomes known to, or is realized by the perpetrator (e.g., Lev 4:14, 23, 28; 6:4), sacrifices of purification or reparation can be offered. In both cases, there is an implicit assumption that the offerer not only acknowledges the error but enters the ritual in an attitude of repentance.

The Day of Atonement

Concerns for ridding the community of the consequences of both unintentional and intentional sins converge on the Day of Atonement (Leviticus 16). Two different kinds of sin had to be dealt with: those that were forgivable and those that were unforgivable. As already noted, certain crimes could only be expiated by the death of the perpetrator, However, not all perpetrators could be found out, nor was the legal system always able to call them to account for their high-handed actions.

The solution is found in sacrifice and in scapegoating. The two-pronged approach of the Day of Atonement ritual allowed it to address the effects of the sins that could be expiated and those that could not. Two goats were used. One goat was sacrificed for "the uncleanness of the people of Israel, and because of their transgressions, all their sins" (16:16). A second goat was sent alive into the wilderness "for Azazel." This was done after the high priest confessed over it "all the iniquities of the people of Israel, and

18. Moore, *Judaism*, 1:497.

19. Mark Boda, *A Severe Mercy: Sin and Its Remedy in the Old Testament* (Siphrut 1; Winona Lake: Eisenbrauns, 2009), 62–67.

all their transgressions, all their sins" (Lev 16:21). These formulas are almost identical, except that the sacrificial goat is for "uncleanness" (*ṭum'ōt*), while the scapegoat is sent away on account of "iniquities" (*'ăwônōt*).

The semantic range of "iniquities" is larger than "uncleanness." It connotes sins that may have been committed deliberately (i.e., with a "high hand"). Unforgivable sins committed by defiant Israelites could not be dealt with by the cult. Even so, the effects of these deadly sins had to be expunged from the holy place. The scapegoat ritual solved this problem by sending the effects of these sins out of the camp.

Where and to whom were they sent? Leviticus 16:10 indicates that the goat bearing the iniquities of the people is sent to "Azazel." The identity of Azazel is debated in biblical scholarship. However, as unorthodox as it may seem in a thorough-going monotheistic text, it is quite plausible that Azazel was the name of a desert demon.[20] Priestly theology occasionally drops other hints of a belief in demonic spirits (e.g., Lev 17:7), but, in general, P distinguishes itself from other religions in the ancient Near East by refusing to credit evil deeds or consequences to demonic agencies. Certainly, it betrays no knowledge of the extensive mythology of demonic power (i.e., Satan and his angels) that characterizes Hellenistic Judaism. In Levitical thought, the only being really capable of compromising YHWH's creative order is a human being.[21] This is underscored by P's purification rituals and sacrifices, which are directed at providing sacrificial remedies for ritual and moral problems involving people—not demons.

Underlying rituals such as those for the Day of Atonement is the belief that the effects of sin can be contagious. One metaphor for this belief is electricity.[22] Everyone knows what happens when a positive and a negative electric charge come close enough to make a circuit. The negative flows to the positive and sparks fly. If your finger gets in the way, you will get a shock. If the current is strong enough, the effects can be lethal. Consequently, it was important to insulate the positive realm from contact with the negative.

This metaphor is not perfect, because in Priestly theology both the holy and the unclean are capable of charging something or someone that touches them. For example, touching a holy object like the altar imparted holiness (Exod 29:37). Touching something unclean, like a corpse, compromised a person's ability to enter sacred space. Similarly, violation of divine privileges,

20. Milgrom, *Leviticus 1–16*, 1020–21.

21. Milgrom, *Leviticus 1–16*, 43.

22. Milgrom (*Leviticus 1–16*, 270) uses the metaphor of electromagnetism.

such as the misuse of God's name or eating blood, also made a person in need of purification.

Another problem with the electricity metaphor is that it does not say where the negative charge resides. Does the impurity (negative charge) lie with the person who made the error or is it lodged elsewhere, i.e., in the holy precincts? Scholars have different views on this question. An influential opinion holds that purification offerings were intended to cleanse the sanctuary from the effects of sin and impurity.[23] Others think that both objects (the sanctuary) and persons were in need of expiation. While purification sacrifices made affected persons clean, the sanctuary itself needed to be purified on the annual Day of Atonement.[24]

Developments

Problems of sin and atonement attracted a large amount of attention in the late Second Temple period.[25] For example, matters of purity and impurity were of great importance among the sect at Qumran, self-exiled as they were from the temple cult.[26] It is not surprising, therefore, that the Jewish thinkers who constituted the early church were intently concerned about matters of sin. This was focused on their efforts to interpret the meaning of the crucifixion of Christ, both as an *ʾāšām* (reparation offering) and a *ḥaṭṭāʾt* (purification sacrifice).[27]

For example, the death of the righteous sufferer in Isa 53:10 is called an *ʾāšām* (reparation sacrifice). Explicit associations between Jesus and Isaiah's suffering servant are made in the Gospels (e.g., Matt 8:17; Luke 22:37; John 12:38). Interpretative possibilities implicit in the Priestly concept of the reparation sacrifice also appear in the prayer from the cross in Luke 23:34, "Father, forgive them; for they do not know what they are doing." While the textual origins of this statement are uncertain, the prayer is related to a

23. Milgrom, *Leviticus 1–16*, 254–58.

24. Roy E. Gane, *Cult and Character: Purification Offerings, Day of Atonement, and Theodicy* (Winona Lake: Eisenbrauns, 2005), 142–43; see also Boda, *A Severe Mercy*, 68–69.

25. See the survey in Miryam T. Brand, *Evil Within and Without: The Source of Sin and Its Nature as Portrayed in Second Temple Literature* (Journal of Ancient Judaism Supplements 9; Göttingen: Vandenhoeck & Ruprecht, 2013).

26. See, e.g., Klawans, *Impurity and Sin*, 67–91.

27. Bruce Chilton, *A Feast of Meanings: Eucharistic Theologies from Jesus through Johannine Circles* (NovTSup 72; Leiden: Brill, 1994), 109–17.

motif in apostolic teaching which claims that the rulers of Jerusalem killed Jesus in ignorance (Acts 3:17). In effect, by making Jesus's death a crime of ignorance, Jesus's prayer of forgiveness connects with the Priestly category of deliberate sins that can be forgiven. Though it was deliberate, the crucifixion is not regarded as a high-handed sin. Atonement through confession and repentance are possible for those guilty of unknowingly crucifying Christ.

The most thorough-going attempt to deal with the sacrificial meaning of the death of Jesus is found in the book of Hebrews, especially chapters 8–10. Here Jesus's death is connected to the rituals of the Day of Atonement. Over the years, many exegetes have tried to explain what the writer of Hebrews wants to say in making this association. Not surprisingly, there is lack of agreement about various points.[28] Nevertheless, Hebrews—no less than other New Testament writings—builds on typical Jewish ideas about atonement and forgiveness. As the quintessential high priest, Christ has effected a form of the *ḥaṭṭā't* (purification sacrifice) for the forgiveness of sins. His sacrifice is capable of dealing with both unintentional and intentional transgressions—provided that the one seeking atonement is determined to be loyal to the God of Israel (cf. Heb 10:26).

28. Surveyed in Willis, *Leviticus,* 48–49.

CHAPTER 15

Hazards of the Holy Life 2: Food, Death, Sex, and Birth

Read: Leviticus 11–15; Numbers 19; 31

Why does a woman become ritually unclean twice as long if she gives birth to a girl instead of a boy (Lev 12:5)? For that matter, why does childbirth render a woman ritually unclean at all? The Torah has no comparable rules for men who have killed in battle. The closest biblical law is Num 31:19: "Camp outside the camp for seven days; whoever of you has killed any person or touched a corpse, purify yourselves and your captives on the third and on the seventh day." These repeat the rules for touching a corpse set out in Num 19:10–13. But they are less stringent than the ritual restrictions surrounding childbirth.

Priestly purification rituals regarding matters of food, death, sex, and birth are difficult to understand. This chapter briefly describes how biblical purity rules represent a way to express Israel's commitment to cultivating healthy relationships with the source of life, YHWH. It begins with an overview of purity thinking in Priestly law before turning to consider issues related to eating, death, and birth. Some observations on the early church and ritual purity end the chapter.

Purity and Impurity in Priestly Law

"Purity" rules are implicated in the maintenance of social relationships.[1] Purity thinking, therefore, is vitally concerned with controlling boundaries, preserving hierarchies, and promoting social cohesion—in a word, community-making. It can be argued that every society has its own system of purity rules, behaviors, and conditions that make some people either temporarily or permanently unable to participate in society. For example, Western society quarantines persons with communicable diseases such as tuberculosis or Ebola. Fear of contact with persons in certain social categories, such as those who suffer mental illness or have a different ethnic background, is also deeply entrenched in modern cultures. Perhaps one of the chief differences between antiquity and the contemporary Western world is that purity thinking was more systematized in ancient societies, whereas it is applied in a more fragmentary way in modernity.

Purity thinking was widespread in the ancient world. It was a concern for priests and kings, the palace and the temple. This should not be surprising, since purity thinking is closely related to power. The metaphor used in the last chapter was electricity: it is dangerous to visit an electric-generating station without proper precautions. Both the gods and the king were considered powers for life in the ancient world; but persons who did not approach them properly put their very lives at risk.

The priestly purity system operates with pairs of binary opposites:

holy (*qādôš*)	vs.	profane (*ḥōl*)
clean (*ṭāhôr*)	vs.	unclean (*ṭāmēʾ*)

What is holy (*qādôš*) belongs to God and the divine character. It is separate (one of the core ideas of holiness) from what is common or profane (*ḥōl*). Not everything that is profane is incapable of communion with the holy; but it is important to be ritually clean (*ṭāhôr*) in order to enter into sacred space. Becoming unclean (*ṭāmēʾ*) invalidates a person's capacity to interact positively with the holy. As the last chapter explained, uncleanness was regarded as something that was contagious. It can be transferred by touch. Therefore, it had to be controlled and counteracted ritually.

What is noteworthy about the ritual impurities dealt with in this chap-

1. Mary Douglas, *Purity and Danger: An Analysis of Concepts of Pollution and Taboo* (London: Routledge & Kegan Paul, 2003), xiii.

Figure 7. This relief comes from the palace of Assurnasirpal II, one of the great Neo-Assyrian kings (883-859 BCE). The king is depicted sitting on his throne drinking. On either side are eunuch attendants (note the lack of beards). At the edge of the panel stand protective spirits extending signs of purity towards the king (note, e.g., the pails of lustral water). The effect was to convey the idea of the throne room as a pure space, participating in the aura of the holy. Art and Picture Collection, The New York Public Library. "The king on his throne attended by eunuchs and winged figures." New York Public Library Digital Collections. Accessed October 11, 2016. http://digitalcollections.nypl.org/items/510d47e4-1363-a3d9-e040-e00a18064a99

ter is that there is no suggestion of any violation of law or ethical norm. Touching corpses and giving birth, for example, are normal human activities; they are not sins and were not regarded as such in ancient Israel. So why are certain unavoidable human conditions or activities subject to purification and sacrifice? Some scholars think that Priestly purity rules have their origins in the need to emulate the nature of God ("the imitation of God").[2] According to this view, purity concerns center on the need to reflect key features of the divine character (e.g., life and order), while eschewing their symbolic opposites (e.g., death and chaos).[3] Other scholars see the problem in terms of social control, symbolized by the control of certain key bodily functions.[4]

2. E.g., Lance Hawley, "The Agenda of Priestly Taxonomy: The Conceptualization of טמא and שקץ in Leviticus 11," *CBQ* 77 (2015): 242.

3. E.g., Jacob Milgrom, "Rationale for Cultic Law: The Case of Impurity," *Semeia* 54 (1989): 103–10; Jacob Neusner, "The Religious Meaning of Bodily Excretions in Rabbinic Judaism: The Halakhah on Leviticus Chapter Fifteen: *Zabim* and *Niddah*," *Review of Rabbinic Judaism* 3 (2000): 67–91.

4. Both opinions are summarized in Hanna Liss, "Ritual Purity and the Construction

Both positions need to be taken into account. Issues of relationship to the divine character and boundary control assert themselves throughout biblical purity laws.

The interest in connecting with the divine nature has more than one dimension. Rituals surrounding food, death, sex, and birth, and helped focus the community on the importance of maintaining movement towards the holy and away from its opposites. However, Israel was constrained to recognize not only the potential for "the imitation of God" but also its limits. YHWH was free of the contingencies experienced by human beings, who need to sustain their lives by eating and reproducing; moreover, YHWH was not touched by death. Consequently, purity rituals became ways of recalling Israel's need for dependency on the one at the center of the sphere of life. As explained by Hanna Liss, they showed how the values of the sanctuary intruded into ordinary life.[5]

Another metaphor for understanding purity concerns is provided by the concept of "boundary failure." This anxiety finds expression in biblical law through the need to avoid experiences of *abjection,* a state which connotes the visceral abhorrence that human beings feel towards experiences that compromise their sense of self.[6] It is experienced as the intrusion of unwanted ambiguities that threaten a sense of social competence and cultural agency.[7] These concerns became important to Israel's thinkers in the exilic and postexilic eras.

The purity system in Leviticus developed out of practices that existed prior to the exile. In addition, as noted in Chapter 12, its canonical shaping offered a way to preserve an identity threatened by the "melting pot" of the Neo-Babylonian and (subsequently) the Persian and Hellenistic Empires. Israel's loss of control over its own boundaries was a traumatic experience. Its system of purity rules has to be seen in the light of Israel's experience as a victim of colonialism. In fact, biblical purity thinking represents a form of resistance to social subordination by a foreign power.[8] Food rules and cultic

---

of Identity: The Literary Function of the Laws of Purity in the Book of Leviticus," in *The Books of Leviticus and Numbers*, edited by Thomas Römer (BETL 215; Leuven: Peeters, 2008), 332–33.

5. Liss, "Ritual Purity," 353.

6. Julia Kristeva, *Powers of Horror: An Essay on Abjection* (New York: Columbia University Press, 1982), 90–112.

7. Martha J. Reineke, *Sacrificed Lives: Kristeva on Women and Violence* (Bloomington: Indiana University Press, 1997), 26–32.

8. Daniel Smith-Christopher, "Reassessing the Historical and Sociological Impact of the Babylonian Exile (597/587–539 BCE)," in *Exile: Old Testament, Jewish, and Christian Con-*

restrictions around sex and death allowed exiled and subjugated Israel to construct behavioral boundaries that could protect its cultural integrity in an alien environment. Maintenance of the exiled community's unique sense of self required vigilance, a vigilance that was acted out by careful attention to the limits set out by food rules and matters related to reproduction, disease, and mortality.

Laws on Food, Death, Sex, and Birth

Food

The Structure of Leviticus 11

Impure animals		Purification procedures			
2–8	quadrupeds				
9–12	fish				
13–19	birds				
20–23	flying insects				
		24–40	touching carcasses:[9]		
				24–28	forbidden quadrupeds
				29–38	eight land swarmers
				39–40	permitted quadrupeds
41–45	land swarmers				
46–47	summary statement				

Several themes come together in the food laws, including concerns:

- to avoid ingesting blood
- to avoid touching corpses
- to esteem wholeness or completeness
- to esteem right worship

ceptions, edited by James M. Scott (Journal for the Study of Judaism Supplement 56; Leiden: Brill, 1997), 36.

9. The text of Leviticus 11 is widely regarded as showing signs of revision: vv. 24–40 have been inserted into the chapter by a writer from the Holiness School (Jacob Milgrom, *Leviticus 1–16* [AB 3: New York: Doubleday, 1991], 691–92; Israel Knohl, *The Sanctuary of Silence: The Priestly Torah and the Holiness School* [Minneapolis: Fortress, 1995], 69).

A great deal has been written on the logic underlying biblical food rules.[10] Scholars have differing opinions about the degree to which are they capable of explanation. To the extent that the biblical food rules can be explained, elements of the imitation of God and social control both appear.

Predatory behavior is manifested by carnivorous animals. Ethically, the preference for domesticated vegetarian animals conveys an implicit discomfort with violence and bloodshed. A similar theme appears in the creation narrative in Genesis 1, which is generally regarded as belonging to the Priestly source. It conveys God's abhorrence with bloodshed by portraying the original intention of creation as one in which all animals were vegetarian (Gen 1:29–30). Its preference for herbivores connects with a belief that predatory violence does not reflect God's character (cf. the cause for the flood in Gen 6:11–12).[11] Cultivating this discomfort through the observance of Priestly food rules can lead to a heightened sensitivity regarding the gravity of violence and bloodshed in human relationships as well.[12]

A major concern of the food laws is to ensure that Israel only consumes the domesticated herbivores that can be offered on the altar or game animals that resemble them. While exclusion of the pig is based on the fact that it does not chew the cud, this rule probably reflects long-standing anxieties about swine in Israel. One source of these was likely the prominent place pigs had in the worship of underworld deities.[13] Therefore, the avoidance of swine also reflects concerns related to boundary maintenance: Israel was not to worship any deity but YHWH.

With respect to fish, only those with both fins and scales are allowed as food. This criterion reflects a concern for wholeness, another divine characteristic. Animals with scales and fins are the most prominent water creatures and, hence, those that most clearly belong to the class of fish. In addition, there may be an appreciation of the fact that fish with scales and fins move constantly through running water. In Priestly thought, running water is ritually clean (e.g., Lev 14:5).[14]

10. See the bibliography in Hawley, "Priestly Taxonomy," 233.

11. Genesis 6:11–12 is usually attributed to P's version of the flood; see Norman K. Gottwald, *The Hebrew Bible: A Socio-Literary Introduction* (Philadelphia: Fortress, 1985), 470.

12. Jacob Milgrom, "The Biblical Diet Laws as an Ethical System: Food and Faith," *Int* 17 (1963): 288–301; *Leviticus 1–16*, 650–52.

13. Milgrom, *Leviticus 1–16*, 652.

14. Milgrom, *Leviticus 1–16*, 836–37.

Death

The Structure of Numbers 19

1	Introductory heading
2–10	Preparation of the ashes of the red heifer
11–13	Purification for those who have touched a corpse
14–20	Additional purifications:
	– living in or entering a tent where someone has died (v. 14)
	– liquids in open vessels in such a tent are unclean (v. 15)
	– touching a human corpse in the open field (v. 16a)
	– touching a human bone or a grave (v. 16b)
	– purifications in these cases (vv. 17–20)
21–22	Summary instructions

The rituals related to corpse contamination reflect key aspects of the divine character while also serving the needs of boundary maintenance. As the location of the lord of life, YHWH's precincts were not be touched by the effects of human mortality. The remedy for corpse contamination seems to have a whiff of sympathetic magic about it, because the products of death are used to undo contact with the dead.[15] The ashes of a red heifer are mixed with water to create a cleansing wash that must be administered to affected persons on the third and seventh day after they have been contaminated by contact with a human corpse.

The rules for corpse contamination also mark Israel's sacrificial system as unique in comparison with its neighbors, because these rules were so stringent. Even being present in the same dwelling where someone has died is sufficient to communicate uncleanness—as does touching a grave. Underlying these prohibitions, one can detect a strong polemic against cults of the dead, which were common in the religions of Canaan and elsewhere in the ancient Near East.[16]

15. Baruch A. Levine, *Numbers 1–20* (AB 4; New York: Doubleday, 1993), 471.

16. Levine, *Numbers 1–20*, 472–77.

Sex

The Structure of Leviticus 15[17]

1–2b			Narrative introduction
A	2b–15		Irregular genital discharge in a male
B	16–17		Regular genital discharge in a male
C	18		Uncleanness in intercourse.
B'	19–24		Regular genital discharge (menstruation) in a woman
A'	25–30		Irregular genital discharge in a woman
31–33			Summary statements

This chapter shows organization by ring structure. Each paragraph about genital discharge deals with problems of contagion and ritual solutions. Milder problems in vv. 16–24 are framed by more serious issues in vv. 2–15 and 25–30. Serious cases demand not only time limitations and washing but also sacrifice.

In the case of a man who has an emission of semen for any reason (vv. 16–17), he is considered unclean until the evening. Anything made of cloth or skin on which the sperm has landed must be washed and is considered unclean until evening. The woman with whom he has had intercourse also becomes unclean (v. 18). Both of them must wash themselves and observe a waiting period until the beginning of the next day (the evening) before they are eligible to enter sacred space.

The question as to why a discharge of semen should require even a mild form of ritual purification is difficult to answer. Psychological and biological explanations may both have a place. If the normal function of sperm was to induce pregnancy, did the risk that the woman might not be fertilized require a ritual remedy?[18] Was it, therefore, the case that every ejaculation risks some loss of potential life?[19] Does semen emission represent some kind of disruption, a sort of simulacrum of chaos?[20] Or are we on firmer ground to appeal to an experience of human limitation, one in which seminal emission testifies to a boundary between God and human beings because YHWH has no need to reproduce himself?

17. As analyzed in Milgrom, *Leviticus 1–16,* 930–31.

18. Liss, "Ritual Purity," 351–52.

19. Timothy M. Willis, *Leviticus* (AOTC; Nashville: Abingdon, 2009), 135.

20. Erhard S. Gerstenberger, *Leviticus* (OTL; Louisville: Westminster John Knox, 1996), 202.

Cases of irregular genital emissions are regarded as more serious in terms of communicating ritual uncleanness. Both the man and the woman undergo comparable rites of purification. Probably one should assume that absences in ritual prescriptions for these cases are to be filled in from parallel cases. For example, if a man with an irregular or regular genital discharge has to wash himself before he is considered ritually clean (Lev 15:13), this applies to the cases of women as well (see Lev 15:28), although it is not spelled out.[21]

In comparison with many traditional societies, biblical menstrual rules were lenient. The woman was not quarantined or isolated from her home. Moreover, as long as she and others around her were scrupulous about touching with washed hands, the contagion of impurity could be controlled.[22] Rabbinical exegesis concluded that a woman became ritually pure seven days after the end of her period. Apparently, the extension of the time of uncleanness to seven days after the end of her period was inferred from the fact that this time period is called for in the case of the woman whose unusual flow of blood ceases (Lev 15:28). But this is not the only way to read the text. At least one ancient Jewish community, the Karaites, held that a woman's ritual impurity did not extend past the end of her period.[23]

Birth

The Structure of Leviticus 12

1–2a		Heading
2b–4	Main instruction: impurity in the case of birthing a boy	
	5	Ancillary instruction: impurity in the case of birthing a girl
6–7	Purification instructions	
	8	Ancillary instruction: rituals for the poor

As in many other biblical instructions, the law in vv. 2b–5 is framed conditionally (if . . . then). Its sections are marked by different forms of the Hebrew word that means "if." The primary instruction in vv. 2b–4 is marked by the Hebrew particle *kî*; the subclauses in v. 5 and v. 8 are marked by the Hebrew particle *ʾim*.

21. Milgrom, *Leviticus 1–16*, 934–35.
22. Milgrom, *Leviticus 1–16*, 952–53.
23. Milgrom, *Leviticus 1–16*, 935.

According to vv. 2b–4, when a women gives birth to a son, she is subject to two stages of ritual impurity. For the first seven days, the new mother has to observe the same restrictions as if she was menstruating. During the next thirty-three days, the only restrictions on her are that she cannot touch holy objects or visit the sanctuary (forty days in total). Verse 5 adds to the law by considering the case if she gives birth to a girl. Then, both forms of ritual impurity are doubled: menstrual impurity rules apply for fourteen days and for a further sixty-six days she is not to touch holy objects or visit the sanctuary (eighty days in total).

Whether she gives birth to a boy or a girl, when the new mother has completed the period of purification she is to bring sacrifices to the entrance of the tent of meeting. The sacrifices in vv. 6–7 are listed in the order whole burnt offering (*ʿolâ*) and purification (*ḥaṭṭāʾt*). This reflects the organization of the ritual prescriptions in Leviticus 1–5, in which the whole burnt offering is listed before the purification offering. Actually, the order of presentation would have been the reverse: the lamb of the burnt offering would have been presented after the bird for the purification offering.[24] A codicil (v. 8) addresses situations in which the woman was too poor to bring a lamb as a burnt offering (cf. Luke 2:22–24).

To date, no plausible explanation has been offered for the double period of impurity in the case of a woman who gives birth to a girl. Some writers claim there is no sexism implied in the longer timetable when a girl is born.[25] Leviticus 12, however, clearly encodes androcentric values. A male priesthood is responsible for integrating the woman back into the worshipping community. This action fits into a common pattern in agrarian societies in which physical birth had to be supplemented by sacrificial rituals overseen by men. While women had charge over the realm of physical birth, it was male ritual specialists who had the task of restoring the birthing mother into good relationship with social space.[26]

Unlike the motivations that underlie some of the ritual concerns regarding sex in Leviticus 15, the anxieties that attend the birth rituals in Leviticus 12 are easier to comprehend. In antiquity, the most common cause of mortality for adult women was childbirth. Not only was there a risk for fatal hemorrhaging, but the threats of edema and eclampsia in the last trimester

24. John E. Hartley, *Leviticus* (WBC 4; Dallas: Word, 1992), 167.

25. See Milgrom, *Leviticus 1–16*, 751; Jonathan Klawans, *Impurity and Sin in Ancient Judaism* (New York: Oxford University Press, 2000), 39.

26. Nancy Jay, *Throughout Your Generations Forever: Sacrifice, Religion, and Paternity* (Chicago: University of Chicago Press, 1992), 30–40.

and puerperal fever after delivery made birthing a dangerous time. Consequently, many traditional societies surround birth with various rituals and taboos. Birthing women must have been seen as drifting perilously close to the realm of death. Little wonder, therefore, that the Priestly purity system regarded the situation as one demanding sacrificial intervention.

Developments

With the loss of the Second Temple, most of the purity concerns found in Leviticus and Numbers ceased to be operative in the day-to-day lives of Jews. Exceptions to this include the concern for keeping kosher (based on Levitical food rules) and observing the menstrual taboo. Although Christians generally describe the effect of the New Testament dispensation as relieving them from the purity (as opposed to the moral) thinking of Leviticus and Numbers, birth and menstruation have continued to be sources of anxiety in Christianity. This is shown, for example, in the use (over many centuries) of rituals for allowing women who have given birth to reenter sacred space.[27] Moreover, at times church practice has discouraged menstruating women from taking Holy Communion.[28]

In fact, no less than in Priestly theology, issues connected to the imitation of God and boundary maintenance have always been important in Christian circles. Such fundamental human experiences as eating, sex, and mortality call for careful and circumspect actions. Each of them represents an opportunity to work out what it means to be faithful to the divine source of the community's identity and purpose. No less than ancient Israel, the church also knew itself called to be a holy people (1 Pet 1:16).

Jesus's own relationship to purity teachings was rather complex.[29] Nevertheless, Jews in the early church did abandon key concerns of ritual purity, such as those expressed by food rules (Acts 10). This appears to have been motivated by apocalyptic expectation. What would be the status of the law

27. E.g., Susan K. Roll, "The Churching of Woman after Childbirth: An Old Rite Raising New Issues," *Questions liturgiques/Studies in Liturgy* 76 (1995): 206–29; Kathryn Wehr, "Understanding Ritual Purity and Sin in the Churching of Women: From Ontological to Pedagogical to Eschatological," *St. Vladimir's Theological Quarterly* 55 (2011): 85–105.

28. See, e.g., Wehr, "Understanding Ritual Purity," 92; Anita Hannig, "The Pure and the Pious: Corporeality, Flow, and Transgression in Ethiopian Orthodox Christianity," *Journal of Religion in Africa* 43 (2013): 316.

29. James D. G. Dunn, "Jesus and Purity: An Ongoing Debate," *NTS* 48 (2002): 449–67.

when the messianic age dawned? While the majority view in Judaism is that the Torah is eternal and will never be abrogated, some rabbinic thinkers believed that reforms would take place in the messianic age.[30] For example:

- The Messiah will propose new meanings and interpretations of the Torah. (Gen. R. 98:9)
- All sacrifices will be annulled except the sacrifice of thanksgiving. (Lev. R. 9:7)
- In the time of the Messiah a new Torah will be given that will dispense with the dietary laws.[31]

Similar ideas may have led influential leaders in the early church to regard biblical food laws and other markers of ritual purity as nonbinding on the followers of Jesus. In no small measure, differences between first-century Jews who joined the infant church and those who rejected the Christian message turned on models of the messianic hope. Would the messianic age demand a new Torah? If so, what would it look like? And had the messianic age dawned with the resurrected Christ or not?

30. Warren Harvey, "Torah," *EncJud*, 15:1244.

31. Louis Ginzberg, *The Legends of the Jews* (Philadelphia: Jewish Publication Society, 1968), 5:47–48.

CHAPTER 16

The Holiness Code: Crops, Tattoos, and Loving Your Neighbor

Read: Leviticus 18–20

The most well-known passage in Leviticus comes from 19:18b, "you shall love your neighbor as yourself." Parallels to this ethical teaching can be found in many religious traditions around the world. Jesus ranked it as the most important of all the commandments, right after and besides the call to love God with all one's heart, mind, and strength (Mark 12:29–31). But Leviticus 19 addresses other topics which do not seem to have much to do with love of neighbor: cultivating a field with two different crops (v. 19), when to start harvesting fruit trees (vv. 23–25), and prohibitions about getting tattoos (v. 28). What holds the various prescriptions and prohibitions of Leviticus 19 together? How can it swing, seemingly so arbitrarily, from extremely important ethical concerns to ones that appear (at least to a modern mind) rather trivial?

This chapter will attempt to answer this question while also introducing the laws of the so-called "Holiness Code" (H). A key point is that behind the apparent disorganization of Leviticus 19 is a sophisticated approach to the problems of constituting a viable community in sacred space. Analogous relationships between the Body, the Temple, and the Community were worked out in this collection of legal discourse.

The chapter begins by recalling some of the points of Chapter 10, but it will also expand on them. The laws of the Holiness Code (H) share many assumptions with the laws of the Priestly writers discussed in Chapters 11–15 (P). In particular, P and H share an approach to cultivating good relationships with the Holy that relies on patterns of polar opposites. They also share a distinct method of analysis through their affinity with analogical thought patterns (this mode of legal thinking is described below). The laws of H, particularly those in Leviticus 18–20, provide a good illustration of how analogical thinking works. For this reason, the next section of the chapter analyzes these paradigmatic expressions of the worldview of H. The chapter ends with some observations about the importance of binary patterns of thought and analogical thinking to New Testament writers.

The Analytical Method of P and H

In *Leviticus as Literature,* the anthropologist Mary Douglas draws attention to a contrast between "analogical thinking" and "discursive thinking."[1] Discursive thinking is the way we are accustomed to describing relationships in the modern world. In the fields of law or science, for example, we want to know which rules are the most important. We expect to have the premises of any system of rules set out for us so we can understand what principles are of primary importance and how other laws both assume these principles and are derived from them. A good example of a body of regulations based on discursive thinking is the canon law of the Roman Catholic church. Here ancillary rules are derived from and related to statements of general norms that appear at the beginning of sections of church law.[2]

This is not how the laws of Leviticus operate. Leviticus reflects thought patterns that can be found in a number of traditional cultures around the world. A major trait of its thinking is that it forms its vision of relationships by presenting concrete examples rather than by spelling out abstract principles. No less than discursive logic, analogical thinking can also be systematic; but it is systematic in a different way. We can think of discursive thinking as a sort of "vertical" system. It likes its relationships to be set out in hierarchical lines that lead from first principles to secondary applications. Analogical thinking represents a sort of "horizontal" system.[3] What it articulates as norms for one sphere of life can also be true of another, though the connections may not be spelled out.

1. Mary Douglas, *Leviticus as Literature* (Oxford: Oxford University Press, 1999), 15–20. Douglas prefers to discuss an opposition between "analogical thinking" and "rational-instrumental" thinking. That terminology is avoided here, because it may suggest that systems based on analogical thought processes lack logic or rationality.

2. "Code of Canon Law," http://www.vatican.va/archive/ENG1104/_INDEX.HTM (accessed 31 Oct. 2014).

3. Douglas, *Leviticus as Literature,* 15–16.

What Douglas has discerned is that there is a correspondence between the spheres of Body, Temple, and Community in the laws of P and H.[4] These three different areas of human experience can be related on the level of analogy. Laws pertaining to one sphere of human experience have implications for the others, although these inferences may not be made explicit. In fact, this lack of comprehensiveness is one of the stimuli for the development of the oral law and its flowering in the great works of rabbinic Judaism: the Mishnah and the Talmuds.

By way of illustration, consider the prohibition in Lev 19:26, a law found in H: "You shall not eat anything with its blood." This is a food rule. As seen in the last two chapters, similar concerns appear in P because contact with bloody bodies risks ritual defilement. Certain categories of animals are forbidden as food because they are meat eaters. Moreover, it is claimed by H that eating meat fit for sacrifice but which has not been properly drained of blood makes one guilty of bloodshed (Lev 17:4). The rule against eating blood works on the three levels of Body, Temple, and Community. It operates on the bodily level as a food rule. At the same time, this rule has important religious dimensions. As Douglas notes, "blood belongs to God alone."[5] This is a criterion acted out in sacrificial worship again and again. The same rule also helps to define the community of Israel over against other communities: Israel is distinctly God's people because it does not consume blood.

As noted previously, the system of thought running through the laws of P and H rests on a number of binary categories. These polar values have analogical value for generating rules in the spheres of Body, Temple, and Community. Below is a list of significant polarities that operate in the laws of both P and H. This chart picks up the contrast between the clean and the unclean discussed in Chapter 15 and offers a complementary description of the sphere of positive values described in Chapter 12.

Major Polar Values in Priestly Thinking

Positive (+)	Negative (–)
Clean	Unclean
Holy	Unholy
Justice	Injustice

4. Mary Douglas, "Deciphering a Meal," *Daedalus* 101 (1972): 61–81.
5. Douglas, "Deciphering a Meal," 77.

Life	Death
Order	Chaos
Purity	Impurity
YHWH	Idols

The system of binary thought shared by P and H, with its opposition between holiness and defilement, finds its reference point in the character of God, thought of as pure life, pure order, and pure justice. As the people of God, Israel's vocation was to cleave to these positive values ritually and morally. The binary opposition assumed in the laws in P and H stands in contrast to certain ways of thought found in East Asian philosophies. In Priestly thinking, positive and negative do not balance each other; rather, they clash in a potentially violent manner. According to P and H, life depends on ordered relationships with the pure realm of being that is God.

Both P and H are concerned with actions that defile people morally as well as ritually. Where H innovates is through its concern for the defilement of the land (18:25). In addition, it demands that Israel cultivate holiness in every area of life. If Israel cannot control defiling behaviors, the land will sicken and vomit out the people (18:28–29)—a metaphor for exile.

Analogical Thinking in Leviticus 18–20

Leviticus 18–20 provide good illustrations of analogical thinking in biblical law. These chapters also illustrate typical emphases of H. Here, rules about right sexual relationships in chapters 18 and 20 form an envelope (ring composition) around Leviticus 19. For this reason, the following discussion turns first to Leviticus 18 and 20, then to Leviticus 19.

Leviticus 18 and 20

The Contents of Leviticus 18 and 20

18	1–5	Exhortation against following the customs of Egypt and Canaan
	6–18	Laws against incest
	19–23	Other prohibited behaviors (mainly sexual)
	24–31	The penalty for defilement (exile)

20	1–5	Against Molech worship
	6	Against divination
	7–8	Demand for holiness
	9	Reverence for parents
	10–16	Sexual acts that demand the death penalty
	17–21	Sexual acts where the death penalty is indirect
	22–26	The rewards of holiness and the penalty for defiling the land
	27	Against divination

While these laws allow for the possibility of polygamy, most families in Israel were probably monogamous. Only elite males would be able to afford more than one wife.[6]

Leviticus 18 and 20 may be based on independent formulations of a common tradition.[7] This tradition must have originated in the Holiness school, because it mandates stringent punishments for sexual relationships that were not necessarily disapproved of in earlier times. Consider the following:

Variations in the Assessment of Sexual Relations in Biblical Literature

	Unpunished	Punished
marriage to two sisters at the same time	Gen 29:21–29	Lev 18:18
marriage to father's sister	Exod 6:20	Lev 18:12; 20:20
marriage to half sister	Gen 20:12; 2 Sam 13:13	Lev 18:9; 20:17
marriage to dead brother's wife	Deut 25:5–6	Lev 20:21
sex during menstruation	Lev 15:24	Lev 18:19; 20:18

H has proscribed a number of sexual relationships acceptable at one time in ancient Israel. For example, Abraham married his half sister, Sarah (Gen 20:12). By the same token, Tamar tries to forestall rape by her half brother Amnon by assuring him that the king would give her in marriage (2 Sam 13:13). Jacob, of course, married the sisters Rachel and Leah (Genesis

6. C. J. H. Wright, "Family," *ABD* 2:766.

7. Jacob Milgrom, *Leviticus 17–22* (AB 3A; New York: Doubleday, 2000), 1766–68.

29). H regards sex with a woman during her period much more severely than P, which simply makes the man unclean for the same time as the woman (Lev 15:24). It also appears that H prohibits the custom of levirate marriage, in which a man is required to impregnate the widow of his childless brother.[8] Nevertheless, this custom was well established (see Deut 25:5–6 and the book of Ruth).

In general, the sexual rules of Leviticus 18 and 20 mean to preserve clear lines of descent in the family.[9] It is troubling, however, that in their concern to proscribe incest neither Leviticus 18 or 20 contain an explicit prohibition against sex between a father and his daughter. The matter may be addressed obliquely in Lev 18:17 and 20:14, which forbid sex with both a woman and her daughter. In fact, rabbinic authorities used these verses to prohibit father-daughter incest (m. Sanh. 9.1). It is also possible that the prohibition against sex with near kin (*šĕʾēr*) in Lev 18:6 assumes the daughter as a prohibited relationship. The daughter is explicitly named as a member of the category of near kin in Lev 21:2.[10]

The need for clean lines of descent is an expression of the assumption that various kinds of mixing are to be avoided in the areas of Body, Temple, and Community. Note, for example, how the motif of adultery is applied to concerns of both Community and Temple. Adultery is proscribed literally (Lev 18:20; 20:10), but it also becomes symbolic. According to Lev 20:6, turning to divination specialists and wizards is "prostitution" or "whoring" (Hebrew root *z-n-h)*. This usage echoes the imagery of prostitution and adultery as ways of describing illegitimate religious activities in prophetic literature (e.g., Jeremiah 2; Ezekiel 16; Hosea 4). Notice also that idolatry is connected to the list of sexual sins in Lev 18:21–23.

The issue of mixing what needs to be kept separate also appears in Lev 18:22–23 and 20:13–16. Sex with animals violates a chain of being in which human beings are in a hierarchical relationship over animals (cf. Gen 1:28; 9:2—both Priestly texts). Reasons for a prohibition against same sex relationships between males are more obscure. These prohibitions are unique to H, whereas other biblical legal collections also proscribe sex with animals (Exod 22:19 and Deut 27:21). Most likely, the problem is a mixing of the roles of men and women. Leviticus 18:22 and 20:13 appear to reflect

8. Milgrom, *Leviticus 17–22*, 1758; Timothy M. Willis, *Leviticus* (AOTC; Nashville: Abingdon, 2009), 176.

9. Stephen F. Bigger, "The Family Laws of Leviticus 18 in Their Setting," *JBL* 98 (1979): 197–98.

10. Milgrom, *Leviticus 17–22*, 1526–28.

an ancient opinion that it was wrong for a man to allow himself to be penetrated like a woman.[11]

In these sets of laws, the absence of any reference to same sex relationships between women cannot be accidental. Note that both men and women are mentioned in the laws against bestiality. Evidently, sex between women did not violate an important social hierarchy.

Leviticus 19

There is disagreement among scholars about how to discern a coherent structure in Leviticus 19. One common solution, based on attempts to orient the contents of Leviticus 19 to the organization of the Ten Commandments, must be abandoned. Recent reconstructions agree, however, that there is an important chapter division at v. 19.[12] This perception is reinforced by a repetition between v. 18 and v. 34:

> you shall love your neighbor as yourself (v. 18)
> you shall love the alien as yourself (v. 34)

The phrases seem to stand at the endpoint of two halves of Leviticus 19: vv. 1–18 and vv. 19–36.

While it may be difficult to explain its current literary arrangement, the conceptual logic of Leviticus 19 is less problematic. Leviticus 19 is interested in exploring the relevance of various categories of behavior for life in the community. These affect everything from bodily integrity (vv. 27–28) to sacramental obligations to God and temple (vv. 3–8, 30–31). What is new and unexpected from the perspective of the purity regulations reviewed in the last chapter is the extensive attention given to relationships with one's neighbors and fellow community members. These moral and ethical concerns are characteristic of H as opposed to P.

The contents of Leviticus 19 are a good illustration of the ways in which various categories of binary opposites can be expressed in law:

11. Jerome T. Walsh, "Leviticus 18:22 and 20:13: Who is Doing What to Whom?" *JBL* 120 (2001): 208.

12. See Jonathan Magonet, "The Structure and Meaning of Leviticus 19," *HAR* 7 (1983): 151–67; Moshe Kline, "'The Editor Was Nodding': A Reading of Leviticus 19 in Memory of Mary Douglas," *JHebS* 8, art. 17 (2008): 40–41; Willis, *Leviticus*, 166–68.

Categories of Polar Thinking in Leviticus 19

Binary category		Examples
Honor	Shame	honoring parents and the aged, vv. 3, 32
Sacred	Profane	the Sabbath, vv. 3, 30
		fruit trees forbidden until the fifth year, vv. 23–25
YHWH	False gods	no idols, v. 4
		against non-Yahwistic rituals, v. 26b
Generosity	Meanness	care for the poor and the disabled, vv. 9–10, 14
Justice	Injustice	no theft or perversion of justice, vv. 11, 13, 15–16
Love	Hate	love the neighbor and the resident alien, vv. 17–18, 34
Purity	Impurity	avoid illegitimate crop and cloth mixtures, v. 19
Holiness	Defilement	against eating blood, v. 26; prostitution, v. 29
		against using wizards and mediums, v. 31
Life	Death	avoid disfigurement with signs of death, vv. 27–28a
Freedom	Slavery	do not mark your body with a tattoo, v. 28b
Truth	Falsehood	use honest measures, vv. 35–36

The contents of Leviticus 19 constitute a good example of analogical thinking. Motifs related to Body, Temple, and Community are connected. In fact, many of these laws invoke more than one form of binary thinking. For example, the opposition between life and death also includes the illegitimate cultic functionaries mentioned in v. 31, as they specialized in consulting the dead.[13]

Groups of related concerns have been combined in Leviticus 19, although the grouping is easier to see in the first half of the chapter. In Lev 19:1–18, rules about revering God and parents (vv. 3–4) give way to regulations regarding the proper treatment of sacrificial meat (vv. 5–8). Combination of the concepts of eating and justice may explain the transitional status of vv. 9–10. Feeding the poor (vv. 9–10) is a justice issue. The entry of the theme of justice explains the presence of rules about fairness that conclude with v. 18 and the command to "love your neighbor as yourself."

Leviticus 19:19 signals a concern for illegitimate mixtures which dominates many of the rules that follow. The opposition between freedom and slavery furnishes an explanation for the ban against tattooing in v. 28. The verse also serves as a good example of the analogies between Body, Temple, and Community. In the biblical context the prohibition against tattooing is best explained

13. Milgrom, *Leviticus 17–22*, 1700–1702.

as a ban on slave marks (either by branding or impressing the skin with ink). This custom, therefore, disfigures the Body. With respect to the Community, as will be seen in the next chapter, H prohibits Israelites from making slaves of their neighbors (fellow Israelites) in Leviticus 25. However, the same rule also affects temple service. It would be wrong to make once free Israelites bear the marks of slavery when they are called upon to worship the God of the exodus.[14]

Developments

The last chapter suggested that the early church believed that the messianic era authorized revision of the Torah. The decision not to demand observance of purity laws, such as food rules, set it on a collision course with what became normative Judaism. No such dramatic break is detectable with respect to ideas of moral defilement. No less than with Jewish groups such as the Dead Sea Scroll sect and early rabbinic thinkers,[15] moral defilement was an important concern for the early church. In fact, the relationship between holiness and ethics was a cornerstone of teaching in early Christianity. Generally speaking, in the early church holiness meant separation from sin.[16] According to Heb 12:15, an immoral or godless person could defile many.[17] For Paul, no less than Priestly writers, holiness was opposed to all forms of moral defilement (2 Cor 7:1). His insistence that sexual immorality could defile God's temple (conceived as the body of Christ) has a precedent in the worldview of H (cf. 1 Cor 6:12–20).

As in the laws of P and H, systems of binary thought played an important role among early Christian thinkers. Paul, for example, discerned a conflict within himself in which an impulse to sin waged against his desire to do God's will (Rom 7:14–25). His analysis has a parallel in a rabbinic psychology that discerns a conflict between the "good inclination" (*yēṣer haṭṭōb*) and the "evil inclination" (*yēṣer hārāʿ*).[18] Binary categories also appear in Paul's

14. See Milgrom, *Leviticus 17–22*, 1694–95; John Huehnergard and Harold Liebowitz, "The Biblical Prohibition against Tattooing," *VT* 63 (2013): 74.

15. Surveyed in Jonathan Klawans, *Impurity and Sin in Ancient Judaism* (New York: Oxford University Press, 2000), 67–117.

16. Robert Hodgson, Jr., "Holiness (NT)," *ABD* 3:253.

17. Wayne G. McCown, "Holiness in Hebrews," *Wesleyan Theological Journal* 16 (1981): 70.

18. George F. Moore, *Judaism in the First Centuries of the Christian Era* (New York: Schocken, 1971), 1:483–85.

contrast between the "works of the flesh" and the "fruits of the Spirit" in Gal 5:16–23. The early church, in concert with its Jewish roots, urged its members to choose the way of the Spirit and spurn the way of the flesh (Gal 6:8).

Where the Jews who formed the early church can be seen innovating is in the way they synthesized the concerns for Body, Temple, and Community. However one may wish to understand the words of institution attributed to Jesus in his last meal with his disciples, the words "this is my body" (Mark 14:22; 1 Cor 11:24) run together the three themes that play such an important part in the analogical thought system of the laws of P and H.[19] The Community made up of his disciples is both the Body of Christ (1 Cor 10:16–17) and the Temple of God's Holy Spirit (1 Cor 3:16).

19. Douglas, "Deciphering a Meal," 76.

CHAPTER 17

Jubilee: Utopia or Practicality?

Read: Leviticus 25

The institution of the Jubilee is an excellent example of the confluence of conservatism and innovation in biblical law. The Holiness Code (H) reaffirms existing Sabbath traditions and measures for the relief of the poor while also transforming them into a new program of land redistribution in Leviticus 25. After a survey of the structure of Leviticus 25, its two concepts of Sabbatical Year will be described. Underlying them is a theology of land tenure and the need to sanctify time. After describing these ideas, this chapter will turn to analogous concepts in the Gospels.

Structure

The Structure of Leviticus 25

I. Guidelines for Sabbatical and Jubilee Years (2–17)
   - 2–7 The Sabbatical Year
   - 8–17 The Jubilee Year

II. Exhortation to obedience (18–24)

III. Four cases of redemption (25–55)
   - 25–34 Selling land to stay out of debt
   - 35–38 Landless persons
   - 39–46 Debt slavery to a fellow Israelite
   - 47–55 Debt slavery to a non-Israelite

Section I contains instructions for two kinds of seven-year patterns. The first (vv. 2–7) requires that all crop fields in Israel be left fallow every seven years. Encouragement for keeping the national Sabbatical Year appears in vv. 18–24 (Section II). Israel should expect a bumper crop in the sixth year to carry the people over until the harvest is reaped in the eighth year.[1]

A second seven-year pattern is set out in vv. 8–17 for the Year of Jubilee. These rules mandate a redistribution of land so that it returns to its traditional owners. While we now associate a Jubilee with a fiftieth anniversary, scholars debate the timing of the Jubilee Year. The text is ambiguous. It seems that the Jubilee takes place every forty-nine years (v. 8). If so, why is Israel called to hallow the fiftieth year in Lev 25:10? This apparent contradiction can be reconciled, however, by assuming this verse means the fiftieth year after the last Jubilee.[2]

Section III deals with four cases of economic hardship of increasing severity:[3]

1. Verses 25–34 address a case in which a person avoided debt slavery by selling ancestral lands. It is assumed that the nearest kinsman who has the means will buy the land, but that the seller remains economically independent. If he (normally land ownership was in the hands of males) cannot redeem his land before the Jubilee, the land returns to its original owner on the Jubilee. Subconditions in vv. 29–34 deal with differences between houses in cities (which are often not subject to redemption in the Jubilee) and houses in unwalled towns (which are).
2. Verses 35–38 deal with a person who has no land left to sell; but he can remain somewhat independent if he leases land from a kinsman. He is to have the same legal rights as a resident alien. Loans for interest to fellow Israelites are forbidden.

1. Similarly, a double portion of manna fell on the sixth day so that Israel could enjoy the Sabbath in the wilderness, according to Exod 16:22–26. Like Leviticus 25, Exod 16:22–26 is from H. See Israel Knohl, *The Sanctuary of Silence: The Priestly Torah and the Holiness School* (Minneapolis: Fortress, 1995), 17.

2. The debate on dating the Jubilee Year is summarized in Jacob Milgrom, *Leviticus 23–27* (AB 3B; New York: Doubleday, 2000), 2248–50. Milgrom believes that the Jubilee was separate from the end of the seventh Sabbatical Year; but see the calculations in Young Hye Kim, "The Jubilee: Its Reckoning and Inception Day," *VT* 60 (2010): 147–51.

3. This summary is based on Timothy M. Willis, *Leviticus* (AOTC; Nashville: Abingdon, 2009), 211.

3. The third case provides a remedy when persons are so poor that they cannot lease land. So, they have to sell their labor to survive (vv. 39–43). This group is to be treated not as slaves but as hired workers. A distinction is made between Israelites and non-Israelites. Foreigners can be bought or sold as slaves and made to serve on a permanent basis (vv. 44–46).
4. Leviticus 25:47–55 deals with the worst case scenario: an Israelite becomes a debt slave to a non-Israelite, specifically a resident alien (*gēr*). In using the term *gēr*, Lev 25:47 seems to be thinking of people who were ethnically not part of Israel but nevertheless resident in it. Leviticus 25:47–55 insists on the right of Israelites to redemption when a kinsman pays off their loan (whether the *gēr* agrees or not), or at the very least on the Year of Jubilee.

Origins of the Sabbatical Year in Leviticus 25

The Sabbatical Year in Lev 25:2–7 has a parallel in Exod 23:10–11. As noted in Chapter 9, the Sabbatical Year for the land in Exod 23:10–11 was intended as a relief measure for the poor. The law in Exodus does not indicate that all people in ancient Israel were required to fallow their fields at one time.[4] In contrast, Lev 25:2–7 demands that the entire nation leave its fields fallow on the same sabbatical timetable. The reason for doing so differs from Exodus. According to Lev 25:2, it is the land itself that requires a Sabbath. Neglect of the land's Sabbaths will be punished by exile from the land (see Lev 26:34–35).

The modifications made by Leviticus 25 suggest that the Holiness school was aware of Exod 23:10–11.[5] Evidently, it also knew the slave law in Exod 21:2–6.[6] However, Leviticus 25 does not restrict debt slavery to a seven-year period. This can be explained as a result of its refusal to allow Israelites to be reduced to slave status. Instead they are to be treated as hired persons. Any money lent to them is to be interest free and their earnings can be directed entirely towards paying their debts.[7]

4. Milgrom, *Leviticus 23–27*, 2155–56.

5. Milgrom, *Leviticus 23–27*, 2155.

6. Bernard M. Levinson, "The Birth of the Lemma: The Restrictive Reinterpretation of the Covenant Code's Manumission Law by the Holiness Code (Leviticus 25:44–46)," *JBL* 124 (2005): 617–39.

7. Milgrom, *Leviticus 23–27*, 2253.

Scholars debate whether Leviticus 25 is dependent on the laws for debt and slave release in Deut 15:1–18. The dominant assumption is that Leviticus 25 knows Deuteronomy 15; but the reverse has also been argued.[8] Deuteronomy 15:1–3 proposes another kind of type of Sabbatical Year than the one encountered in Exod 23:10–11.[9] The Deuteronomic program of release is not an agricultural institution. It is directed towards the cancellations of loans. The supplementary laws that follow in Deut 15:7–11 make it clear that Deuteronomy is thinking of a national practice that should take place every seven years.

One can demonstrate that Lev 25 and Deut 15:1–18 provide alternate solutions to the same economic problem: debt and landlessness in ancient Israel. Leviticus 25 seems to know the wording of the Deuteronomic law,[10] while promoting its own solution. Unlike Deuteronomy, Leviticus 25 has no concept of an institution of debt release on a seven-year cycle. It provides no explicit statement that debt release will take place even in the Year of Jubilee;[11] but two details suggest that H connects return of the land with debt release. First, Lev 25:10 calls the Jubilee a time of *dĕrôr* (NRSV "liberty"). The Hebrew word *dĕrôr* means "release" and is associated with the freeing of slaves (e.g., Isa 61:1; Jer 34:8). Second, Lev 25:39–46 wants its readers to regard Israelites liable to debt slavery as hired workers. As this passage argues against treating fellow countrymen as slaves, it must know of the practice of debt slavery for nonpayment of loans.

Ancient Near Eastern societies also knew of periodic proclamations of debt release that affected the entire nation. These are well attested in Mesopo-

8. A majority of biblical critics regard the slave laws in both Deut 15:12–18 and Lev 25:39–46 as derived from and responding to details in Exod 21:2–6; e.g., Bernard M. Levinson, "The Manumission of Hermeneutics: The Slave Laws of the Pentateuch as a Challenge to Contemporary Pentateuchal Theory," in *Congress Volume: Leiden 2004*, edited by André Lemaire (VTSup 109; Leiden: Brill, 2006), 281–324. Prominent advocates for the priority of Leviticus 25 to Deuteronomy 15 include Sara Japhet, "The Relationship between the Legal Corpora in the Pentateuch in Light of Manumission Laws," in *Studies in the Bible 1986*, edited by Sara Japhet (ScrHier 31; Jerusalem: Magnes, 1986), 63–89; Milgrom, *Leviticus 23–27*, 2251–57.

9. William S. Morrow, *Scribing the Center: Organization and Redaction in Deuteronomy 14:1–17:1* (SBLMS 49; Atlanta: Scholars, 1995), 99.

10. Not only do both Leviticus 25 and Deuteronomy 15 have the word *dĕrôr*, but they also share vocabulary regarding slavery; see Levinson, "The Birth of the Lemma," 636.

11. Stephen A. Kaufman, "A Reconstruction of the Social Welfare Systems of Ancient Israel," in *In the Shelter of Elyon: Essays on Ancient Palestinian Life and Literature in Honor of G. W. Ahlström*, edited by W. Boyd Barrick and John R. Spencer (JSOTSup 31; Sheffield: JSOT, 1984), 283.

tamia. One name given to these actions in Akkadian (the Semitic language spoken in ancient Assyria and Babylonia) is *mīšaru(m),* a word that can mean "justice." Often when a new king came to the throne he would annul various debts and/or taxes. Debt release was also used by Mesopotamian monarchs as a form of financial stimulus in times of difficult economic conditions.[12] Another Akkadian word for this practice is *andurāru(m),* a cognate of the Hebrew noun *dĕrôr.* Both *andurāru* and *dĕrôr* connote concepts such as "freedom, emancipation, release." However, there are no indications that proclamations of *andurāru* or *mīšaru* were implemented regularly in ancient Mesopotamia. With respect to ancient Near Eastern culture, biblical law innovated by demanding debt release on a sabbatical timetable.

The Year of Jubilee in Israelite History

According to rabbinic tradition, the Jubilee was never practiced during Second Temple times.[13] Nor is there evidence that a national Jubilee was observed in the preexilic period.[14] These facts raise questions about when the Jubilee laws of Leviticus 25 were composed.

Leviticus 25 assumes a tradition of land ownership that reaches back before the monarchical period. The ancient Israelite family was supposed to be a self-sustaining economic unit. It supported itself (at least, partly) on a piece of land believed to be passed down to it from the time Israel established itself in Canaan. The basic unit of agricultural production and social organization was called the *bêt ʾāb.* A literal translation of this phrase would be "father's household," but it can be also translated as "family." Depending on social and economic conditions, the *bêt ʾāb* could constitute an extended family of several generations.[15]

Ideally, the *bêt ʾāb*'s traditional land-holding was "inalienable." It was not supposed to pass out of the family's control. Normally, the eldest son inherited the family property from his father. Other sons might receive some portion of the family real estate, but they were not to receive as much as the firstborn son. Daughters did not inherit property if there were sons

12. Ancient Near Eastern evidence for royal decrees of debt release is surveyed in Moshe Weinfeld, *Social Justice in Ancient Israel and in the Ancient Near East* (Minneapolis: Fortress, 1995), 75–96.

13. Aaron Rothkoff, "Sabbatical Year and Jubilee," *EncJud* 14:580.

14. Milgrom, *Leviticus 23–27,* 2247.

15. C. J. H. Wright, "Family," *ABD* 2:762.

Figure 8. The Jubilee was inaugurated by blowing a shofar, made of a ram's horn. The shofar is still used to sound the beginning of the Jewish New Year and the Day of Atonement, the same day on which the horn was to sound the Jubilee (Lev 25:9). As this dove of peace has discovered, the shofar is not easy to play – nor was the Jubilee easy to implement. Cartoon of "Dove and Shofar." © Steven Greenberg. Used with permission.

(though see the exception in Job 42:15). A crisis occurred when there was no male heir, as indicated in reflections on the legal status of the daughters of Zelophehad (Num 27:1–11; 36:1–12).[16] This was normally resolved by the fact that the family belonged to a larger kinship group called the *mišpāḥâ* ("clan").[17]

As far as the *bêt ʾāb* was concerned, marriage was supposed to be *exogamous,* outside the family; but it was normally *endogamous* with respect to the clan.[18] In other words, members of the family were expected to marry inside the *mišpāḥâ.* This was required to keep the land within its traditional kinship group. If and when the family was reduced to such dire financial straits that it lost control of its land or failed to produce any male heirs, the clan was obliged to help out. Consequently, the land was kept in the clan

16. For different interpretations of these chapters, see Katherine Doob Sakenfeld, "Zelophehad's Daughters," *PRSt* 15.4 (1988): 37–47; David H. Aaron, "The Ruse of Zelophehad's Daughters," *HUCA* 80 (2009): 1–38.

17. Hebrew *mišpāḥâ* is often translated "family." However, in ancient Israel the *mišpāḥâ* was a group of related families that had a claim over a certain territory, hence "clan" would be a better translation. The clan was assumed to belong to a larger (and looser) kinship group called a "tribe"; see Wright, "Family," 761–62.

18. Wright, "Family," 761.

even if it could not be kept in the family; see, for example, Numbers 36 or the social circumstances assumed in the book of Ruth.[19]

The need for land redistribution would have asserted itself when economic and political conditions severely compromised Israel's traditional ideology of land tenure. There are grounds for thinking that localized land redistribution probably did take place in Israel; but programs of local land reform cannot be identified with the national program of the Jubilee.[20] Apparently the inequitable distribution of land first become a national concern during the eighth century BCE. Prophets such as Amos and Isaiah decried the growth of a landless peasantry and the expansion of large estates at their expense.[21] Moreover, the predations of the Assyrian and Babylonian Empires in the late monarchical period would have severely disrupted patterns of traditional land ownership in Israel through various forms of depopulation and confiscation. Since neither the economic nor political conditions of the postexilic period recommend themselves for the conception of the Jubilee,[22] dating the composition of Leviticus 25 requires a time either in the late monarchical period or in the exilic era.

In the postexilic period, those returning from exile committed themselves to a Sabbatical Year of release that combined features of both a fallow year and forgiveness of debts (Neh 10:31), but not the Jubilee. During the Second Temple period, Jews living in the land of Israel continued to observe the seventh year of release.[23] Some time after the Bar Kokhba rebellion (132–135 CE), however, economic and political conditions made the institution too problematic to continue. Efforts have been made to revive the Sabbatical Year of release in modern Israel.[24]

19. Raymond Westbrook, *Property and the Family in Biblical Law* (JSOTSup 113; Sheffield: JSOT, 1991), 68.

20. See Kaufman, "Social Welfare Systems," 280.

21. Milgrom, *Leviticus 23–27*, 2243–44.

22. Milgrom, *Leviticus 23–27*, 2242–43; John S. Bergsma, "The Jubilee: A Post-Exilic Priestly Attempt to Claim Lands?" *Bib* 84 (2003): 225–46.

23. Evidence of Sabbatical Year observance can be found in Josephus, who reports that both Alexander the Great (*Ant.* XI 338) and Julius Caesar (*Ant.* XIV 202) decreed tax releases for Jews in the land of Israel because of the national practice of fallowing the land every seventh year; see Rothkoff, "Sabbatical Year and Jubilee," 583.

24. Rothkoff, "Sabbatical Year and Jubilee," 584–85.

God and the Nature of Time

The concept of the Jubilee Year is an expression of biblical law at its most idealistic and utopian. Regardless as to when Leviticus 25 is dated, there is no reason to think it was ever put into practice. What was its value, therefore, to ancient readers of the Torah? Most likely, Leviticus 25 provided an important expression of two significant theological ideas that Israel needed to commit to as it anticipated a rather uncertain future. The first is connected to the belief that the true owner of the land is YHWH. The second is the importance of the Sabbath as an institution for hallowing time.

As noted in the previous chapter and also in Chapter 10, the emphasis on the holiness of the land is a distinctive characteristic of H as opposed to P. Leviticus 25 is based on the idea that land was given to Israel by YHWH, who was regarded as its true owner (v. 23).[25] He graciously allowed his covenant partners to use it, provided that they keep his commands. As the land was thought to have been apportioned according to tribe, clan, and family at Israel's origins, Leviticus 25 expresses a desire to recreate the time in which everyone will once again be able to "sit under their own vines and under their own fig trees" (Mic 4:4).

The concept of Jubilee and its ideal of land redistribution is, therefore, closely connected to the biblical demand to sanctify time. An emphasis on the holiness of time compels human beings to take seriously the nature of history and how to conform it to the divine will.[26] The sanctification of time also entails recognizing the unique nature of moments in time. Not all time possesses the same quality. Some times are capable of being more redemptive than others.[27]

In prescribing a Sabbath of Sabbaths, Leviticus 25 asks Israel to convert its ordinary time into sanctified time. The Jubilee, therefore, becomes an opportunity to acknowledge God's sovereignty in a special way. Land redistribution participates in the hallowing of time, because the Sabbath ideal prefigures an end to conflict between human beings unequal in social status and between humanity and the earth (see Exod 20:8–11).[28] This is also the impetus for realizing the Jubilee.

25. E. W. Davies, "Land: Its Rights and Privileges," in *The World of Ancient Israel: Sociological, Anthropological and Political Perspectives*, edited by R. E. Clements (New York: Cambridge University Press, 1989), 349–53.

26. Abraham J. Heschel, *The Sabbath* (New York: Farrar, Straus and Giroux, 2005), 8–10.

27. Abraham J. Heschel, *God in Search of Man: A Philosophy of Judaism* (New York: Farrar, Straus and Giroux, 1983), 203–4.

28. See Heschel, *God in Search of Man*, 15–24, esp. p. 23,

The idealism of Leviticus 25 can seem like a utopian dream with no hope of realization. Still, it is connected to a deep sense of the meaning of time that Western civilization owes to the Tanakh. This is the concept of the "future." Alone among the literatures of the ancient world, the Bible holds out the possibility that the future need not be like the past.[29] However human beings feel bound in their current time and space, dreams of freedom and release are not simply false hopes nurtured in an unalterable present. They are signs that God has not finished making the world.

Developments

According to Luke 4:18–19, Jesus inaugurated his ministry with reference to the Jubilee.[30] He opened a synagogue scroll to read:

> The Spirit of the Lord is upon me,
> because he has anointed me
> to bring good news to the poor.
> He has sent me to proclaim release to the captives
> and recovery of sight to the blind,
> to let the oppressed go free,
> to proclaim the year of the Lord's favor.

"The year of the Lord's favor" here alludes to the Year of Jubilee. The imagery of Jubilee appealed to the imagination of the early church because it intersected with two key concepts: release and the inauguration of a new quality of time.

The word for "release" in Isa 61:1 is Hebrew *dĕrôr,* the same concept that lies behind the idea of land and slave release in Leviticus 25. Translated into Greek, *dĕrôr* becomes *aphesis,* a word that means "liberation, release." In fact, *aphesis* occurs two times in the biblical quotation in Luke 4:18. The Septuagint (on which the citation of Luke 4:18 is based) translates Hebrew *dĕrôr* with *aphesis* in the phrase "to proclaim release to the captives" in Isa 61:1. Also, *aphesis* appears in a citation from Isa 58:6 which has been inserted into the quotation from Isaiah 61 as "to let the oppressed go free."[31]

29. Thomas Cahill, *The Gifts of the Jews: How a Tribe of Desert Nomads Changed the Way Everyone Thinks and Feels* (New York: Talese, 1998), 130–32.

30. François Bovon, *Luke 1: A Commentary on the Gospel of Luke 1:1–9:50* (Hermeneia; Minneapolis: Fortress, 2002), 54.

31. Joel B. Green, *The Gospel of Luke* (NICNT; Grand Rapids: Eerdmans, 1997), 210.

The repetition of *aphesis* shows that concepts of liberation and release were important in the ministry of Jesus and his disciples. A clue to their centrality is also found in Matthew's version of the Lord's Prayer: "forgive us our debts as we forgive our debtors" (Matt 6:11). Here (as in the parallel in Luke 11:4), the Greek word meaning "to forgive" is *aphiēmi*. It is one of the common verbs meaning "forgive" in the New Testament, and the noun *aphesis* is related to it. The emphasis on "debts" in Matthew's version of the Lord's Prayer underscores the fact that Jesus's mission was holistic; it was intended to be physically, economically, psychologically, and spiritually redemptive.[32]

Forgiveness of debts was not just a spiritual concern in first-century Judea and Galilee. To the downtrodden poor, it was a real issue in a world of economic hardship and social injustice. In fact, Jesus's program of *aphesis* represented a number of different forms of release. These included literal debt release (see Matt 18:23–35), release from demonic attack and healing from disease (see Luke 13:10–17), as well as the forgiveness of sins.[33] In the hands of Jesus and his followers, the Jubilee was a metaphor for the in-breaking of a new era of salvation. The Jubilee symbolized an era of messianic fulfillment. As in Leviticus 25, this new time would be an epoch of reversals, particularly favoring the poor—however they are to be defined.

Jubilee thinking was deeply embedded in the ancient Jewish thought world. For example, the methods of scriptural interpretation that Luke 4:18–19 relies on reflect traditional methods of Jewish exegesis.[34] In fact, Isaiah 61 was important in the messianic expectations of a number of early Jewish groups, including the Dead Sea Scroll sect.[35] Jesus's proclamation of a time of release hearkens back to Leviticus 25 and through it to the Sabbath ideal. The coming world order he proclaimed was deeply grounded in early Jewish spirituality, even as he offered his contemporaries a new opportunity to sanctify history for the purposes of God.

32. Paul Hertig, "The Jubilee Mission of Jesus in the Gospel of Luke: Reversals of Fortune," *Missiology* 26.2 (1998): 171–72.

33. Green, *Luke*, 210–12.

34. Charles Kimball, "Jesus' Exposition of Scripture in Luke 4:16–20: An Inquiry in Light of Jewish Hermeneutics," *PRSt* 21.3 (1994): 179–202.

35. Hertig, "The Jubilee Mission of Jesus," 167.

Further Reading: Priestly and Holiness Writings

Davies, Douglas. "An Interpretation of Sacrifice in Leviticus." *ZAW* 89 (1977): 387–99.

Douglas, Mary. "Deciphering a Meal." *Daedalus* 101 (1972): 61–81.

———. "Atonement in Leviticus." *JSQ* 1 (1993): 109–30.

———. *Leviticus as Literature*. Oxford: Oxford University Press, 1999.

Feder, Yitzhaq. *Blood Expiation in Hittite and Biblical Ritual: Origins, Context, and Meaning*. WAWSup 2. Atlanta: Society of Biblical Literature, 2012.

Gane, Roy E. *Cult and Character: Purification Offerings, Day of Atonement, and Theodicy.* Winona Lake: Eisenbrauns, 2005.

George, Mark K. *Israel's Tabernacle as Social Space*. AIL 2. Atlanta: Society of Biblical Literature, 2009.

Haran, Menahem. *Temples and Temple-Service in Ancient Israel*. Winona Lake: Eisenbrauns, 1985.

Hurowitz, Victor Avigdor. *"I Have Built You an Exalted House": Temple Building in the Bible in Light of Mesopotamian and Northwest Semitic Writings*. JSOTSup 115. Sheffield: JSOT, 1992.

Janzen, David *The Social Meanings of Sacrifice in the Hebrew Bible*. BZAW 344. Berlin: de Gruyter, 2004.

Jenson, Philip Peter. *Graded Holiness: A Key to the Priestly Conception of the World*. JSOTSup 106. Sheffield: JSOT, 1992.

Klein, Ralph W. "The Tabernacle in the Book of Exodus." *Int* 50 (1996): 264–76.

Knohl, Israel. *The Sanctuary of Silence: The Priestly Torah and the Holiness School*. Minneapolis: Fortress, 1995.

Koester, Craig R. *The Dwelling of God: The Tabernacle in the Old Testament, Intertestamental Jewish Literature, and the New Testament*. CBQMS 22. Washington: Catholic Biblical Associaton of America, 1989.

Levinson, Bernard M. "The Birth of the Lemma: The Restrictive Reinterpretation of the Covenant Code's Manumission Law by the Holiness Code (Leviticus 25:44–46)." *JBL* 124 (2005): 617–39.

Liss, Hanna. "The Imaginary Sanctuary: The Priestly Code as an Example of Fictional

Literature in the Hebrew Bible." In *Judah and the Judeans in the Persian Period*, edited by Oded Lipschitz and Manfred Oeming, 663–89. Winona Lake: Eisenbrauns, 2006.

———. "Ritual Purity and the Construction of Identity: The Literary Function of the Laws of Purity in the Book of Leviticus." In *The Books of Leviticus and Numbers*, edited by Thomas Römer, 329–54. BETL 215. Leuven: Peeters, 2008.

Meshel, Naphtali. "The Grammar of Sacrifice: Hierarchic Patterns in the Israelite Sacrificial System." *JBL* 132 (2013): 543–67.

Milgrom, Jacob. "The Biblical Diet Laws as an Ethical System: Food and Faith." *Int* 17 (1963): 288–301.

———. "Rationale for Cultic Law: The Case of Impurity." *Semeia* 54 (1989): 103–9.

Modéus, Martin. *Sacrifice and Symbol: Biblical Šəlāmîm in a Ritual Perspective*. ConBOT 52. Stockholm: Almqvist & Wiksell International, 2005.

Sommer, Benjamin D. "Conflicting Constructions of Divine Presence in the Priestly Tabernacle." *BibInt* (2001): 41–63.

Walsh, Jerome T. "Leviticus 18:22 and 20:13: Who Is Doing What to Whom?" *JBL* 120 (2001): 201–9.

Watts, James W. "The Rhetoric of Sacrifice." In *Ritual and Metaphor: Sacrifice in the Bible*, edited by Christian A. Eberhart, 3–16. RBS 68. Atlanta: Society of Biblical Literature, 2011.

PART FIVE

Israel in the City

CHAPTER 18

Deuteronomy: Introduction

Uniquely among collections of biblical law, Deuteronomy takes the city seriously as a socially and theologically important institution.[1] Ostensibly, the Covenant Code situates Israel in rural environments with ready access to local altars (Exod 20:24–25), while Priestly law assumes that the nation is settled in close proximity to the sacrificial cult (Numbers 2). But Deuteronomy's Israel typically consists of city-dwellers who do not live close to the only place where sacrifice was permitted. For these reasons, Deuteronomy modifies some important legal and religious traditions.

The following chapters of this book describe a number of Deuteronomy's innovative features:

- It radicalized preexisting commitments to YHWH as the sole God of Israel (Chapter 19).
- It transformed older institutions of sacrifice (Chapter 20).
- It reformed the legal system (Chapter 21).
- It revised important customs in family law (Chapter 22).

This chapter begins by describing the structure of Deuteronomy. Then it will touch on matters related to its distinctive literary style. After reviewing problems related to dating the book, it will close with some notes on Deuteronomy's influence on the literature of late Second Temple Judaism.

1. See Don C. Benjamin, *Deuteronomy and City Life: A Form Criticism of Texts with the Word City (*ʿîr*) in Deuteronomy 4:41–26:19* (Lanham: University Press of America, 1983), 17–18.

The Meaning of "Deuteronomy"

"Deuteronomy" literally means "a second/repeated law." The word originated with the Septuagint's translation of a phrase in Deut 17:18, which requires the king to have "a copy of the law." The Hebrew name for the book is based on the fact that, reflecting an ancient custom of giving titles to books by referring to their opening lines, it begins with the phrase *ʾēllê haddĕbārîm*, meaning "these are the words." Jewish scholarship often refers to Deuteronomy as *Dĕbārîm* ("[the] words").

Structure

It is difficult to describe the structure of Deuteronomy because different patterns of organization can be found in it. The following will consider three distinct literary outlines:

1. Story
2. Law book
3. Treaty

1) Deuteronomy as a story

Deuteronomy represents itself as the "farewell discourses" of Moses.

As a story, Deuteronomy can be divided into four narrative scenes:[2]

1:1–4:43	The words of Moses
4:44–28:68	The instructions of Moses
29:1–32:52	The covenant speeches of Moses
33:1–34:12	The final blessings of Moses

Each of these has a distinct heading. "The words of Moses" recounts the journey of Israel from Mount Horeb, where it received the law, to the plains of Moab, where it stands "today" (Deut 4:8). A second section recounts Mo-

2. This division is based on Norbert Lohfink, "Bund als Vertrag im Deuteronomium," *ZAW* 107 (1995): 218–20.

ses's instructions to the people. The third section relates Moses's actions and words as covenant mediator. The fourth section tells of final blessings, the appointment of Joshua, and the death of Moses.

2) Deuteronomy as a law book

Another way of looking at the organization of Deuteronomy is to think about it as an ancient Near Eastern law book. While not every legal collection has the same structure, a classical Mesopotamian composition such as the Laws of Hammurabi shows a literary arrangement that can also be applied to Deuteronomy:

Prologue	1–11
Laws	12–26
Epilogue	27–34

According to this layout, Deuteronomy begins with a number of introductory speeches in chapters 1–11. They recount YHWH's past history with the people (1–3) and then urge the people to obey the instructions of their God (4–11). An extensive body of law is found in Deuteronomy 12–26, which is followed by material about the acceptance of these laws by Israel (27–34).

3) Deuteronomy as a treaty document

In comparison to other biblical texts, Deuteronomy stands out because of the fullness of its use of various elements commonly found in ancient Near Eastern treaties (not every treaty contains all of these elements):

The Treaty Formulary in Biblical Texts[3]

	Exodus 19–24	*Joshua 24*	*Deuteronomy*
Preamble	19:3b; 20:2a	2a	1:1–6a; 5:6a

3. From Moshe Weinfeld, *Deuteronomy and the Deuteronomic School* (Oxford: Clarendon, 1972), 66.

Historical prologue	19:4; 20:2b	2b–13	1:6b–3:29; 5; 9:7–10:11
Basic stipulation of allegiance	19:5–6a; 20:3–6	14–18	4:1–24; 6:4–7:26; 10:12–22
Covenant clauses	20:7–17; 21–23	23	12–26
Invocation of witnesses	–	22, 27	4:26; 30:19; 31:28
Blessings and curses	–	19–20	28
Oath–imprecation	–	–	27:11–26; 29:10–29
Document deposit	–	–	10:1–5; 31:24–25
Periodic reading	–	–	31:9–13
Copies	–	26	17:18–19; 31:26

The treaty form was previously mentioned in Chapters 3 and 6, where it was associated with the covenantal idea. In Deuteronomy, the treaty metaphor is used to express the belief that Israel had no king but YHWH. In other words, Israel was to be a theocracy, whose supreme ruler was God alone.

Much of Deuteronomy can be connected to elements in the treaty paradigm. The book contains parallels to the preamble, in which the parties to the treaty are named. The recapitulation of Israel's past history with God recalls the motif of the historical prologue. After a basic call to loyalty, the various expectations that the overlord has imposed on the vassal are set out (covenant stipulations). Curses and blessings are divine rewards and punishments for keeping or breaking the covenant. Sometimes, treaties contain clauses that stipulate when they are to be read and where copies are to be stored; these are also found in Deuteronomy.

Due to its extensive connections with the treaty metaphor, Deuteronomy is the collection of biblical law most conscious of itself as Scripture. Deuteronomy 31:26 imagines that the ark of the covenant will contain not only the Ten Commandments (cf. 10:1–5), but a copy of the entire law that Moses has mediated to Israel. This covenant document is to be read in the hearing of all Israel every seven years (31:10).

The Rhetoric of Deuteronomy

One of Deuteronomy's distinctive features is a repertoire of phrases and themes that recur in its speeches and laws. Often, when scholars use the adjective "Deuteronomic," they are identifying stylistic features that have links to phraseology characteristic of the book of Deuteronomy. Major categories of Deuteronomic rhetoric include the following:[4]

Examples of Deuteronomic Rhetoric

1. THE STRUGGLE AGAINST IDOLATRY
   "to go after/follow other gods" (e.g., Deut 8:19; 13:2; 28:14)
2. CENTRALIZATION OF WORSHIP
   "the place that the LORD will choose" (e.g., Deut 12:14; 14:23; 16:2)
3. EXODUS, COVENANT, AND ELECTION
   "to choose" (e.g., Deut 7:6; 10:15; 14:2)
   "remember that you were a slave in Egypt" (e.g., Deut 5:15; 15:15; 24:18)
4. OBSERVANCE OF THE LAW AND LOYALTY TO THE COVENANT
   "to learn to fear the LORD" (e.g., Deut 4:10; 31:12)
   "with all the heart and soul" (e.g., Deut 4:29; 6:5; 10:12)
5. INHERITANCE OF THE LAND
   "the land as an inheritance (to possess)" (e.g., Deut 15:4; 19:10; 26:1)
6. RETRIBUTION AND MATERIAL MOTIVATION
   "so that it may be well with you" (e.g., Deut 5:16; 12:25)
   "to perish/be uprooted from the land" (e.g., Deut 11:17; 28:21; 29:28)

This distinctive style influenced other biblical books as well, especially the Deuteronomistic History (DtrH), which includes Joshua, Judges, 1–2 Samuel, and 1–2 Kings, and the book of Jeremiah. Since Jeremiah and the DtrH use phrases that show derivation from their form in Deuteronomy, scholars often distinguish between a "Deuteronomic" style and later "Deuteronomistic" language. Here are some examples of Deuteronomistic phrases:

> "the city/Jerusalem that the LORD has chosen"
> 1 Kgs 8:44; 11:13, 32, 36; 14:21; 2 Kgs 21:7; 23:27
>
> "(the place that the LORD will choose) to put his name there"
> Deut 12:5, 21; 14:24; cf. 1 Kgs 9:3; 11:36; 14:21; 2 Kgs 21:4, 7

Compare these examples with the chart above. Whereas Deuteron-

4. See Weinfeld, *Deuteronomy and the Deuteronomic School,* 320–49.

omy never names the "place the LORD will choose," the DtrH identifies it as Jerusalem. Also, the DtrH prefers the phrase "to put his name there" to Deuteronomy's formula "to make his name dwell there." Occasionally, Deuteronomistic phrases appear in Deuteronomy (e.g., Deut 12:5). This shows that Deuteronomy and Deuteronomistic literature influenced each other as their canonical forms were developing.[5]

Dating Deuteronomy

The book of Deuteronomy has been called "the Archimedean point of the Pentateuch."[6] The phrase refers to the ancient Greek philosopher's discovery of the principle of the lever. Archimedes is supposed to have said, "Give me a lever long enough and a fulcrum on which to place it, and I shall move the world." It may be strange to think of a biblical book as a fulcrum, but Deuteronomy has been used in the world of critical scholarship to get leverage on many important issues. For example, the ability to date Deuteronomy allows for relative dating of other legal and literary traditions. Those that have been used or altered by (a version of) Deuteronomy must have existed previously. Biblical writings dependent on Deuteronomic texts must have been written later.

A great deal of energy has been expended in order to determine what the original version of Deuteronomy looked like. A technical term taken from German is often used to refer to this hypothetical document: *Urdeuteronomium* ("original Deuteronomy"). Scholars want to know when *Urdeuteronomium* was composed and how to account for the literary history of the book until it reached its canonical form.

The book of Deuteronomy was built up over time. Of the three patterns of literary organization described above, the narrative outline is the latest. The fact that Deuteronomy 1–3 rehearses material found in Numbers 20–31 suggests that their primary purpose is to integrate the book of Deuteronomy into the historical narrative that flows from Exodus to Numbers.[7] The same can be said for Deuteronomy 34, which recounts the death of Moses. The composition of these chapters is connected to processes associated with

5. Raymond F. Person, *The Deuteronomic School: History, Social Setting, and Literature* (SBLStBL 2; Atlanta: Society of Biblical Literature, 2002), 6.

6. Moshe Weinfeld, *Deuteronomy 1–11* (AB 5; New York: Doubleday, 1991), 16–17.

7. See, e.g., Richard D. Nelson, *Deuteronomy* (OTL; Louisville: Westminster John Knox, 2002), 36.

creating the Pentateuch, which probably reached something close to its canonical form by the end of the Persian period.

How much older was *Urdeuteronomium* and what did it consist of? Most scholars agree that the primary layer of Deuteronomic law contained many, if not all, of the laws connected to the centralization of sacrifice and related reforms. Therefore, the earliest edition of Deuteronomy probably included (at least) versions of Deut 12:13–19; 14:22–27, 28–29; 15:1–3; 19–23; 16:1–17, 18–20; 17:8–13; 18:1–6; 19:2–7; 26:1–10. The grammatical syntax used in writing these laws tips the balance in favor of a treaty form for *Urdeuteronomium.* Throughout the rules related to the centralization of worship, the overlord/YHWH is consistently referred to in the third person ("he") and the vassal/Israel in the second person ("you"). This grammatical usage corresponds to the syntax common in Iron Age treaty texts. It is not found in ancient Near Eastern legal collections or law books.[8]

If Deuteronomy was originally a kind of treaty document, then it must have had some of the other elements typical of the genre. One can probably find the preamble of *Urdeuteronomium* and a basic call to loyalty in Deuteronomy 6. In fact, Deut 6:4 contains the confession of faith that represents the basic commitment of Judaism to this day: "Hear, O Israel: The LORD is our God, the LORD alone."[9] A version of Deuteronomy 28 probably ended *Urdeuteronomium* with covenant blessings and curses.

The original Deuteronomy was expanded over the years, as more rhetorical material was added by way of introduction and conclusion and more laws were added to chapters 12–26. Consequently, Deuteronomy acquired the form of a law book. Later, the law book pattern was obscured as Deuteronomy was integrated into the pentateuchal canon.

Three models are possible for dating *Urdeuteronomium* based on how its treaty affinities are analyzed.

1) By and large, historical prologues are missing from Iron Age treaties (cf. Deuteronomy 1–3), as are combinations of curses and blessings (cf. Deut 28:1–19). These are fairly common, however, in the Late Bronze Age treaties made by the Hittite Empire with subordinate rulers in the northern Levant.

8. William S. Morrow, "A Generic Discrepancy in the Covenant Code," in *Theory and Method in Biblical and Cuneiform Law: Revision, Interpolation and Development*, edited by Bernard M. Levinson (JSOTSup 181; Sheffield: JSOT, 1994), 138.

9. Deuteronomy 6:4 is difficult to translate. For options, see Nathan MacDonald, *Deuteronomy and the Meaning of 'Monotheism'* (FAT/2 1; Tübingen: Mohr Siebeck, 2003), 62–70.

Figure 9. Esarhaddon's Succession Treaty (also known as the "Vassal Treaty of Esarhaddon") was imposed on the provinces and vassals of the Neo-Assyrian world in 672 BCE in order to ensure that the crown prince, Assurbanipal, would become the next king of the Assyrian Empire. Photograph of the Vassal Treaty of Esarhaddon. From, D. J. Wiseman, The Vassal Treaties of Esarhaddon, Part 1 (Iraq 20; London: British School of Archaeology in Iraq, 1958), 1. Copyright the British Institute for the Study of Iraq (Gertrude Bell Memorial). Used with permission.

Consequently, some scholars argue that Deuteronomy must be largely based on that tradition, because of its parallels to Hittite treaty rhetoric.[10]

2) Deuteronomy comes from the late monarchical period (eighth-seventh century), because it shows dependency on the treaty rhetoric of the Neo-Assyrian Empire. A prominent example is the idiom "to speak defection or rebellion" *(dabbēr sārâ)* in Deut 13:5 . This is equivalent to the Akkadian expression *dabābu surrāte,* which describes the actions of rebellious treaty partners in Neo-Assyrian documents.[11] Other linguistic usages in Deuteronomy also seem to be derived from Neo-Assyrian models.[12]

The long list of curses in Deuteronomy 28 is not typical of Hittite treaties. Lengthy curse sections, however, are common in Neo-Assyrian treaties and loyalty oaths. The most exhaustive list of curses is found in Esarhaddon's

10. E.g., Meredith G. Kline, *Treaty of the Great King. The Covenant Structure of Deuteronomy: Studies and Commentary* (Grand Rapids: Eerdmans, 1963); Joshua Berman, "CTH 133 and the Hittite Provenance of Deuteronomy 13," *JBL* 130 (2011): 25–44.

11. Weinfeld, *Deuteronomy and the Deuteronomic School,* 99.

12. William S. Morrow, "'To Set the Name' in the Deuteronomic Centralization Formula: A Case of Cultural Hybridity," *JSS* 55 (2010): 365–83.

Succession Treaty (EST). Also known as the "Vassal Treaty of Esarhaddon," it was imposed on the provinces and vassals of the Neo-Assyrian world in 672 BCE in order to ensure that the crown-prince Assurbanipal would become the next king of the Assyrian Empire. A number of scholars think that there are specific links between the EST and Deuteronomy.[13] A suggestive parallel is found in the curse section:

Parallels between Deuteronomy and Esarhaddon's Succession Treaty

Deut 28	Theme	EST §
26	carcasses as food for animals	41
27	skin inflammations	39
28–29	madness, blindness, dismay	40
30	fiancée raped, loss of home	42

Except for the alteration of EST §§ 41 and 39, the same material is found in the same order in Deuteronomy.

Moreover, there is another Iron Age treaty that has combined elements typically found in the Hittite treaty tradition and in Neo-Assyrian formulas.[14] It was found at Sefire, in present-day Syria, written in different versions on stone pillars. The Sefire treaties are dated to the mid-eighth century BCE. This parallel makes a case for viewing Deuteronomy as a composition of the late monarchical era.

13. See William S. Morrow, "The Paradox of Deuteronomy 13: A Postcolonial Reading," in *»Gerechtigkeit und Recht zu Üben«* (Gen 18, 19): *Studien zur altorientalischen und biblischen Rechtsgeschichte, zur Religionsgeschichte Israels und zur Religionssoziologie,* edited by R. Achenbach and M. Arneth (BZABR 13; Wiesbaden: Harrasowitz, 2009), 229. However, a number of recent studies deny any close relationship between Deuteronomy and the EST, e.g., Markus Zehnder, "Building on Stone? Deuteronomy and Esarhaddon's Loyalty Oaths (Part 1): Some Preliminary Observations," *BBR* 19 (2009): 341–74; Kenneth A. Kitchen and Paul J. N. Lawrence, *Treaty, Law and Covenant in the Ancient Near East* (Wiesbaden: Harrassowitz, 2012), 3:230–32; Carly L. Crouch, *Israel and the Assyrians: Deuteronomy, the Succession Treaty of Esarhaddon, and the Nature of Subversion* (ANEM 8; Atlanta: SBL, 2014), 47–92.

14. William S. Morrow, "The Sefire Treaty Stipulations and the Mesopotamian Treaty Tradition," in *The World of the Aramaeans,* vol. 3: *Studies in Language and Literature in Honour of Paul-Eugène Dion,* edited by P. M. Michèle Daviau, John W. Wevers, and Michael Weigl (JSOTSup 326; Sheffield: JSOT, 2001), 84–89.

3) While dating *Urdeuteronomium* to the late monarchy has held a majority position in critical biblical studies, a number of scholars have preferred an exilic date.[15] Among the evidence that might support this position are the following observations:

- Normally, one would expect a monarch in the ancient Near East to initiate this kind of sweeping innovation; but no credit is given to the king for promoting the reforms of Deuteronomy.[16]
- Some important parallels to Deuteronomic legal process appear in Neo-Babylonian trial records.[17]
- The treaty between Carthage and Philip of Macedon made in 215 BCE shows that affinities between Northwest Semitic treaties and Hittite models survived past the Iron Age.[18]

Of the three criteria listed, the most cogent is the lack of reference to a human monarch as lawgiver. Yet, the meaning of this absence is not obvious. Other unexpected absences also appear in Deuteronomy. For example, the book never mentions the name of YHWH's chosen place. However, the derivative and slightly later Deuteronomistic History has no problem identifying Jerusalem as God's chosen city (e.g., 1 Kgs 11:36).

As the Covenant Code, on which Deuteronomy relies (see Chapter 20), has no clear reference to a king, there may be a theological convention of regarding YHWH as the true ruler of Israel that a preexilic Deuteronomy did not want to call into question. In this regard, it is important to note that there were preexilic groups who regarded the premonarchical era with nostalgia, For example, the early prophecies of Jeremiah (late seventh century BCE) depict the exodus as a time when Israel was faithful to YHWH, while also criticizing its rulers (e.g., Jer 2:2–8). Jeremiah's prophetic imagination seems to be breathing the same air that inspired the first edition of Deuteronomy.

15. E.g., David H. Aaron, *Etched in Stone: The Emergence of the Decalogue* (New York: T. & T. Clark, 2006), 182–84; Juha Pakkala, "The Date of the Oldest Edition of Deuteronomy," *ZAW* 121 (2009): 388–401.

16. Pakkala "The Date of the Oldest Edition of Deuteronomy," 392–94.

17. Bruce Wells, *The Law of Testimony in the Pentateuchal Codes* (BZABR 4; Wiesbaden: Harrassowitz, 2004), 132.

18. See Michael L. Barré, *The God-List in the Treaty between Hannibal and Philip V of Macedonia: A Study in the Light of the Ancient Near Eastern Treaty Tradition* (Baltimore: Johns Hopkins University Press, 1983), 101–2.

Scholars have also noted northern Israelite traditions contained in the book, including the exodus motifs.[19] The most economical way of accounting for many of these affinities is to assume that northern legal and theological traditions made their way into Judah after the destruction of the kingdom of Israel by Assyria in 720 BCE. These traditions were assimilated by scribes from Judah intent on promoting reforms in the religion of the southern kingdom.[20]

Biblical tradition associates the book of Deuteronomy with the reign of King Josiah (ca. 640–609 BCE). 2 Kings 22–23 wants readers to understand that King Josiah's religious and political reforms were inspired by a discovery of "the book of the law" (*sēper hattōrâ;* see 2 Kgs 22:8, 11). This phrase implies that Josiah based his reforms on the book of Deuteronomy.[21] Nevertheless, scholars continue to debate the historical truth of Josiah's reforms and its connection to the book of Deuteronomy.[22]

Developments

If one looks at a standard edition of the Greek New Testament and counts the number of times books from the Pentateuch are quoted, Deuteronomy stands out because there are approximately fifty direct citations. The second most popular book is Exodus (about forty citations). The same picture appears among the biblical manuscripts found at Qumran. The Dead Sea Scrolls are the closest thing we have to a Jewish library from the first century CE. When manuscripts of the Pentateuch are counted, they distribute themselves as follows:

19. E.g., Weinfeld, *Deuteronomy 1–11,* 44–47.

20. See Weinfeld, *Deuteronomy and the Deuteronomic School,* 158–71.

21. Only Deuteronomy is called the "book of the law" in the Pentateuch (see Deut 29:21; 30:10; 31:26).

22. For some cautious reconstructions of the events in 2 Kings 22–23 which argue for a core of authentic historical memory, see Christoph Uehlinger, "Was There a Cult Reform under King Josiah? The Case for a Well-Grounded Minimum," in *Good Kings and Bad Kings,* edited by Lester L. Grabbe (LHBOTS 393; New York: T. & T. Clark, 2005), 279–316. The motif of finding a scroll to justify a cult reform is regarded quite suspiciously by some scholars; e.g., David Henige, "Found but Not Lost: A Skeptical Note on the Document Discovered in the Temple under Josiah," *JHebS* 7, art. 1 (2007): 1–17.

Torah Scrolls in the Dead Sea Scrolls

Genesis	20
Exodus	16
Leviticus	13
Numbers	7
Deuteronomy	30

These statistics may come as a surprise to modern readers, who are more easily oriented to biblical narrative than to law. Certainly, in the church much more attention is given to Israel's storyline than to the legal portions of the Pentateuch. In the first century CE, however, people took a different view. There were three probable reasons for this esteem for Deuteronomy among early Jewish thinkers.

1) More than any other biblical book, Deuteronomy spells out the importance of Israel's covenant with God. Various groups in late Second Temple times claimed to be God's true (new) covenant community, including both the Dead Sea Scroll sect and the early church.[23]
2) Deuteronomy holds out hope. Despite all its threats and dire warnings, Deuteronomy also tells its readers that God is never going to give up on his people, because the covenant relationship that God wants with his people can and will be restored (e.g., Deut 4:25–31). This would have been extremely important to the people of Judea, living under the oppressive thumb of a foreign ruler.
3) Finally, Deuteronomy states that God's will for Israel has been revealed in written form. As no other book in the Pentateuch, Deuteronomy validates the scriptural idea and sets the written text up as the charter document for Jewish faith and life. It also promotes the study of Torah as a central obligation (e.g., Deut 6:6–9). Thus it undergirds the unfolding tradition of exegesis and commentary so central to rabbinic Judaism.[24]

23. E.g., 1QpHab 2:3–4 and Heb 10:16–17.

24. Jacob Weingreen, *From Bible to Mishna: The Continuity of Tradition* (Manchester: Manchester University Press, 1976), 143–54.

CHAPTER 19

Covenant Theology and Religious Intolerance: Israel and the Canaanites

Read: Deuteronomy 7 and 13; Joshua 1–11

Few biblical motifs are as upsetting as the command to exterminate the Canaanite nations in Deuteronomy 7. The Scriptures shared by church and synagogue appear to authorize the destruction of whole populations. Did Israel's early thinkers believe that genocide was the will of God?

An answer to this question has to recognize that it operates on two levels. One is historical, the other ideological. On the one hand, as noted in Chapter 3, there is no reason to think that ancient Israel emerged as a distinct ethnic and religious entity in the land of Canaan through a decisive one-time action of military invasion. On the other hand, the fiction of the extermination of the Canaanites served important rhetorical functions. It reinforced a polemic against idolatry and idolatrous culture that is deeply embedded in Deuteronomy's covenant theology.

This chapter seeks to explain the ideology behind Deuteronomy 7. For that reason, it is necessary to examine Deuteronomy 13 also. It is important to notice that the same penalties administered to the Canaanite nations awaited apostate Israel as well. The chapter begins by briefly surveying the structures of Deuteronomy 7 and 13. It then turns to a discussion of the theological underpinnings of these chapters. These observations will help explain their origins and also shed some light on postbiblical developments.

Structure

Deuteronomy 7

The "charter" for Deuteronomy's treatment of the Canaanite nations is found in Deuteronomy 7:

The Structure of Deuteronomy 7

1–6	Basic Command
	– put the seven Canaanite nations to the ban (vv. 1–3)
	– do not intermarry with them (v. 4)
	– destroy the material culture of idolatry (v. 5)
	– motivation (v. 6)
7–11	Exhortation I: The character of YHWH
	– motivation (vv. 7–10)
	– command (v. 11)
12–16	Exhortation II: Obedience produces blessing
	– motivation (vv. 12–15)
	– command (v. 16)
17–24	Exhortation III: Assurance of military success
	– motivation (vv. 17–24)
	– command (vv. 25–26)

Various divisions of this chapter are possible. The table above shows that the demand not to have anything to do with idolatrous culture is basic to the chapter (vv. 1–5). This demand has three different components. One is to exterminate the Canaanite nations by putting them "to the ban" (*ḥērem*). This term denotes an act of total destruction of the populace. A second is to avoid intermarriage, and a third is to destroy the material culture of idolatry. All three criteria appeal to the fact that Israel has a special relationship with God: it is a holy people (v. 6).

The basic demand is reinforced by three sections that encourage obedience. Each has a similar structure: a span of motivating material leads to a reiteration of the basic commandments with which the chapter begins. Logically, the opening instructions of the chapter stand in tension with each other. If the Canaanite nations are exterminated (vv. 1–3), how does the problem of intermarriage exist (v. 4)? But this contradiction is mitigated in v. 22, which represents the conquest as a gradual process.

Deuteronomy 13

According to Deuteronomy 13, the extreme penalty awaits anyone in Israel who commits an act of apostasy. It highlights three situations:

vv. 1–5	the false prophet
vv. 6–11	the close family member or friend
vv. 12–18	the apostate town

The penalty for enticing someone to worship a god other than YHWH is death (vv. 5, 9–10). In the case of an idolatrous town, its entire populace is subject to the ban (*ḥērem*). The people are to be put to the sword, their property and livestock destroyed, and the site left as a perpetual ruin (vv. 15–17).

Covenant Theology and Exclusive Worship in Deuteronomy 13

It may come as a surprise to realize that, strictly speaking, Deuteronomy does not articulate a monotheistic theology. In fact, Deuteronomy never says it is wrong for non-Israelites to worship divine beings other than YHWH.[1] It is only wrong for Israel to do so; and it is wrong for anyone to do so in the land of Israel. To that end, God's people have to occupy an idol-free land, free from social intercourse with idol-worshipping peoples, and free from any visual or material representation of their god.

To appreciate Deuteronomy's worldview, it is helpful to distinguish the concepts "monotheism,""henotheism," and "polytheism." The cultures surrounding ancient Israel were polytheistic. They believed in a plurality of gods and goddesses who could be worshipped and propitiated. Henotheism insists that one's loyalty and worship ought to be directed towards a single deity. It does not necessarily hold the opinion that there are no other gods or divine realities in the cosmos, only that Israel has no business with them. Monotheism goes beyond henotheism to deny the reality of any other deity

1. Jeffrey H. Tigay, *Deuteronomy* (JPS Torah Commentary; Philadelphia: Jewish Publication Society, 1996), 470.

besides the one Israel worships. The first biblical thinker to explicitly articulate a monotheistic worldview was the late exilic prophet called the "Second Isaiah" (e.g., Isa 45:5–7).

The background to Deuteronomy's insistence on henotheism can be found in prophetic protests against Israelite popular religion in the Iron II period. Like the legendary Canaanites, a significant part of the population in preexilic Israel expressed itself in a religious culture that included sacred poles, pillars, and other divine images.[2] Against these trends stood the "YHWH-alone" movement.[3] It was an iconoclastic faction that insisted on the exclusive veneration of YHWH by Israel, without any visible representations (i.e., idols).

Deuteronomy shows affinities with the YHWH-alone movement through its insistence on Israel's exclusive relationship with God. It was also influenced by the covenantal idea and its manifestation in ancient Near Eastern politics. Kings demanded that their subjects show them exclusive loyalty. These politically exclusive relationships were ratified under oath to the gods by vassal treaties and loyalty oaths (see Chapter 6).

A useful explanation for the origins of Deuteronomy 13 is that it reflects a loyalty oath directed to YHWH.[4] The political underpinnings of Deuteronomy's insistence on exclusive loyalty to YHWH as its king are visible in ancient Near Eastern parallels to the demands set out in Deuteronomy 13, for example Esarhaddon's Succession Treaty (672 BCE):

> If you hear any evil, improper, ugly word which is not seemly nor good to Assurbanipal, the great crown prince designate, son of Esarhaddon, king of Assyria, your lord, either from the mouth of his enemy or from the mouth of his ally, or from the mouth of his brothers or from the mouth of his uncles, his cousins, his family, members of his father's line,

2. William G. Dever, "The Silence of the Text: An Archaeological Commentary on 2 Kings 23," in *Scripture and Other Artifacts: Essays on the Bible and Archaeology in Honor of Philip J. King,* edited by Michael D. Cogan, J. Cheryl Exum, and Lawrence E. Stager (Louisville: Westminster John Knox, 1994), 160; Robert Karl Gnuse, *No Other Gods: Emergent Monotheism in Israel* (JSOTSup 241; Sheffield: Sheffield Academic, 1997), 179.

3. Morton Smith, *Palestinian Parties and Politics That Shaped the Old Testament* (New York: Columbia University Press, 1971), 29–30; Gnuse, *No Other Gods,* 75–77. A pre- or proto-Deuteronomistic expression of YHWH-alone ideology can be found in Exod 23:20–33.

4. Christoph Koch, *Vertrag, Treueid und Bund: Studien zur Rezeption des altorientalischen Vertragrechts im Deuteronomium und zur Ausbildung der Bundestheologie im Alten Testament* (BZAW 383; Berlin: de Gruyter, 2008), 289–93.

> or from the mouth of your brothers, your sons, your daughters, or from the mouth of a prophet, an ecstatic, an inquirer of oracles, or from the mouth of any human being at all, you shall not conceal it but come and report it. (EST §10)[5]

What kind of religion demands such total devotion to its god that even close family members are to be put to death for violating this primary commitment (Deut 13:6–11)? There is a similarity between what is expected of Israel by YHWH and what is expected of the vassals of Assyria by Esarhaddon: unconditional loyalty on pain of death.

Deuteronomy 13:12–18 metes out destruction for an apostate town. This also has parallels in Iron Age politics. For example, this is what Assurbanipal says he did to those who rebelled against him in Lower Egypt:

> As for Sais, Mendes, and Tanis, which had rebelled and made an agreement with Taharka, these same cities I conquered. I put their inhabitants to death with the sword. Their corpses I impaled on stakes. I flayed their skins and covered the city walls with them. (Annals of Assurbanipal Prism B §10; ca. 667 BCE)[6]

The ferocity of the Neo-Assyrian loyalty oath tradition responds to the fact that the Neo-Assyrian Empire was far-flung and difficult to control. The ferocity of the loyalty oath to YHWH also communicates the urgency of maintaining Israel's spiritual center even when physical access to it was limited. There is no shortage of evidence that ancient Near Eastern kings dealt harshly with rebels and oath breakers. Frequently, they paid for their disloyalty with their lives. The same logic was applied by the writers of Deuteronomy to Israel's relationship with YHWH. Even so, it is not clear that exilic Israel was able or even willing to literally apply the death penalty to cases of apostasy. As Chapter 14 noted, death penalty language in biblical law has rhetorical as well as juridical functions.

5. Translation from Simo Parpola and Kazuko Watanabe, eds., *Neo-Assyrian Treaties and Loyalty Oaths* (SAA 2; Helsinki: Helsinki University Press, 1988), 33.

6. Translation based on Rykle Borger, *Beiträge zum Inschriftenwerk Assurbanipals* (Wiesbaden: Harrassowitz, 1996), 214.

The Origins of Deuteronomy 7

Both Deuteronomy 7 and 13 reflect the fact that Judah's scribes continued to rewrite and expand Deuteronomy during the exilic period and after. Deuteronomy 13 interrupts a more primary connection between the centralization laws in Deut 12:13–28 and their continuation in 14:22–29. It is widely regarded as belonging to a revision of *Urdeuteronomium*.[7] There are also many grounds for thinking that Deuteronomy 7 belongs to a later edition of the book.[8] Both the insertions of Deuteronomy 7 and 13 were probably contemporary with efforts to (re)write the Deuteronomistic History (DtrH) during the exilic period.[9] As the stories of Joshua's conquest of Canaan belong to the DtrH (Joshua 1–11), we might expect that they share a common theological and social outlook with Deuteronomy 7.

A few weeks after Jerusalem was captured in 587/6 BCE, the temple, royal palace, and homes of the aristocracy were burned to the ground. In addition, there was wide-ranging destruction of the fortress towns, which were pillaged and despoiled. Portions of the population of Judah and Jerusalem were forcibly deported by the Babylonian Empire in order to suppress the country's capacity to rebel. By any account, a sizable number of elite citizens, temple and military officials, and artisans was involved. Estimates vary, as one must also guess about the total size of Judah and Jerusalem at this time. It is possible, however, that at this time Judah's population was reduced by about half as a result of war, famine, deportation, and escape as refugees.[10]

Both Deuteronomy 7 and the conquest narratives in Joshua 1–11 reflect

7. Koch, *Vertrag, Treueid und Bund*, 130–33.

8. Michael Fishbane, *Biblical Interpretation in Ancient Israel* (Oxford: Clarendon, 1985), 199–20; Alexander Rofé, "The Laws of Warfare in the Book of Deuteronomy: Their Origins, Intent and Positivity," *JSOT* 32 (1985): 28–29.

9. Discussions of the origins of the DtrH are complex; this discussion follows Raymond F. Person (*The Deuteronomic School: History, Social Setting, and Literature* [SBLStBL 2; Atlanta: Society of Biblical Literature, 2002], 28) in his conclusion that, even if there was an attempt to write a version of the DtrH in late monarchical times, the earliest version that probably can be recovered from the biblical record dates to the exilic era. For an exilic dating of Deuteronomy 7, see William S. Morrow, "Deuteronomy 7 in Postcolonial Perspective: Cultural Fragmentation and Renewal," in *Interpreting Exile: Interdisciplinary Studies of Displacement and Deportation in Biblical and Modern Contexts,* edited by Brad E. Kelle, Frank R. Ames, and Jacob L. Wright (AIL 10; Atlanta: Society of Biblical Literature, 2011), 277–78.

10. Rainer Albertz, *Israel in Exile: The History and Literature of the Sixth Century B.C.E.* (SBLStBL 3; Atlanta: Society of Biblical Literature, 2003), 90.

the trauma of the destruction of Judah and Jerusalem by the Babylonians.[11] The challenge to Judah's sense of self-definition created by this catastrophe cannot be overstated. From the perspective of Judah's intellectuals, the exile increased the threat of cultural annihilation. It directly challenged their commitment to create a society that honored YHWH alone. Their response was to go on the offensive. They took materials and traditions available to them to produce law and narrative that would reinforce a commitment to YHWH, the God of Israel.

In addition to resemblances between Deuteronomy 13 and the Neo-Assyrian loyalty oath, another tactic used by the Deuteronomic thinkers was to tell a particular story about Israel's origins in the land of Canaan. As Chapter 3 noted, scholars are generally agreed that the extermination of the Canaanites commanded in Deuteronomy 7 and portrayed in Joshua is a fiction. Nevertheless, it was a valuable instrument for encouraging fidelity to YHWH under extremely threatening conditions.

The Deuteronomist's story of Israel's destruction of Canaan served a couple of different purposes. One was to provide an explanation for Israel's loss of the land by drawing implicit parallels with the Canaanites. However they actually vanished from the historical record, the disappearance of the peoples that once lived in Canaan was "remembered" as an act of God.[12] Another motif for writing Joshua 1–11 was to reinforce the perspective that successfully living as God's people meant not repeating the mistakes of the past.

To that end, the Deuteronomist's account of the conquest of Canaan blends memories of two forms of military violence. On the one hand, the conquest narratives recall the fate of various nations in the Levant (including Israel and Judah) who were crushed and exiled from their homelands by the Assyrian and Neo-Babylonian war machines. On the other hand, it complemented this recollection of foreign invasion and deportation with a model of holy warfare well known in the Northwest Semitic world: the *ḥērem*. In a military context, the *ḥērem* represents a vow in which the aspiring victor promises to dedicate all the spoils of war to a god in exchange for military success.[13]

11. For applications of trauma theory to Deuteronomy 7 and parallels, see William S. Morrow, "Putting the Neighbors in Their Place: Memory and Mindscape in Deuteronomy 2:10–12, 20–23," in *History, Memory, Hebrew Scriptures,* edited by Ian D. Wilson and Diana V. Edelman (Winona Lake: Eisenbrauns, 2015), 69–71; and "Deuteronomy 7 in Postcolonial Perspective," 283–89.

12. Tigay, *Deuteronomy,* 471–72.

13. Susan Niditch, *War in the Hebrew Bible: A Study in the Ethics of Violence* (New York: Oxford University Press, 1993), 29–37.

The *ḥērem* motif helped emphasize the exclusive nature of Israel's relationship with YHWH that Deuteronomy sought to create (cf. Deut 7:2), concerned as it was, primarily with religious identity rather than ethnic purity. The objective of the Deuteronomic conquest narrative was not to distinguish foreigners from Israelites/Judeans but to distinguish proper worship of YHWH from what it regarded as foreign and unacceptable religious proclivities.[14] It seems to reflect, therefore, a genre of foundation stories found elsewhere in the Mediterranean world. These stories tell of a violent migration into a land, even though archaeological and historical evidence suggests that the storytellers were native to the region. It appears that this sort of violent foundation story was told to emphasize the distinctiveness and superiority of a new form of social and political organization from older models.[15]

In fact, the myth of conquest promoted by the YHWH-alone tradition was directed at fellow Israelites. "Canaanite" was a cipher for a polytheistic or idol-worshipping Israelite. According to the YHWH-alone theology, a polytheistic Israelite was no Israelite at all.[16] Clearly, a sense of social apprehension and the idea that Israel's boundaries can be compromised by dangerous insiders permeates the book of Deuteronomy.[17] Deuteronomy 7 participated in this anxiety; but it also offered readers a solution by calling on them to express their exclusive loyalty to YHWH in the most uncompromising terms.

The Deuteronomic polemic against idolatry projected Judah's experiences of devastation and loss at the hands of the Assyrians and Babylonians onto the early history of Israel. The conquest of Canaan provided a narrative strategy so that Judah's thinkers could digest the psychological and cultural trauma of these military and social catastrophes.[18] The chart below shows that Judah's theologians analyzed the reasons for the exile in parallel with the reasons for Canaan's destruction.

14. Kenton L. Sparks, *Ethnicity and Identity in Ancient Israel: Prolegomena to the Study of Ethnic Sentiments and Their Expression in the Hebrew Bible* (Winona Lake: Eisenbrauns, 1998), 235–36.

15. Guy Darshan, "The Origins of the Foundation Stories Genre in the Hebrew Bible and Ancient Eastern Mediterranean," *JBL* 133 (2014): 706–7.

16. Morrow, "Deuteronomy 7 in Postcolonial Perspective," 289.

17. Louis Stuhlman, "Encroachment in Deuteronomy: An Analysis of the Social World of the D Code," *JBL* 109 (1990): 631.

18. Morrow, "Putting the Neighbors in Their Place," 70–71.

Reasons for the Destruction of Canaan and Israel/Judah

Cause	Canaan	Israel/Judah
Idolatry	Exod 23:23–24	2 Kgs 17:15, 19; Jer 11:10
Immorality	Lev 18:24	Jer 23:14
Social injustice	Deut 9:4–5	2 Kgs 21:16; Jer 22:13–17
Child sacrifice	Deut 18:9–12	2 Kgs 17:17; 21:6

Like the Canaanites, Israel and Judah also lost their hold on the land as a result of military conquests from external forces: the Assyrians and the Babylonians. These national disasters were explained as the consequence of sin. In fact, 2 Kgs 21:11 describes the sins of King Manasseh as "more wicked than all the Amorites did."

But why did Deuteronomic writers target a symbol instead of attacking the actual perpetrators of Judah's exile, namely the Babylonians? Israel's thinkers refused to acknowledge any cause for the destruction of Jerusalem other than the wrath of YHWH against his rebellious people. According to the prophetic witness (e.g., Jeremiah 1–24; Ezekiel 1–11), Israel and Judah had been destroyed for their persistent disloyalty to YHWH. This was symbolized by telling the story of the destruction of Canaan.

Developments

The history of Jewish exegesis shows attempts to mitigate the force of Deuteronomy 7. For example, some commentators took the verses in Josh 11:19–20 to mean that all of the Canaanite cities were given the chance to surrender to Joshua. Thereby they sought to defuse the unconditional language of Deut 7:1–3.[19]

Yet, maintaining the uncompromising covenant values represented by Deuteronomy 7 and 13 has been key to the survival of the Jewish people during centuries of statelessness and political disenfranchisement. The same could be said for Christian communities which have been subject to intense persecution over long periods of time, such as the Amish or the Coptic Church in Egypt. As a charter for groups that wish to preserve their identity as disenfranchised minorities, the ideology of Deuteronomy 7 and 13 has

19. Tigay, *Deuteronomy*, 472.

proven its value. Its uncompromising symbol system justifies the necessity of continuing vigilance so that the faith community can survive under severe duress.

Nevertheless, one confronts a serious problem in regarding Deuteronomy 7 and 13 as charter documents for a state that demands that its members create a culture wholly dedicated to the biblical God. The religious viewpoint of Deuteronomy is puritanical and uncompromising. In fact, a number of scholars have connected Deuteronomy 13 with the ideology of the religiously intolerant state.[20] Its provisions have been regarded as "abhorrent" and irreconcilable with modern concepts of right and wrong.[21]

Here national policies directed against the suppression of the indigenous religions of North America provide a potent counterexample to the survival value of Deuteronomy 7 for a beleaguered minority. These policies were actively promoted by Christian readers of a Bible that included Deuteronomy. From them Christians derived a political mandate that was intolerant of religious pluralism and actively strove to suppress it using the powers of the state.

Therefore, texts such as Deuteronomy 7 and 13 can have both a positive and a negative value. Deuteronomy 7 was never intended to set in motion a program of physical genocide. However, its commitment to religious exclusivity carries within it the seeds of cultural repression, as does Deuteronomy 13. A great deal depends on the conditions under which these texts are read. In this regard, it is worth noting that Deuteronomy 13 was revolutionary in its day. By transforming the ancient Near Eastern loyalty oath tradition into an unconditional pledge of faithfulness to YHWH, it holds an important place in the development of the biblical attitude towards the state, for it effectively denies to any state or political power the right to an obedience that belongs to God alone.

What constitutes the kingdom/rule of God on earth and what is its relationship to the political power of the state? This question has continued to make itself felt in the history of biblically informed communities. The same conundrum was highlighted by an early rabbi, who taught his followers to "render unto Caesar what belongs to Caesar and unto God what belongs to God" (Mark 12:17).

20. E.g., Paul E. Dion, "Deuteronomy 13: The Suppression of Alien Religious Propaganda in Israel during the Late Monarchical Era," in *Law and Ideology in Monarchic Israel*, edited by Baruch Halpern and Deborah W. Hobson (JSOTSup 124; Sheffield: JSOT, 1991), 206.

21. Jeffries M. Hamilton, "How to Read an Abhorrent Text: Deuteronomy 13 and the Nature of Authority," *HBT* 20 (1998): 12.

CHAPTER 20

Revolution: Centralization of the Cult

Read: Deuteronomy 12–16; 18:1–8

Imagine that a bishop decreed that only one church in the diocese could be used to celebrate mass. Celebration of Holy Communion in any other place was illegitimate. As a result, many priests would become unemployed; nevertheless, the bishop had no plan except to put them on welfare. This scenario may sound far-fetched; but it is analogous to what the writers of Deuteronomy proposed with their reforms to the worship life of ancient Israel. With a stroke of the pen, they were prepared to dispense with long-standing practices in traditional religion.

This chapter begins by surveying some of the major shifts in religious practices proposed by Deuteronomy. The chapter then turns to a discussion of the underlying political and theological motivations entailed in cult centralization. It ends with a consideration of groups in the first century CE who developed strategies that allowed them to do without temple worship altogether.

Deuteronomy's Reforms to Israel's Legal and Religious Life

In proposing its reforms, Deuteronomy was conscious of preexisting law and custom.[1] This theme will be discussed in the present chapter and the next two; it has also been anticipated in Chapter 9, which noted how Deut

1. William S. Morrow, *Scribing the Center: Organization and Redaction in Deuteronomy 14:1–17:1* (SBLMS 49; Atlanta: Scholars, 1995), 210–14.

15:12–18 modified aspects of the slave law in Exod 21:2–6. The following chart lists significant cases in which laws of the Covenant Code were taken over and modified by a Deuteronomic writer:[2]

Cases of Deuteronomy's Dependence on Law in the Covenant Code

Exodus	Deuteronomy
20:24	12:13–19, 20–28[3]
21:2–6	15:12–18[4]
21:13–14	19:1–13[5]
22:25–27	24:10–13[6]
23:4–5	22:1–4[7]

Deuteronomy's religious reforms were aimed at shoring up a threatened cultural identity. The last chapter showed that this threat was connected with the subjection of Judah to various international powers beginning with the Neo-Assyrian Empire. However, that is to read between the lines. One must also take seriously the social condition of Israel as the book presents it. In the land of promise, Israel will live in cities that cannot be the locations of sacrificial activity. For Deuteronomy, exclusive commitment to YHWH means that there can only be one legitimate place of sacrifice. This created challenges in terms of keeping the faith community unified and focused.

In order to promote their agenda of national unity, the writers of Deuteronomy were prepared to reorganize or alter preexisting religious institutions. The following discussion takes Deuteronomy at face value and assumes that the text means to create the reforms it prescribes. But it is worth asking

2. This list is confined to what may be regarded as the most indisputable cases where Deuteronomy has revised a legal text that is clearly from the Covenant Code.

3. Bernard M. Levinson, *Deuteronomy and the Hermeneutics of Legal Innovation* (New York: Oxford University Press, 1997), 28–38.

4. Moshe Weinfeld, *Deuteronomy and the Deuteronomic School* (Oxford: Clarendon, 1972), 282–83.

5. Eckart Otto, *Das Deuteronomium: Politische Theologie und Rechtsreform in Juda und Assyrien* (BZAW 284; Berlin: de Gruyter, 1999), 253–57.

6. Christoph Levin, "The Poor in the Old Testament," in *Fortschreibungen: Gesammelte Studien Zum Alten Testament*, edited by Christoph Levin (BZAW 316; Berlin: de Gruyter, 2003), 329.

7. Otto, *Das Deuteronomium*, 282–83.

whether Deuteronomy was actually trying to normalize a situation that had already arisen in monarchical Judah. For example, the assaults of the Assyrian Empire compromised older patterns of settlement because much of Judah's territory had been destroyed or confiscated.[8] Deuteronomy's reforms may have been a necessary response to this state of affairs.

Deuteronomy's religious reforms are mainly found in chapters 12–16. They intersect with and frame laws aimed at defining the rights and duties of key officials in the state (see the next chapter). While reference is made to *Urdeuteronomium* below, no attempt will be made to reconstruct its original contents.

Cultic Centralization Laws in Deuteronomy 12–26

Chapter	Theme
12	Centralization of worship
. . .	
14:22–29	Tithes
15:1–18	Seven-year limits for debts and slavery
15:19–23	Firstlings
16:1–17	Festival laws
. . .	
16:21–17:1	Unacceptable cultic practices
. . .	
18:1–8	Rights of priests
. . .	
26:1–15	Tithe ceremonies

1. *"The place the* LORD *your God will choose"* *Deut 12:14; 14:23; 16:2*

Deuteronomy seeks to limit sacrificial activity to "the place where the LORD your God will choose." Consequently, Deuteronomy's religious reform program is often called cult centralization. Religious reforms of this magnitude are ascribed to both King Hezekiah (2 Kgs 18:22) and King Josiah (2 Kgs 22:8–23:25). Scholars continue to question the historical accuracy of these

8. Nadav Na'aman, "Sojourners and Levites in the Kingdom of Judah in the Seventh Century BCE," *ZABR* 14 (2008): 274–75.

reports, their connection to the book of Deuteronomy, and their relationship to archaeological discoveries made in modern Israel.[9]

One of the fuller expressions of the cult centralization formula is, "the place the LORD your God will choose in one of your tribes" (cf. 12:5, 14). Although some scholars debate the meaning of the phrase "in one of your tribes," the majority opinion is that Deuteronomy has in mind the selection of a single legitimate place for sacrifice in all of Israel.[10] This interpretation is supported by a consideration of the Deuteronomic reforms described below.

Behind the Deuteronomic reforms lay a system of traditional religious observances which assumed the presence of many cult centers, not just one. For example, 12:13–19 alludes to the altar law that begins the Covenant Code (Exod 20:24).[11] Exodus's altar law permits sacrifice at any place where YHWH reveals himself. In this, it agrees with biblical traditions that associate sacrifice with several places of divine revelation: for example, Shechem (Gen 12:7), Bethel (35:1–15), Ophrah (Judg 6:24–27), Shiloh (1 Samuel 3), and Gibeon (1 Kgs 3:4–5). Deuteronomy 12:13–19, however, insists that God will choose only one place in the land of promise as the legitimate place of sacrifice.

2. *The Priesthood*
Deut 12:19; 14:28–29; 18:1–8; cf. 2 Kgs 23:8–9

Deuteronomy assumes that Israel's conventional plurality of shrines was served by members of the tribe of Levi. Unlike other tribes, according

9. For pessimistic assessments of the biblical ascriptions of centralization to either Hezekiah or Josiah see, Lisbeth S. Fried, "The High Places (*bāmôt*) and the Reforms of Hezekiah and Josiah: An Archaeological Investigation," *JAOS* 122 (2002): 437–65; and Diana Edelman, "Hezekiah's Alleged Cultic Centralization," *JSOT* 32 (2008): 395–434. More positive assessments can be found in Christoph Uehlinger, "Was There a Cult Reform under King Josiah? The Case for a Well-Grounded Minimum," in *Good Kings and Bad Kings*, edited by Lester L. Grabbe (LHBOTS 393; New York: T. & T. Clark, 2005), 279–316; and Ze'ev Herzog, "Perspectives on Southern Israel's Cult Centralization: Arad and Beer-Sheba," in *One God—One Cult—One Nation*, edited by Reinhard G. Kratz and Hermann Spieckermann (BZAW 405; Berlin: de Gruyter, 2010), 169–99.

10. The question revolves around whether the phrase "the place the LORD your God will choose" is used distributively or exclusively in Deuteronomy. For a defense of the distributive idea, see Frederick E. Greenspahn, "Deuteronomy and Centralization," *VT* 64 (2104): 227–35. For a defense of the majority opinion, see Morrow, *Scribing the Center*, 52–54; Bill T. Arnold, "Deuteronomy and the Law of the Central Sanctuary *noch einmal*," *VT* 64 (2014): 236–48.

11. Levinson, *Deuteronomy and the Hermeneutics of Legal Innovation*, 28–36.

to tradition the Levites were to have no part of the land of Israel (Deut 10:9). They were maintained by the tithes that Israel was required to give to YHWH.

The Deuteronomic reforms affected the priesthood in fundamental ways. The laws of centralization assume that Israel would no longer bring tithes to a local shrine. Consequently, Deuteronomy makes a number of provisions to address the problem of supporting members of the tribe of Levi.

- It adds the Levites to the list of landless people that Israel should support. Deuteronomy 14:29; 16:11, 14; 26:12 regard the Levite as a distressed person who belongs to the same social category assigned to widows, orphans, and resident aliens.
- It invents a second tithe, to be offered every three years (see below).
- It permits dispossessed Levites to travel to the place of legitimate sacrifice in order to benefit from the sacrificial cult.
- It finds new roles for the Levites in a reformed judicial system (see the next chapter).

Unfortunately, it is not clear what Deuteronomy means when it uses the term "Levite." According to Priestly law, the tribe of Levi was the sole tribe allowed to take care of the sanctuary and preside over the sacrificial cult. Still, not every Levite was a priest. Only one clan of the tribe of Levi was allowed to preside over the sacrifices: the descendants of Aaron. All other Levites were placed in a subordinate role (see Numbers 18).

Some scholars think that Deuteronomy reflects a situation prior to the division of the tribe of Levi into lower and higher divisions. The Levites it mentions were actually the priests who presided over YHWH-shrines outside the legitimate cult place. The loss of their cult places left them without their traditional means of support. They were given permission, however, to preside with their brother priests in the chosen place. Later developments would strip them of equality with the Jerusalemite priesthood and assign them a subordinate role in the cult. The results of this evolution are reflected in law now found in Leviticus and Numbers.[12]

Some scholars, however, think that Deuteronomy recognizes divisions among the Levites.[13] Deuteronomy expected members of the priestly clan to

12. E.g., Rainer Albertz, *A History of Israelite Religion in the Old Testament Period* (OTL; Louisville: Westminster John Knox, 1994), 1:221; 2:430–31.

13. J. G. McConville, *Law and Theology in Deuteronomy* (JSOTSup 33; Sheffield: JSOT, 1984), 152; Rodney K. Duke, "The Portion of the Levite: Another Reading of Deuteronomy 18:6–8," *JBL* 106 (1987): 193–201.

preside over sacrifice at the central place (18:1–3), but it adjusted the social welfare system to address the impoverished state of subordinate Levites (cf. 12:19; 14:29; 18:6–8).

3. *Profane Slaughter*
Deut 12:13–27; cf. Lev 17:1–13

As noted in Chapter 13, traditionally the slaughter of any domestic animal for food was considered a sacrificial act. Normally, it was done at an altar with the blood ritually disposed by the presiding priest, a member of the tribe of Levi. As a result of cult centralization, sacrificial aspects of killing domestic animals for meat had to be revised. It was too difficult to drive animals for sacrifice to a single altar for the whole country (Deut 12:20–27). Consequently, the religious aspects of slaughtering domestic animals for food were transformed into the beginnings of the kosher system of food preparation developed in rabbinic Judaism. Now, only the blood had to be disposed of—no longer at an altar, but simply poured into the earth (Deut 12:16). A sign of the changed context is the note about the person permitted to eat the meat. Ritual cleanness was no longer required (12:15), because the meat consumed was not sacrificed.

4. *Tithes*
Deut 14:22–29; cf. Lev 27:30–33; Num 18:21–32

According to Priestly tradition (Lev 27:30–33), tithes of agricultural products should be offered in kind. When they are exchanged, 20 percent of the value must be added to them. In either case, they are to be given to the sanctuary (Num 18:21–32). Altered provisions are visible in Deut 14:22–27. Pilgrims who live at a distance from the central sanctuary are not penalized for bringing the tithe in silver instead of in kind. Additionally, use of the tithe also changes. Formerly, it was intended solely for the support of the personnel of the central sanctuary. Now, it also becomes the means for a family meal.[14] This development probably represents an incentive for worshippers to make the journey to the central sanctuary.

14. McConville, *Law and Theology*, 73–74; Christopher J. H. Wright, *Deuteronomy* (NIBCOT 4; Peabody: Hendrickson, 1996), 186.

Along with changing the conditions for offering the tithe, Deuteronomy requires a second tithe every three years. This tithe is not to be brought to the sanctuary; it is set out in the city square as a gift to sustain the poor. Deuteronomy makes a point of including the Levites in the list of disadvantaged persons who are to benefit from the second tithe (14:29).

5. *Firstlings*
Deut 15:19–23; cf. Exod 22:29–30; Lev 27:26–27

The automatic sanctity of firstling animals is challenged in Deuteronomic law.[15] Traditionally, these animals were to be sacrificed to YHWH shortly after they were born (Exod 22:30). Deuteronomy innovates in two ways. First, it permits firstling sacrifices to be offered once a year because they have to be driven to the central shrine. Blemished animals, however, can be eaten at home, like any other animal. Neither the deity nor his representatives are to be compensated in such a case (cf. Lev 27:26–27).

This revision is as breathtaking as the permission for secular slaughter discussed above. Here, a long-standing conception of what constitutes the holy is rejected. For Deuteronomy, it is first and foremost the people of Israel that are holy (e.g., Deut 7:6; 14:21).

6. *Pilgrim Festivals*
Deut 16:1–17; cf. Exod 12:1–13:16; 23:14–17; 34:18–24; Leviticus 23

Critics debate whether Deut 16:1–17 is built on a knowledge of the festival rules in Exod 23:14–17 or 34:18–24.[16] In either case, modifications of previous pilgrim traditions and law occur. One of the most striking is the fusing of the Passover sacrifice with the Festival of Unleavened Bread.

Much has been written about the significance of Deut 16:1–8 for reconstructing the history of the Passover sacrifice.[17] Discussion of the Passover in Chapter 13 suggested that the conversion of the Passover into a type of thanksgiving offering had already taken place in monarchical times. Con-

15. Morrow, *Scribing the Center*, 123.

16. Shimon Gesundheit, *Three Times a Year: Studies on Festival Legislation in the Pentateuch* (FAT 82; Tübingen: Mohr Siebeck, 2012), 147–56.

17. See summaries of past scholarship in Gesundheit, *Three Times a Year*, 97–98.

scious of the need to centralize all sacrificial actions, Deuteronomy turned Passover into the sacrifice that inaugurates the Festival of Unleavened Bread. This innovation, however, is not reflected in Priestly law, which affirmed a more traditional pattern in which Passover precedes the beginning of the Festival of Unleavened Bread (cf. Lev 23:5–6).

A significant marker of Deuteronomy's transformation of Israel's pilgrim feasts into centralized ceremonies is the emphasis on joy. This motif occurs in, e.g., 12:12; 16:11 and 14 and is characteristic of the spirituality of Deuteronomy. Knowledge that all of Israel is gathered at the central sanctuary is to lead to a new awareness of solidarity between God's people and with YHWH.[18] Nevertheless, the relationship between cult centralization and celebrations of social solidarity is somewhat problematic. Poor persons and women, for example, would find it more difficult to attend Deuteronomy's pilgrim festivals given the distances that had to be travelled.[19]

7. Sacred Symbols
Deut 16:21–22; cf. Gen 28:18–22

Raising standing stones or pillars (*maṣṣēbôt*) as a gesture of devotion was a custom of long standing in ancient Israel. For example, Jacob is said to have done so when he established Bethel as a place of worship (Gen 28:22).

There is evidence that standing stones played an important part in official religion during monarchical times, as is apparent in the construction of the fortress shrine of Tel Arad.[20] This cultic structure appears to have been deliberately dismantled at the end of the eighth century BCE, just prior to the invasion of Judah by Assyria. Although the fortress was restored in the seventh century, the shrine was never used again. Its decommissioning and lack of reuse may be associated with a campaign to centralize worship in Jerusalem in monarchical times.[21] Does the fact that two incense altars were buried among the cultic paraphernalia of Arad's shrine point to the

18. Georg Braulik, "The Joy of the Feast," in *The Theology of Deuteronomy* (N. Richland Hills: BIBAL, 1994), 52–55.

19. Harold V. Bennett, *Injustice Made Legal: Deuteronomic Law and the Plight of Widows, Strangers, and Orphans in Ancient Israel* (BIW; Grand Rapids: Eerdmans, 2002), 118.

20. Ze'ev Herzog, "Arad," *Oxford Encyclopedia of the Bible and Archaeology,* edited by Daniel M. Master (New York: Oxford University Press, 2013), 1:40.

21. Herzog, "Perspectives on Southern Israel's Cult Centralization," 173–78; but see Edelman, "Hezekiah's Alleged Cultic Centralization," 406–11.

Figure 10. Standing stone (at the back left) and incense altars (in the front) at the shrine in the fortress of Tel Arad (eighth century BCE).

possibility that YHWH was worshipped there along with another deity? The prohibition against the sacred pole and standing stones in Deut 16:21–22 is an expression of a desire for the exclusive worship of YHWH, and one that was entirely without images.

The Theology of Cult Centralization

Some scholars wish to connect the Deuteronomic reforms with policies for political stabilization implemented during the reign of King Josiah (ca. 640–609). However, the perspective conveyed here does not depend on a historical reconstruction of that kind. *Urdeuteronomium* can be read as a utopian program whose agenda was never fully realized during the monarchical period.

Religious reform and political expediency probably went together in Deuteronomy's agenda for reform. By the late monarchical period, Judah had experienced a number of disruptions in its traditional social fabric. Deuteronomy's program of cult centralization responded to these pressures with measures which sought to reunify a threatened society through its advocacy of the exclusive worship of YHWH at a single authorized cult site. Some of these tactics were mentioned in the previous two chapters. The use of motifs drawn from international law and the polemic against Canaanite culture were intended to create a society with a single-minded devotion to YHWH.

An important theme in Deuteronomy's rhetoric of cult centralization is that YHWH's chosen place is the place "where he makes his name to dwell." Some commentators have suggested that this phrase points to a theology of divine presence they call the "name theology." According to this theory, Deuteronomy intends a polemic against an older perspective, which held that YHWH literally dwelled in the temple. By contrast, Deuteronomy advocated a more abstract and transcendent theology, which limited God's presence in the temple to the power of the divine name.[22]

The concept of a name theology in Deuteronomy has been challenged in recent years. A doctrine of the "real presence" of YHWH in the temple seems presupposed by Deuteronomy's statements that cultic actions are to take place "in the presence of/before the LORD" (e.g., 14:23; 15:20; 16:11).[23] Moreover, there are other ways of interpreting the emphasis on the chosen place as the dwelling place of YHWH's name. For example, there are indications that Deuteronomy's name-motif relies on Neo-Assyrian idioms. In this case, the concept of name symbolizes royal presence.[24] The fact that the chosen place is the locale where YHWH's name dwells is an indicator of its centrality as the place where God is present on earth.

22. See the survey of past scholarship in Sandra L. Richter, *The Deuteronomistic History and the Name Theology* (BZAW 318; Berlin: de Gruyter, 2002), 26–31. A classic statement of the position that Deuteronomy advocates a name theology is found in Weinfeld, *Deuteronomy and the Deuteronomic School*, 191–209.

23. Ian Wilson, *Out of the Midst of Fire: Divine Presence in Deuteronomy* (SBLDS 151; Atlanta: Scholars, 1995), 192–95.

24. Richter, *Name Theology*, 211.

Developments

Deuteronomy's boldness in revising traditional concepts of worship provides a potent illustration of the dynamism of biblical law. In order to stabilize the identity of YHWH's holy people, venerable traditions of the past were subject to scrutiny. Fidelity to YHWH was an over-arching value. For that reason, Deuteronomy was prepared to make radical adaptations to the traditional ways temple and sacrifice were connected in ancient Israel.

During the first century CE various Jewish groups in Judea were also prepared to challenge preexisting practices connected to temple and sacrifice in order to promote their agendas for fidelity to the God of Israel. For example, as a result of a breach with the temple authorities, the sectarian group at Qumran withdrew from participating in the sacrificial cult altogether. Consequently, they developed a form of community that made attendance at the temple temporarily irrelevant. They did so by creating an alternative way of life, based on their own concepts of holiness and moral purity.[25]

The protorabbinic group (e.g., the Pharisees) also prepared the way for a normative Judaism that would thrive, despite having no access to a temple. While observant Jews continued to hope for the restoration of the temple after its destruction in 70 CE, they developed a culture of worship and study that did not depend on sacrifice. As other chapters in this book have indicated, this entailed esteeming Torah study as equivalent to temple service, redefinitions of the concept of purity, and the prominence given to repentance for atonement from sin. In addition, sacrifice was interpreted symbolically in rabbinic exegesis.[26]

The Jesus group also created forms of community that did not depend on access to a physical temple. In this they were following existing trends in Judaism, as well as innovating. As in Deuteronomy, the holiness of God's people was emphasized. Now understood as the community of Jesus's disciples, the temple became a metaphor for the body of Christ (e.g., 1 Cor 6:19). Sacrifice was interpreted symbolically through the redemptive actions of Jesus. These innovations, however, were not intended to mark the early church as a community discontinuous from Jewish tradition. On the contrary, they were regarded as necessary to preserve the spirit of ancient Israelite religion, even if—like Deuteronomy—early Christians were prepared to rewrite its letter.

25. Eyal Regev, "Abominated Temple and a Holy Community: The Formation of the Notions of Purity and Impurity in Qumran," *DSD* 10 (2003): 243–78.

26. Max Kadushin, *The Rabbinic Mind*, 3rd ed. (New York: Bloch, 1972), 300.

CHAPTER 21

Justice at the Gates: Capital Crimes and Judicial Reform

Read: Deuteronomy 16:18–25:19

Deuteronomy's preferred way of naming the places where Israel lives is "your gates" (NRSV "your towns"). This phrase reflects two different aspects of the places where Deuteronomy's addressees typically live. First, it assumes that Israel dwells in walled villages, towns, and cities physically accessed by gates. Second, city gates functioned as places where justice was typically enacted in ancient Israel (e.g., Gen 23:10; Ruth 4:1–2; Jer 38:7–10).[1] Locating the town as a place of justice accords it a spiritual significance even after it has been stripped of sacrificial functions by cult centralization.

This chapter begins by discussing the organization of the laws in Deut 16:18–25:19. It then turns to a description of some of the legal reforms these chapters contain. Finally, there is a discussion of the ways in which Deuteronomy reflects exegetical trends that paved the way for the emergence of normative Judaism.

Structure

The last chapter noted that rules about defining the rights and duties of key functionaries in the nation were interlocked with rules about cultic

1. Bernard M. Levinson, *Deuteronomy and the Hermeneutics of Legal Innovation* (New York: Oxford University Press, 1997),

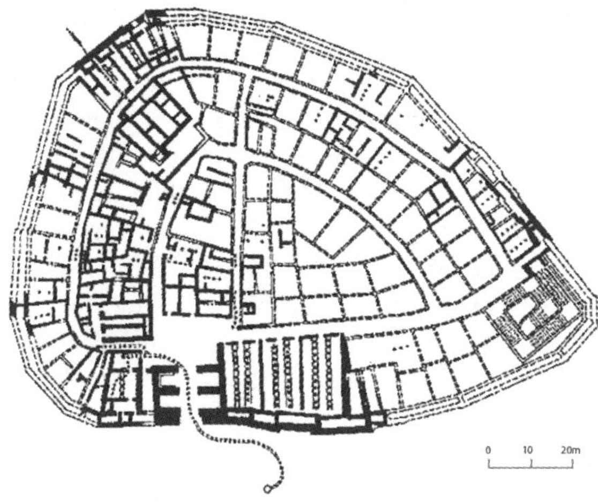

Figure 11. Plan of the Iron Age city of Beersheba at the end of the eighth century BCE. The city gate is in the lower left-hand corner. In between the gate chambers there were benches for people to sit. The gate opened into a plaza, a convenient place for public meetings for the administration of justice. Drawing taken from Ze'ev Herzog, *Archaeology of the City: Urban Planning in Ancient Israel and Its Social Implications* (Monograph Series of the Sonia and Marco Nadler Institute of Archaeology 13; Emery and Claire Yass Archaeology Press, Institute of Archaeology, Tel Aviv University: Tel Aviv 1997) p. 247, fig. 5.31. © Institute of Archaeology of Tel Aviv University. Used with permission.

organization.[2] Rules regarding important agents in the community occur in Deut 16:18–18:22:

The Organization of Deuteronomy 16:18–18:22

16:18–20	Judicial appointments
. . .	
17:8–13	Consultation processes for judges
17:14–20	The law of the king
18:1–8	Rights of priests
18:9–22	Authentic and illegitimate religious intermediaries

2. See also Levinson, *Hermeneutics of Legal Innovation*, 135–36.

The rules for judges and priests explicitly intersect with the theme of cult centralization.

Legal materials found in Deut 19:1–26:15 cover a wide range of concerns. They include capital crimes, rules of war, family law, relief for the poor, community membership, illegitimate mixtures, and economic justice. They end with instructions about tithes that look back to the centralization laws found earlier in Deuteronomy 14.

Finding a pattern in the organization of chapters 19–25 is not easy. One set of solutions involves connecting the contents of this material to the second table of the Ten Commandments.[3] However, some of the suggested connections are rather vague, and the quest to identify close links between the Decalogue and the organization of Deuteronomy 19–25 ultimately breaks down. An attractive solution to the organization of Deuteronomy 19–25 is based on the discovery of a series of alternating themes in these chapters:[4]

Literary Organization in Deuteronomy 19–25

A	Capital crimes	19:1–13
B	Legal procedures	19:15–21
A	Capital crimes	21:1–9
C	Family law	21:15–21
A	Capital crimes	21:22–23
C	Family law	22:13–30; 24:1–4
B	Legal procedures	25:1–3
C	Family law	25:5–10
B	Legal procedures	25:11–12

This scheme has been subject to supplementation and revision in the process of creating the canonical form of chapters 19–25. An explanation for the current disposition of the laws in Deuteronomy 19–25 can also benefit from a description of techniques used to organize texts on the basis of shared

3. E.g., Stephen Kaufman, "The Structure of Deuteronomic Law," *Maarav* 1 (1979): 105–58.

4. Based on Eckart Otto, *Das Deuteronomium: Politische Theologie und Rechtsreform in Juda und Assyrien* (BZAW 284; Berlin: de Gruyter, 1999), 235, 252.

features and themes. These are sometimes called principles of "immanent organization." Among these techniques one finds:

- movement from the general to the particular
- chronological order
- arrangement according to social group
- association through repetitions on the level of syntax and phraseology

Immanent organizational techniques have been identified in various collections of biblical law.[5]

Besides methods of immanent organization, there is also evidence that the contents of Deuteronomy 19–25 are built on older law. In these cases, Deuteronomic authors may have been constrained in the way they arranged the collection by their source material. As in Chapter 20, this chapter and the next will note uses of pre-Deuteronomic legal sources.

Legal Reforms in Deuteronomy

Space prevents a full discussion of the ways in which Deuteronomy sought both to alter and reinforce existing legal and religious traditions in Israel. This section will limit itself to four major topics:

1. appointment of a professional judiciary
2. introduction of rules of evidence
3. establishment of cities of refuge
4. modifications to legal procedures involving capital crimes

1) Appointment of a professional judiciary

Judicial functions were distributed over a variety of officials in preexilic Israel.[6] Heads of families (e.g., Gen 38:24), town and tribal elders (e.g., Deut 22:13–21), military commanders and royal appointees (e.g., 2 Chr 19:4–11),

5. E.g., Lyle M. Eslinger, "More Drafting Techniques in Deuteronomic Laws," *VT* 34 (1984): 221–26; William S. Morrow, *Scribing the Center: Organization and Redaction in Deuteronomy 14:1–17:1* (SBLMS 49; Atlanta: Scholars, 1995), 14–17

6. Hector Avalos, "Legal and Social Institutions in Canaan and Ancient Israel," *CANE* 1:621–23.

and the king himself (e.g., 1 Kgs 3:16–28) all engaged in adjudicating legal disputes.[7]

This multifaceted situation is reflected in the parallel traditions reporting the appointment of judges in the Pentateuch: Exod 18:13–26; Num 11:16–25; Deut 1:9–17. The Exodus passage reflects a quasi-military organization. Numbers, however, refers to both elders and officials in its story of the distribution of the Mosaic spirit. This may reflect a juridical practice in which local elders and royal appointees collaborated in making legal decisions.[8] Deuteronomy adapts the pre-Deuteronomic tradition in Exodus 18 with an emphasis on wisdom,[9] which is a characteristic motif in Deuteronomic thought.[10]

What is the point, therefore, of demanding the appointment of judges and officers in Deut 16:18–20; 17:8–13? Given the multilayered situation described above, it seems redundant. Surely, appointments of this kind were part of Israel's legal culture throughout much of the monarchical period, as well as later?

A key to its interests begins with the recognition that Deuteronomy's law on the appointment of judges uses language drawn from the rhetoric of cult centralization. Local judges are to be appointed "in your towns" (16:18); but they are to have recourse to "the place that the LORD your God will choose," if the case is too hard to handle (17:8, 10). Here, the intent is not to set up a court of appeal but to refer to experts in the law (v. 11) in order to render a difficult decision. These experts consist of priests and a judge with special training who reside at the central sanctuary.[11]

The Deuteronomic reforms can be related to a diminished importance of the assertory (declaratory) oath in Israel's legal processes. The assertory oath was a kind of self-curse taken in the presence of divine symbols which called on the god(s) to punish the oath-taker if he or she was not telling the truth. It was an important component for determining legal guilt or

7. Raymond Westbrook and Bruce Wells, *Everyday Law in Biblical Israel: An Introduction* (Louisville: Westminster John Knox, 2009), 35–37.

8. Westbrook and Wells, *Everyday Law,* 38.

9. Richard D. Nelson, *Deuteronomy* (OTL; Louisville: Westminster John Knox, 2002), 20.

10. Moshe Weinfeld, *Deuteronomy and the Deuteronomic School* (Oxford: Clarendon, 1972), 260–74.

11. Alexander Rofé, "The Organization of the Judiciary in Deuteronomy (Deut. 16.18–20; 17.8–13; 19.15; 21.22–23; 24.16; 25.1–3)," in *The World of the Aramaeans,* vol. 1: *Biblical Studies in Honour of Paul-Eugène Dion*, edited by P. M. Michèle Daviau, John W. Wevers, and Michael Weigl (JSOTSup 324; Sheffield: Sheffield Academic, 2001), 99–101.

innocence in many of the cultures of the ancient Near East. For example, a legal process using this procedure can be found in the law for stored goods in Exod 22:7–9. In Israel and Judah, the shrines and high places tended by local Levites would have been the appropriate places to make an assertory oath in the Iron I period and during most of the monarchical era. As a result of cult centralization, the closure of these sacred locales created a serious problem for the administration of justice. Deuteronomy's reorganization of the justice system in 16:18–20; 17:8–13 is plausibly connected to the loss of opportunities to make the assertory oath.[12]

Arguably, however, another motivation behind Deut 16:18–20 is to create an opportunity for displaced Levites to participate in the collective life of the people. The people are commanded in v. 18 to " appoint judges (*šōpĕṭîm*) and officials (*šōṭĕrîm*)" While the Hebrew word for "judge" (*šōpēṭ*) is well known, the word for "officer" (*šōṭēr*) is less common. In fact, the Hebrew root *š-ṭ-r*, from which the word for "officer" is generated, seems to be derived from a Mesopotamian (Akkadian) word meaning a "scribe" or "someone who is able to write."[13] Therefore, the word *šōṭēr* can connote a scribe.

In 16:18, the words "judge" and "officer" may actually refer to the same official: a scribally trained person.[14] During monarchical times, the priesthood was one of the notable offices that required literate functionaries.[15] Therefore, it is reasonable to imagine that one source of Deuteronomy's appointed judiciary would be displaced Levites, who would be able to preside over local legal cases as both judges and officers.

Unfortunately, Deuteronomy does not define the relationship between the office of appointed judge and the legal competence of the city elders. A number of laws in Deuteronomy mention only city elders as the public body involved in making legal decisions (Deut 19:12; 21:20; 22:16–18; 25:8). It appears that the city elders' powers were limited to the local community. When cases proved beyond the elders' ability to resolve, other authorities became involved.[16] This would be an occasion for the appointed judge to intervene, especially if a legal opinion was required from the central sanctuary (17:8–9). There is also evidence that appointed judicial authorities and

12. Levinson, *Hermeneutics of Legal Innovation*, 117.

13. Rofé, "Organization of the Judiciary," 96–98.

14. Rofé, "Organization of the Judiciary," 98–99.

15. Aaron Demsky, *Literacy in Ancient Israel* [Hebrew] (Biblical Encyclopedia Library; Jerusalem: Bialik Institute, 2012), 217–52.

16. Timothy M. Willis, *The Elders of the City: A Study of the Elders-Laws in Deuteronomy* (SBLMS 55; Atlanta: Society of Biblical Literature, 2001), 307.

city elders could hold juridical authority simultaneously and even exercise overlapping legal powers.[17]

2) *Rules of evidence*

While pre-Deuteronomic passages such as Exod 23:1 demonstrate that witnesses appeared in ancient Israelite trial procedures, the importance of witnesses is underscored in Deuteronomic law (17:6–7; 19:15–20). Why does Deuteronomy feel the need to emphasize the use of witnesses in legal procedures? A plausible answer has to do with the reduced value of the assertory oath for Deuteronomy. Deuteronomy's insistence on the use of multiple witnesses was probably motivated by several factors. One is mentioned above: cult centralization made the assertory oath more difficult to administer.

One can also can detect a shift in legal procedure that parallels developments in Mesopotamia. Neo-Babylonian trial records from the sixth–fifth centuries (the exilic and early postexilic eras in Israelite history) show that the formal assertory oath had a diminished importance from earlier times.[18] The oath of innocence taken before the gods did not disappear in Neo-Babylonian times, but it was not considered determinative in cases of law. Mesopotamian judges preferred to make their decisions on a rational basis, using evidence taken from human witnesses.[19]

Similar conclusions are warranted for Deuteronomy. Certain details remain unclear in 17:8–13. Scholars debate whether the litigants were expected to make their way to the central judiciary in the case of a difficult trial or only the judges. Likewise, it is not clear that Deuteronomy expected the use of the assertory oath to continue in the central sanctuary. [20] What is apparent, however, is that those who had recourse to the central judiciary were travelling for instruction from legal experts (vv. 10–11). Like their

17. Bruce Wells, "Competing or Complementary? Judges and Elders in Biblical and Neo-Babylonian Law," *ZABR* 16 (2010): 88–89.

18. Bruce Wells, F. Rachel Magdalene, and Cornelius Wunsch, "The Assertory Oath in Neo-Babylonian and Persian Administrative Texts," *RIDA* ser. 3, 57 (2010): 15–16.

19. Bruce Wells, *The Law of Testimony in the Pentateuchal Codes* (BZABR 4; Wiesbaden: Harrassowitz, 2004), 128–30. A detailed description of Neo-Babylonian trial procedures appears in F. Rachel Magdalene, *On the Scales of Righteousness: Neo-Babylonian Trial Law and the Book of Job* (BJS 348; Providence: Brown University, 2007), see esp. ch. 4.

20. See the discussion and a possible solution in Levinson, *Hermeneutics of Legal Innovation*, 127–30.

Neo-Babylonian counterparts, the writers of Deuteronomy favored rational means for deciding the outcomes of trials and were less disposed to see cases settled by an oath before God.[21]

3) Cities of refuge

Homicide was regarded as a crime against the family. The penalty was death, and it was to be carried out by a relative of the deceased. Yet, as Chapter 7 noted, there was a provision for adjudication in the case of unintentional homicide. An accused person could seek asylum at a local altar until his case could be decided (Exod 21:13–14). This system of legal protection was undone by Deuteronomy's program of cult centralization. How were persons innocent of the crime of premeditated murder to protect themselves when there was no shrine to seek for asylum—except far away from where they lived? They could be hunted down and killed by the family's "blood redeemer" (*gōʾēl haddām*) without a trial. Deuteronomy's solution is to create cities of refuge to which murder suspects could flee until their case could be adjudicated.[22] Its innovations are consciously building on and also modifying Exod 21:13–14.[23]

The law of the cities of refuge is found in Deut 19:1–13. It consists of two parts. Initially, three cities of asylum are to be established (vv. 2–3); in the future, if the nation's territory expands, three other cities of asylum are to be established (vv. 8–10). The parallel legislation in Num 35:9–15 appears to be built on the Deuteronomic law.[24]

4) Legal procedures involving capital crimes

Deuteronomy's concern to manage legal processes involving capital punishment manifests itself in 17:2–7; 21:1–9, 18–21, 22–23; 22:13–27; and 24:16. The focus here concentrates on those cases that regulate city and family law by

21. Wells, *Law of Testimony,* 130.

22. Pamela Barmash, "Blood Feud and State Control: Differing Legal Institutions for the Remedy of Homicide during the Second and First Millennia B.C.E.," *JNES* 63 (2004): 185.

23. Otto, *Das Deuteronomium,* 253.

24. Baruch A. Levine, *Numbers 21–36* (AB 4A; New York: Doubleday, 2000), 568; Jeffrey Stackert, *Rewriting the Torah: Literary Revision in Deuteronomy and the Holiness Legislation* (FAT 52; Tübingen: Mohr Siebeck, 2007), 68–70.

demanding their legal processes be supervised by higher authorities. It is not clear from the wording of these laws that this supervision came from Deuteronomy's appointed judiciary. Still, these laws show the town being used as a legal body of decision-making to which family heads must respond. This detail is commensurate with Deuteronomy's assumption that its addressees live in towns and that appointed judicial authorities reside there.

a. Deuteronomy 21:1–9

Like the Holiness school, Deuteronomy regards homicide as an action that defiles the land. At the basis of 21:1–9 is a ritual for cleansing the land from defilement by the corpse of a murder victim in an unsolved crime. These rules seem to be build on pre-Deuteronomic custom or law.[25]

The provisions in Deut 21:1–9 have a complex literary history, however. As this legal paragraph developed over time, it came to involve multiple judicial authorities. The elders represent their respective groups or territories. The judges represent the legal system appointed in the town. The priests appear in a later layer of the law as witnesses that the ritual was carried out properly. As in the cases of 21:18–21 and 22:13–27, we can see a trend in Deuteronomic law to control local authorities by demanding their accountability to larger systems of law.

b. Deuteronomy 21:18–21

In this case, the law deals with an incorrigible adult whose refusal to comply with the larger interests of the family makes him a danger to everyone. He is exactly the kind of person likely to kill a member of another family or clan in a drunken rage.[26] If that happens, his actions will then harm his own family by drawing them into a blood feud. Such an action could easily spiral into a vendetta that could last for generations. The law arises, therefore, out of an ancient tribal society with few external legal controls.

Deuteronomy attempts to check the family's power by demanding that they make their case before a larger assembly of decision makers. No longer autonomous in the realm of law, the heads of the family (here father

25. Willis, *The Elders of the City*, 149–50.

26. Douglas A. Knight (*Law, Power, and Justice in Ancient Israel* [LAI; Louisville: Westminster John Knox, 2011], 195) sees the issue differently. He thinks Deut 21:18–21 involves the adult child who refuses to care for his parents in their old age.

and mother) must submit their cause "to the elders of his town at the gate" (21:19). Ultimately, it is the heads of the community who decide if execution in such a case is justified. And it is the community that must carry out the extreme penalty (v. 21).[27]

c. Deuteronomy 22:13–27

Further discussion of family and marriage law will continue in the next chapter. The problems that Deut 22:13–27 addresses concern women who are engaged or recently married. A woman who is betrothed commits adultery if she has sex with someone other than her fiancé. The penalty for this was death, as it was for adultery itself (Lev 20:10).

Deuteronomy effectively places limits on the ability to engage in lynch law. The "men of the town" must be involved in the execution of the woman who falsely claimed to be a virgin on her wedding night (22:21). This presupposes a formal process of adjudication.[28]

In the case of a charge of rape, evidence must also be judged in a forum above the family. The town will stone both the betrothed woman and her partner if it is found that they had sex in the town, where the woman could have cried out for help. But benefit of the doubt accrues to the woman who claims she was raped in the countryside. Such cases have to be decided and executed at the city gate by and in the presence of the leaders of the community (22:22–27).

Developments

It may seem a small gain to insist that execution for adultery could be undertaken only after the accusations were proven in a public judicial procedure. However, Deuteronomy's modification of traditional family law represents a tiny step towards insistence on due process. The same could be said for the case of the wayward son in 21:18–21. These are small strides towards demanding legal procedures that are more rational and collectively controlled than pre-Deuteronomic legal tradition allowed.

The trend towards mandating uniform practice across the nation and

27. Elizabeth Bellefontaine, "Deuteronomy 21:18–21: Reviewing the Case of the Rebellious Son," *JSOT* 13 (1979): 13–31.

28. Avalos, "Legal and Social Institutions," 619.

the preference for rational modes of jurisprudence continued into the late Second Temple period and beyond. By the first century CE, many Jewish groups were involved in extensive efforts to develop the raw materials of Scripture into comprehensive visions of the community's obligations to God and the neighbor. To no small degree, these labors continued the inspiration of Deuteronomic exegesis and reasoning. The result was not simply biblical commentary, however; it also led to the production of new forms and expressions of Torah.

In fact, Deuteronomic exegesis and legal innovation anticipate the rabbinic movement in Judaism. Jacob Weingreen has called attention to resonances between Deuteronomy and the processes that gave rise to the Mishnah. Both works restate older law, revise long-standing legal practices, and generate new law. Resemblances also can be found in their exegetical methods. As a result of these observations, Weingreen labels Deuteronomy a "proto-Mishnah."[29] Among protorabbinic thinkers (e.g., the Pharisees), a substantial body of new law and community organization emerged through those methods leading to the production of the oral Torah culminating in the Mishnah (ca. 200 CE).

The Jews involved in creating the early church also had another authority to set alongside their reading of the scriptural tradition. They found the equivalent of an oral Torah in the life and words of Jesus. The first disciples shared with their coreligionists a deep esteem for Torah; but they found its ultimate expression in Christ incarnate. Even in this case, however, it would be incorrect to drive too great a wedge between the spirituality of the nascent Jesus movement and the Jewish thinkers that created the Mishnah and its literary developments. Jacob Neusner has called attention to the importance of the incarnational spirit in rabbinic literature. While the means were different, Judaism arrived at its own full encounter with the personality of God, incarnated in the stories and traditions of the Babylonian Talmud (ca. 500 CE).[30]

29. Jacob Weingreen, *From Bible to Mishna: The Continuity of Tradition* (Manchester: Manchester University Press, 1976), 143–54.

30. Jacob Neusner, "Is the God of Judaism Incarnate?" *RelS* 24 (1988): 213–38.

CHAPTER 22

The Limits of Social Solidarity: Women in Deuteronomic Law

Read: Deuteronomy 21–25

Two questions occupy this chapter:

1. Why does Deuteronomy have more law governing family relationships than other biblical law collections?
2. How are we to understand the place of women in connection to Deuteronomy's rhetoric of social solidarity?

Answers to these questions have to grapple with the social background and ideological commitments of Deuteronomic law. Both of these aspects of Deuteronomy have already been noted, but they are worth reiterating here.

First, Deuteronomy assumes that Israel has become urbanized. While urbanization was growing throughout the monarchical period, it received a substantial impetus from the devastating conquests of Assyria in the eighth century and Babylonia in the sixth century. These national disasters had destructive effects on the traditional structures of Israelite society as the people of Judah were forced into new configurations of town and city life.[1] Deuteronomy's interest in the urban reality, therefore, went hand in hand with the need to address challenges to the cohesion of traditional family structures. This is one reason that Deuteronomy 21–25 contains many rules regulating family life (see the chart in Chapter 21).

1. Nadav Na'aman, "Sojourners and Levites in the Kingdom of Judah in the Seventh Century BCE," *ZBAR* 14 (2008): 276.

A second characteristic of Deuteronomy is its demand for exclusive loyalty to YHWH. We should not be surprised, therefore, to find Deuteronomic law searching for various means to reinforce its commitments to undivided fidelity to YHWH. One of those was found in the regulation of female sexuality. In this respect, Deuteronomy belongs to a long tradition of patriarchal (male-centered) law-making that uses the female body as a site for the regulation of social values and norms.[2]

As indicated in the introduction, this book intends a sympathetic appraisal of biblical law. Unfortunately, a sympathetic reading strategy is difficult to sustain entirely. For example, we have already had to grapple with Deuteronomy's rhetoric of religious intolerance in Chapter 19. In addition, modern readers are likely to take offense at the androcentrism that manifests itself throughout biblical legal collections.[3] The goal of this chapter is not to explain away Deuteronomy's androcentric perspective but to explore it in its historical and cultural context. Discussion of Deuteronomic laws on marriage will follow some general observations about patriarchal authority in ancient Israel. The next section addresses the status of women in the context of Deuteronomy's rhetoric of social solidarity. The chapter concludes with some brief observations on developments in late Second Temple times.

Patriarchal Authority and the Family

Chapter 17 introduced the concept of the *bêt ʾāb,* "the father's household" or "family." A key interest of the Bible's political thought is to protect the father's household against encroachment by larger concentrations of political power. This is one reason that human kingship is regarded with suspicion by biblical thinkers. However, there is little to suggest that they questioned asymmetries in the distribution of power within the family.

It is common to label the social system that biblical laws represent as "patriarchal." That is, they encode asymmetrical power relationships that favor men over women. Even so, social reality in the ancient world had its nuances. Recent feminist biblical scholarship suggests that it is more appro-

2. Carol Smart, *Feminism and the Power of Law* (New York: Routledge, 1989), 113.

3. For a summary of studies on the subordinate status of women in biblical law, see Cheryl B. Anderson, *Women, Ideology, and Violence: Critical Theory and the Construction of Gender in the Book of the Covenant and the Deuteronomic Law* (JSOTSup 394; London: T. & T. Clark, 2004), 74–76.

priate to talk about "heterarchy" (alternate governance structures) than patriarchy. This does not deny the fact that social hierarchies existed in Israelite society; but these power relationships were not always linear or one-sided.[4] Women in ancient Israel exercised significant agency within the household, including the ownership of property (Prov 31:16). In the public sphere, they could possess various offices including judge (Judg 4:4–14), community advisor (2 Sam 20:14–22), and prophet (2 Kgs 22:14–20). Queens exercised political power, and there is evidence for women's formal activity in the cult as singers, dancers, and instrumentalists.[5]

Nevertheless, male privilege generally trumped female agency in biblical law. Some of these emphases are visible in Deuteronomy's rules on rape.[6] They also appear in the only biblical law that demands physical mutilation for a criminal action.

Deuteronomy 25:11–12 concerns a woman who tries to help her husband in a fight with another man. This is probably a hypothetical case, which comes from scribal circles rather than from real life, as there is a similar rule from the Middle Assyrian laws (MAL) written down in the Late Bronze Age: "If a woman should crush a man's testicle during a quarrel, they shall cut off one of her fingers" (MAL A 8).[7] Physical mutilation is a common legal punishment in the MAL, but Deut 25:11–12 is unique in biblical law. Why should the woman's hand be cut off? Sandra Jacobs suggests that 25:11–12 has to be read in conjunction with 23:1, which states that no male with crushed sexual organs can be admitted as a full member of Israel's worshipping community. By attempting to wound her husband's opponent in the genitals, the woman is threatening his ability to enter sacred space. This law communicates the priority of male to female in the distribution of social power, for the woman is obligated to ensure that her actions do not impair the privileges of any male in the community.[8]

4. Carol L. Meyers, "Was Ancient Israel a Patriarchal Society?" *JBL* 133 (2014): 27.

5. Meyers, "Was Ancient Israel a Patriarchal Society?" 23.

6. Suzanne Scholz, *Sacred Witness: Rape in the Hebrew Bible* (Minneapolis: Fortress, 2010), 109–17.

7. "The Middle Assyrian Laws," trans. Martha Roth (*COS* 2.132:354).

8. Sandra Jacobs, *The Body as Property: Physical Disfigurement in Biblical Law* (LHBOTS 582; London: T. & T. Clark, 2014), 177–78.

Marriage in Deuteronomy

Deuteronomy 22:13–29 addresses various cases of sexual misconduct connected with marriage. While it may be based on a number of legal traditions, its canonical form shows signs of careful organization:[9]

The Organization of Deuteronomy 22:13–29

13–19	recently married woman falsely accused of not being a virgin
20–21	recently married woman convicted of not being a virgin
22	married woman caught in adultery
23–24	betrothed woman caught having sex in the town
25–27	betrothed woman caught having sex in the country
28–29	rape of an unbetrothed woman

The previous chapter suggested that these laws reflect a legal reform in which family law was subordinated to adjudication by city authorities. One can also see the importance of evidence-based procedures, because none of these laws permit the use of the assertory oath as a means to prove one's innocence.

Typically, marriage was a contractual relationship that involved two stages—a pattern widespread in the ancient Near East. In the first phase, a young woman became betrothed to her husband-to-be. The commitment was sealed by the payment of a bride-price (*mōhār*) given to the woman's father by the prospective husband. The amount (either in money or in kind) was negotiated between the two families. While she was betrothed, the woman remained with her parents.[10] Although it was certainly frowned on, sex between a betrothed woman and her intended was not considered a crime, but sex between a betrothed woman and any other man was a form of adultery (cf. Matt 1:18–19).

When the marriage was to be consummated, the bride went to live with the groom. This was the second phase in effecting the marriage. The woman

9. Cynthia Edenburg, "Ideology and Social Context of the Deuteronomic Women's Sex Laws (Deuteronomy 22:13–19)," *JBL* 128 (2009): 43–48.

10. Tikva Frymer-Kenski, "Israel," in *A History of Ancient Near Eastern Law*, edited by Raymond Westbrook (HdO 72; Leiden: Brill, 2003), 2:1007.

brought her share of the family inheritance (the dowry) into the marriage. A dowry usually consisted of cash and/or moveable property. Often the father of the bride would give his daughter the bride-price he had received when the marriage was first arranged along with her dowry.[11]

The terms of the marriage were set out in a contract. Although ancient Near Eastern marriage contracts frequently contain penalty clauses that affect either party if they leave the marriage, biblical sources suggest that the right of divorce belonged solely to the husband.[12] However, even without that formal right, a wife could press for divorce by leaving her husband's house and returning to her family. Her husband did not have the power to compel her to return.[13] If the husband divorced his wife, he was required to give her a certificate of divorce (Deut 24:1).

In the Deuteronomic marriage laws, a great deal of responsibility falls on the woman to keep the relationship intact.[14] For example, the onus is on the married woman accused of not being a virgin on her wedding night to prove her innocence. A successful defense means that her husband forfeits the right to divorce her (22:19). If she cannot defend herself, she is presumed guilty and executed (vv. 20–21). The same onus is found in laws on rape in the town (22:23–24). It is assumed that if the girl did not cry out for help she consented to sex, even though there are valid reasons (such as fear for her life) that might lead a woman to remain silent when she was being raped.[15]

Deuteronomy 22:28–29 also addresses a case of rape.[16] The violation of the young woman's virginity has economic as well as social consequences, as the ability of the family to demand a good bride-price would be lost when it became known that the girl was not a virgin. The perpetrator, therefore, must pay a substantial fixed bride-price, marry the woman, and give up the right to divorce her. It does not sit well with modern sensibilities to require

11. Raphael Patai, *Sex and Family in the Bible and the Middle East* (Garden City: Doubleday, 1959), 57.

12. Ben-Zion Schereschewsky, "Divorce," *EncJud*, 6:123–25.

13. Patai, *Sex and Family*, 116–17.

14. Edenburg, "Ideology and Social Context," 44.

15. Anderson, *Women, Ideology, and Violence*, 89.

16. Jeffrey H. Tigay, *Deuteronomy* (JPS Torah Commentary; Philadelphia: Jewish Publication Society, 1996), 209. Tigay sees a significant difference in wording between the law regarding the seduction of the virgin in Exod 22:16–17 and Deut 22:28–29. However, Carolyn Pressler (*The View of Women Found in the Deuteronomic Family Laws* [BZAW 216; Berlin: de Gruyter, 1993], 37–38) does not regard the difference between those accounts as having much legal significance.

a woman to marry her rapist; but demanding marriage without divorce extends some protection to the woman. It gave her security when she might be left socially vulnerable and shielded her from accusations of sexual impropriety such as alluded to in 22:13–19.[17]

The penalty for adultery in Deut 22:22 is death; as in the parallel in Lev 20:10, both the man and the woman are executed. This law is harsher than comparable customs indicated elsewhere in the Tanakh. For example, Prov 6:35 suggests that a husband could accept monetary compensation in such a case. The idea an adulteress would be dismissed from a marriage with a bill of divorce is implied in Isa 50:1–2 and Jer 3:8.[18] Nevertheless, Deut 22:22 does not allow the offended husband to demand monetary compensation nor does it address any extenuating circumstances.[19]

Assessment of the meaning of Deuteronomy's marriage laws involves several lines of evidence. First, the Deuteronomic stance can be compared with other biblical texts. As has been seen, it is not certain that traditional biblical culture automatically invoked the death penalty for adultery. Second, one can consult ancient Near Eastern legal collections, which are also ambiguous on this question. In some cases, the husband had the right to invoke a lesser penalty.[20] Finally, marriage contracts in extrabiblical sources also shed light on this aspect of Deuteronomic law.

While many marriage contracts are preserved in cuneiform sources, the following discussion focuses on a marriage contract from the archive of Aramaic documents left by the ancient Jewish military colony on the island of Elephantine near modern Aswan in Egypt. As noted above, biblical sources suggest only the husband had the right to divorce according to biblical law. But this restriction is not found in the marriage contract of Mibtahiah, a Jewish woman who lived in Elephantine, as seen in an extract from her document of wifehood dated October 14, 449 BCE. At this time Mibtahiah was a widow contracting a second marriage with a man named Esḥor through the mediation of her father.

> Tomorrow or the next day, should Mibtahiah stand up in an assembly and say, "I hated Esḥor my husband," silver of hatred is on her head . . . Tomorrow or the next day, should Esḥor stand up in an assembly and

17. Pressler, *The View of Women*, 42–43.

18. Frymer-Kenski, "Israel," 1010.

19. Anderson, *Women, Ideology, and Violence*, 91.

20. Edenburg, "Ideology and Social Context," 48–56.

> say, "I hated my wife Mibtahiah," her bride-price will be lost and all that she brought in in her hand she shall take out.[21]

Both parties have the right to terminate the marriage, and both bear a monetary penalty ("silver of hatred") if they do; but there are no other legal ramifications. This extrabiblical evidence needs to be evaluated carefully, because the culture in which Mibtahiah contracted this marriage was under the rule of Persian law, not the authority of the Second Temple. Nevertheless, it ought to give one pause about concluding that Deuteronomic law accurately represented the legal culture of early Judaism.

Deuteronomy's marriage laws were generated as much out of ideological concerns as out of social necessity or legal practice. This can be seen from the fact that several of Deuteronomy's marriage laws use a special formula that employs the phrase "so you shall purge the evil from your midst" (22:21, 22, 24). Similar Deuteronomic formulas also appear in cases demanding the death sentence for idolatry (13:5; 17:7), willful disobedience of the central judiciary (17:12), intentional homicide (19:13), false testimony in court (19:19), and kidnapping a free Israelite in order to sell him as a slave (24:7).

A common denominator to these laws is an offense against social solidarity.[22] They involve an analysis of criminal activity that also appears in the Holiness Code, where idolatry, murder, and adultery are considered criminal actions that defile the land. In Deuteronomy, they defile the community. They must be expiated by putting the perpetrator to death.

Marriage in Deuteronomy, therefore, has multiple meanings. In terms of its metaphorical value, analogy can be seen with the covenant relationship common in prophetic literature. Several prophets compare God's covenantal relationship with Israel to a marriage (e.g., Hosea 1–3). Deuteronomy also uses imagery drawn from the realm of domestic life to portray God's relationship with Israel. This is suggested by the motif of divine jealousy associated with punishment for idolatry (Deut 4:24; 5:9; 6:15). Probably, Deuteronomy's marriage laws were drafted not only to reinforce the family structure but also to reinforce Israel's loyalty to YHWH.[23] The regulation of women's bodies recommended itself in a system that was interested in strengthening Israel's relationship with God. In both cases, and in analogous ways, the

21. "Document of Wifehood," adapted from the translation by Bezalel Porten (*COS* 3.63:155–56).

22. Edenburg, "Ideology and Social Context," 57.

23. Edenburg, "Ideology and Social Context," 60.

female agent in the marital/covenant relationship was given a primary responsibility for keeping the relationship intact.

Deuteronomy's Rhetoric of Social Solidarity

From a modern perspective, Deuteronomy's failure to advocate more fully for the rights of women is disappointing. In other spheres of life, Deuteronomy is capable of making rather bold modifications of traditional legal practice. A dramatic illustration of Deuteronomy's capacity for readjusting social mores in the interests of justice occurs in 23:15–16. A regular feature of ancient Near Eastern treaties is the demand that fugitive slaves and renegade servants be returned to the country from which they came. In contrast, Israel is not to return foreign slaves to their owners.[24] They are permitted to settle freely "in any one of your towns." Returning them to their owners amounts to oppression (v. 16).

In fairness, Deuteronomy does not fundamentally call into question the institution of slavery. However, its ethical viewpoint demanded that the socially disadvantaged be looked upon with sympathy. A similar rhetoric seldom appears with respect to the status of women. Nevertheless, the potential exists in Deuteronomy. After all, the book demands of Israel "Justice, and only justice, you shall pursue"(16:20).

Deuteronomy's reluctance to address women's rights contrasts with a humanitarian tendency noticeable in a number of the laws in Deuteronomy 21–25.[25] For example, Chapter 9 cited instances in which Deuteronomic law sought to limit the right of the creditor to force the payment of a loan (24:10–13) while advancing the interests of the freed debt slave (15:12–18). One could also note its concern for the welfare of animals (22:1–4, 6–7) and laws that demand attention to the needs of the landless: widows, orphans, and resident aliens (e.g., 24:17–22).

Deuteronomy's humanitarian laws are connected to its concern to promote social solidarity. This is apparent in Deuteronomy's favorite phrase for members of the community, "your brother." Unfortunately, a translation such as the NRSV has leveled the distinction between "neighbor" (*rēaʿ*) and

24. Richard D. Nelson, *Deuteronomy* (OTL; Louisville: Westminster John Knox, 2002), 280.

25. A classic description of Deuteronomic "humanism" is found in Moshe Weinfeld, *Deuteronomy and the Deuteronomic School* (Oxford: Clarendon, 1972), 282–97.

"brother" (*ʾāḥ*) in Deuteronomy, although these ideas correspond to different words in Hebrew. Deuteronomic law can refer to the "neighbor" (e.g., 19:14; 23:25; 24:10) just as the Covenant Code does (e.g., Exod 22:7, 26). Where it distinguishes itself from the older law collection, however, is in its use of the word "brother" to refer to a fellow Israelite. This usage never appears in the Covenant Code. For example, the opponent-at-law who has lost his animal in Exod 23:4–5 (i.e., "your enemy") is called "your brother" in Deut 22:1–4.[26]

Deuteronomy's concept of "brotherhood" emphasizes Israel's sense of shared kinship (implicit in the Hebrew concept of "brother"). It is meant to reinforce a perception of social solidarity among Deuteronomy's addressees. So, for example, it is forbidden to lend money at interest to a brother kinsman in 23:19 (NRSV "another Israelite"). Even corporal punishment is regulated to avoid humiliating "your brother" (25:3). Nevertheless, the status of "brotherhood" is not generally extended to women in Deuteronomic law.[27] The sole exception is found with respect to the male or female who sells himself into debt slavery. According to Deut 15:12, such a person is "your kinsman/brother" (NRSV "a member of your community").

Developments

The last chapter indicated that Deuteronomic thinking set in motion trends that had far-reaching effects in the emergence of both rabbinic Judaism and early Christianity. These entailed both innovations and extensions in the concept of Torah. Among them, one should consider the ways in which the concept of the "neighbor" was developed by the early Jesus group (cf. the parable of the "Good Samaritan" in Luke 10:29–37). This innovation can claim a precedent in Deuteronomic thought, which also sought to redefine social boundaries by its rhetoric of social solidarity.

The literature on the concept of the "neighbor" in the New Testament is quite large, and it cannot be summarized here. Suffice it to note that generations of biblical commentators, preachers, and theologians have agreed that Jesus and his first followers sought to extend the idea of "neighbor" beyond its traditional boundaries. Unfortunately, there is little to show that the early church thought of women when it revised the category of neighbor.

26. Gerhard von Rad, *Deuteronomy* (OTL; Philadelphia: Westminster, 1966), 140–41.

27. For further commentary on the exclusion of women from Deuteronomy's humanitarian ethic, see Pressler, *The View of Women*, 113–14.

There are indications that the symbol system which formed the first Christians contained a potential for emancipating women's agency in the divine economy.[28] Nevertheless, contrasts between a woman-positive Jesus movement and a patriarchal rabbinic Judaism are to be avoided.[29] To the degree that the primitive church was woman-positive, its ethics were commensurate with the biblical commitment to justice. As with the thinkers who produced the book of Deuteronomy, however, history shows that early Christianity failed to develop the logic of its symbol system when it came to emancipating women or children. It would take the emergence of very different social structures to afford both church and synagogue opportunities to appropriate the liberating dynamics of the scriptural tradition in new ways, ones which would lead them to reassess their commitments to justice for women.

28. See, e.g., Elizabeth Schüssler Fiorenza, *In Memory of Her: A Feminist Theological Reconstruction of Christian Origins* (New York: Crossroad, 1983); Anne Jensen, *God's Self-Confident Daughters: Early Christianity and the Liberation of Women* (Louisville: Westminster John Knox, 1996).

29. Amy-Jill Levine, "The Disease of Post-Colonial New Testament Studies and the Hermeneutics of Healing," *JFSR* 20 (2004): 91–99.

Further Reading: Deuteronomy

Benjamin, Don C. *Deuteronomy and City Life: A Form Criticism of Texts with the Word City (*'ir*) in Deuteronomy 4:41–26:19*. Lanham: University Press of America, 1983.

Crouch, Carly L. *Israel and the Assyrians: Deuteronomy, the Succession Treaty of Esarhaddon, and the Nature of Subversion*. ANEM 8. Atlanta: SBL, 2014.

Dion, Paul-Eugène. "Deuteronomy 13: The Suppression of Alien Religious Propaganda in Israel during the Late Monarchical Era." In *Law and Ideology in Monarchic Israel,* edited by Baruch Halpern and Deborah W. Hobson, 147–217. JSOTSup 124. Sheffield: JSOT, 1991.

Edenburg, Cynthia. "Ideology and Social Context of the Deuteronomic Women's Sex Laws (Deuteronomy 22:13–19)." *JBL* 128 (2009): 43–60.

Japhet, Sara. "The Relationship between the Legal Corpora in the Pentateuch in Light of Manumission Laws." In *Studies in the Bible 1986*, edited by Sara Japhet, 63–89. ScrHier 31. Jerusalem: Magnes, 1986.

Kaufman, Stephen A. "The Structure of Deuteronomic Law." *Maarav* 1 (1979): 105–58.

Kline, Meredith G. *Treaty of the Great King: The Covenant Structure of Deuteronomy. Studies and Commentary.* Grand Rapids: Eerdmans, 1963.

Levinson, Bernard M. *Deuteronomy and the Hermeneutics of Legal Innovation.* New York: Oxford University Press, 1997.

MacDonald, Nathan. *Deuteronomy and the Meaning of 'Monotheism.'* FAT/2 1. Tübingen: Mohr Siebeck, 2003.

McConville, J. G. *Law and Theology in Deuteronomy*. JSOTSup 33. Sheffield: JSOT, 1984.

Moran, William J. "The Ancient Near Eastern Background of the Love of God in Deuteronomy." *CBQ* 25 (1963): 77–87.

Morrow, William S. *Scribing the Center: Organization and Redaction in Deuteronomy 14:1–17:1*. SBLMS 49. Atlanta: Scholars, 1995.

———. "The Paradox of Deuteronomy 13: A Postcolonial Reading." In *»Gerechtigkeit und Recht zu* Üben« (Gen 18, 19): *Studien zur altorientalischen und biblischen Rechtsgeschichte,* edited by R. Achenbach and M. Arneth, 227–39. BZABR 13. Wiesbaden: Harrasowitz, 2009.

———. "'To Set the Name' in the Deuteronomic Centralization Formula: A Case of Cultural Hybridity." *JSS* 55 (2010): 365–83.

———. "Deuteronomy 7 in Postcolonial Perspective: Cultural Fragmentation and Renewal." In *Interpreting Exile: Interdisciplinary Studies of Displacement and Deportation in Biblical and Modern Contexts*, edited by Brad E. Kelle, Frank R. Ames, and Jacob L. Wright, 275–94. AIL 10. Atlanta: Society of Biblical Literature, 2011.

Otto, Eckart. "Aspects of Legal Reforms and Reformulations in Ancient Cuneiform and Israelite Law." In *Theory and Method in Biblical and Cuneiform Law: Revision, Interpolation and Development*, edited by Bernard M. Levinson, 160–96. JSOTSup 181. Sheffield: Sheffield Academic, 1994.

Pakkala, Juha. "The Date of the Oldest Edition of Deuteronomy." *ZAW* 121 (2009): 388–401.

Pressler, Carolyn. *The View of Women Found in the Deuteronomic Family Laws*. BZAW 216. Berlin: de Gruyter, 1993.

Rofé, Alexander. "The Organization of the Judiciary in Deuteronomy (Deut. 16.18–20; 17.8–13; 19.15; 21.22–23; 24.16; 25.1–3)." In *The World of the Aramaeans*. Vol. 1: *Biblical Studies in Honour of Paul-Eugène Dion*, edited by P. M. Michèle Daviau, John W. Wevers, and Michael Weigl, 92–112. JSOTSup 324. Sheffield: Sheffield Academic, 2001.

Schwartz, Baruch J. "Reexamining the Fate of the Canaanites in the Torah Traditions." In *Sefer Moshe: The Moshe Weinfeld Jubilee Volume*, edited by C. Cohen, Avi Hurowitz, and Shalom M. Paul, 151–70. Winona Lake: Eisenbrauns, 2004.

Stackert, Jeffrey. *Rewriting the Torah: Literary Revision in Deuteronomy and the Holiness Legislation*. FAT 52. Tübingen: Mohr Siebeck, 2007.

Stuhlman, Louis. "Encroachment in Deuteronomy: An Analysis of the Social World of the D Code." *JBL* 109 (1990): 613–32.

Weinfeld, Moshe. *Deuteronomy and the Deuteronomic School*. Oxford: Clarendon, 1972.

Willis, Timothy M. *The Elders of the City: A Study of the Elders-Laws in Deuteronomy*. SBLMS 55. Atlanta: Society of Biblical Literature, 2001.

Summary Observations

This chapter is not written as a report of the book's conclusions. In fact, I hope that this book does not conclude. My dream is that it opens conversations that will continue well into the future. It is worth, however, summarizing some of its dominant perspectives.

It was important to sample each of the law collections to show how its premises were worked out. I trust, however, that the preceding chapters also showed how the collections' details fit into agendas of community-making. Whether located at the foot of the holy mountain, in the rural village, the tabernacle, or the city, each collection of pentateuchal law was written in order to convey a vision of what it meant to live as God's people. To that end, it seems appropriate to return to the traits of canonical criticism that were introduced in Chapter 1. They provide a convenient template for restating the major thrusts of this book's argument. These principles are addressed here, however, in a different order than they were listed above.

1. The underlying purpose of Scripture is to enable communities to *monotheize* in a particular time and place.

As explained in Chapter 1, to monotheize means to bring every sphere of life under the aegis of God. We can see that motif in all of the law collections examined. While their laws tend to be representative rather than exhaustive, matters typically divided between "sacred" and "secular" in the modern world stand closely together. Of course, the word "monotheize" risks being an anachronism. Israel's lawmakers did not necessarily believe that YHWH was the only deity that existed. The theological presuppositions of the book of Deuteronomy are a case in point. Nevertheless, all of the biblical law collections assumed that Israel could only live with integrity with YHWH if it worshipped no other gods and if it brought its entire life under what sociologist Peter Berger called the "sacred canopy."[1]

The Ten Commandments expressed its monotheizing program through the device of the "two tables" of the law. The Covenant Code used sophisticated forms of ring composition so that instructions for right worship enveloped law and ethics that touched on the integrity of the person, possessions, and economic welfare. One of the contributions of Holiness thinking was to extend Priestly ideology into the sphere of morality. As was seen in Chapter 16, this was accomplished through a form of analogical reasoning that united Body, Temple, and Community. Finally, Deuteronomy's treaty form was expanded over time into a law book that described how an urban Israel was to pursue righteousness in every sphere of life.

2. Scripture contains a plurality of voices.

The foregoing observations support the recognition that the major biblical law collections do not speak with a single voice. To put this observation into terms somewhat compatible with church history, it seems to me the Covenant Code breathes an atmosphere I associate with the primitive Anabaptist tradition. Its vision of Israel is decentralized, rural, and quite indifferent to the state. By contrast, when I read materials from P, I get a distinct whiff of a religion that emphasizes priestly hierarchy, the real presence of God, and the significance of the sacrificial. These are traits I associate with the more sacramentally inclined forms of Christianity. Deuteronomy, on the other hand, smacks of the Reformed tradition. Its thoroughgoing covenantal theology is reminiscent of my Presbyterian heritage.

Of course, one should not (and cannot!) push these analogies too far. We must not read church history into the Old Testament. On the other hand, perhaps it is worth noting that there is precedent for alternate models of Christian faith communities in Scripture. And, just as the identity markers of contemporary Christian denominations are not entirely interchangeable, neither are the social metaphors around which the biblical law codes were organized.

At present, there is a debate among biblical scholars as to how to think about the differences between the various law collections, For example, was

1. Peter Berger, *The Sacred Canopy: Elements of a Sociological Theory of Religion* (Garden City: Doubleday, 1967).

Deuteronomy intended to displace the Covenant Code or complement it?[2] As I have presented the differences between the major pentateuchal law collections, there is room for both perspectives. They both challenge and supplement each other's vision of the ideal community of faith. What I find especially informative, however, is that the differing community models presented in the Torah have not been erased by the editors of the Tanakh. Its accommodation of a plurality of voices allows for the idea that no one form of Israel was valid for all time and in all places.

Certainly, some cultural assumptions are common to all three of the major law collections. These include important religious ideas and also social conventions. Religiously, all have a place for sacrifice. Socially, it is clear that males have a prominence in public religious life and in legal precedent that women lack. We have also seen that slavery is not called into serious question and that there are a number of ways in which biblical law reflects ideas of due process shared with ancient Near Eastern neighbors.

Even so, the Old Testament's law collections had different emphases and felt free to alter preexisting traditions and institutions in order to promote Israel's collective life. This is most dramatically communicated by the reforms of Deuteronomy (see Chapters 20 and 21). With one sweep of the hand, this biblical book was prepared to do away with many venerable traditions in the religion of Israel.

Other modifications can also be seen. For example, Chapter 10 and 16 noted how the Holiness school extended the Priestly concept of holiness to the people and the land of Israel. The Covenant Code, H, and Deuteronomy all innovate differently with respect to sabbatical institutions for the relief of the poor. The Covenant Code's demand to fallow local fields every seven years was not followed in Deuteronomy, which proclaimed a national seven-year cancellation of debts instead. Leviticus 25, however, adapted both institutions (Chapter 17). Against the Covenant Code, it demanded a single fallow year on a national basis. Against Deuteronomy, it does not allow for the cancellation of debts before the Jubilee.

2. E.g., Joshua Berman ("Supersessionist or Complementary? Reassessing the Nature of Legal Revision in the Pentateuchal Law Collections," *JBL* 135 [2016]: 201–22) suggests that the relationship between the biblical law collections is basically complementary. Opposed are the viewpoints of Bernard M. Levinson, *Deuteronomy and the Hermeneutics of Legal Innovation* (New York: Oxford University Press, 1997), 153; and Jeffrey Stackert, *Rewriting the Torah: Literary Revision in Deuteronomy and the Holiness Legislation* (FAT 52; Tübingen: Mohr Siebeck, 2007), 218. Both Levinson and Stackert think that Deuteronomy was written to replace the Covenant Code.

3. Scripture allows for both community stability and adaptability.

The two points above combine to support this third observation. Each biblical law collection allows for the community to maintain its stability as a representative of the Mosaic tradition, while also permitting it to adapt to unprecedented challenges and cultural situations. Several features could be discussed here by way of illustration. I will focus on the metaphor of YHWH's kingship and the ways in which the sacrificial cult was redefined both in biblical and postbiblical times.

In framing its vision of the functional faith community, the Covenant Code assumed that YHWH was a king who had no need of the human institutions that often supported human monarchies. It knows of neither palace nor temple. The Priestly writings (including those of the Holiness school), however, were impressed by the necessity of centering the community on a visible manifestation of divine presence: the tabernacle, which assumed aspects of both palace and temple. Deuteronomy also appealed to the institutions of human monarchy. While it acknowledged the importance of the temple, it borrowed from the political instruments of the ancient Near Eastern state (i.e., treaty and law book) to communicate its vision to an urbanized Israel. In other words, what remained stable was the concept of the kingship of God; but this metaphor was capable of being adapted to serve various community configurations.

Particularly dramatic distinctions between the Covenant Code, Priestly law, and Deuteronomy appear in their attitudes towards the practice of sacrifice. In this regard, the Covenant Code allows for the possibility of a plurality of sacrificial sites whose number is not fixed. Moreover, it appears to be indifferent to the need for a priestly caste to preside over the sacrificial cult. This is implied both by the absence of any reference to priests in its laws and also by its literary position. It is set down prior to the foundation story of the Levites as the priestly tribe in Exodus 32. Priestly law, on the other hand, assumes there is a fixed place for the sacrifice of domestic animals overseen by the descendants of Aaron. The Holiness school considered it an act of apostasy to offer a sacrificial animal otherwise.

In contrast to the Covenant Code, Deuteronomy insists on the restriction of sacrifice to a single place. This requires Deuteronomy to authorize the people to treat firstling sacrifices and the slaughter of domestic animals in new ways. The cult need not be compensated for unfit firstlings, and ritual impurity is no longer a barrier to the consumption of domestic animals because they no longer have to be sacrificed at an altar.

Postbiblical Jewish communities continued to wrestle with the place of sacrifice in the Mosaic tradition. In fact, first-century Jews found various ways of living without a functioning temple. For example, the Qumran sect developed a sense of legitimacy through the observance of purity laws, even after it had been expelled from (or left) the Jerusalem temple. Both rabbinic Judaism and the early church were able to survive the destruction of the Second Temple because their symbol systems did not require animal sacrifice. Rabbinic Jews did so by developing Torah study as an alternate site of divine presence, while the first Christians found a new Torah in the person of Jesus. Despite these adaptations, none of the groups mentioned above thought of themselves at variance with the Mosaic tradition. On the contrary, they regarded their innovations—as different as they were from one another—as logical and necessary adaptations in order to preserve a stable identity as the people of God.

4. Canon and community are inextricably bound.

Two points can be made here. The first is connected to the idea that Scripture and community have a reciprocal relationship with each other. The second is that the relationship into which God calls people is always and simultaneously a gift and an obligation. In the Bible, ethical and legal discourse articulate the meaning of the relationship that God has graciously bestowed on Israel.

Canonical criticism makes the claim that there is a reciprocal relationship between the written standards that are called Scripture and the community that knows itself through them. The great scholar of comparative religions Wilfred Cantwell Smith makes a similar point in his book *What is Scripture?*: "The true meaning of Scripture is the solid historical reality of the continuum of actual meanings over the centuries to actual people."[3] This insight is true not only for the Bible as a whole, but also for the various parts that make it up. Canon implies community; and the community selects as its written standards literature that enables it to reaffirm and recreate its identity through time.

That is one of the reasons this book has frequently used the motif of "community-making" when discussing the dynamics of biblical law. Underlying the scriptural imperative is the desire to create and sustain viable

3. Wilfrid Cantwell Smith, *What Is Scripture? A Comparative Approach* (Minneapolis: Fortress, 1993), 89.

relationships with God and neighbor. A study of the history of biblical law reveals the fact that Israel needed to maintain a stable identity as God's people and to adapt to new and challenging cultural and historical situations. The articulation, development, and canonization of biblical law helped them do that.

For that very reason, these scriptural writings remain important in the present. The interplay between the need to find a stable identity as God's people and the necessity of adapting to new times and new cultural situations has continuing importance. Therefore, one needs to think rather carefully about how biblical law collections might continue to function as Scripture in the church. In my opinion, the scriptural authority question operates on two levels. One is on the level of content, and the other is on the level of method.

The survey of biblical law undertaken in the previous chapters has tried to describe both the contents of biblical law collections and also their methodology (i.e., ways of doing theology). I doubt that many modern readers will find their ethical sensibilities mollified by close study of the contents of biblical law presented in this book. For example, many will have no interest in living in faith communities where the ordinary ethical actor is assumed to be a land-owning male, where animal sacrifice is accepted as the norm for worship, and where the institution of slavery is left unchallenged. The temptation, therefore, will be to abandon biblical law as incapable of addressing the contemporary church.

Unfortunately, such a decision is premature as long as it refuses to take into consideration not simply the contents of biblical law collections but also their methodology. Here the observation made above, that relationship entails both gift and obligation, comes into its own. This is a truth that is deeply reflected in biblical law.[4] Nor is it contradicted by the experience of the New Testament. On the contrary, the very act of proclaiming the gospel leads naturally to ethical and regulatory discourse. This is visible in the teachings of Jesus (e.g., the Sermon on the Mount), the letters of Paul (e.g., Romans 12–14), the Epistle of James, the admonitions of Hebrews 12, etc.

From this perspective, the method used in biblical collections calls out for careful study and consideration. Each of these biblical texts bases its legal discourse on the fact that YHWH has graciously called Israel into relationship with himself. This experience of unmerited grace is not contrary to instructional discourse; it actually demands articulation through Torah.

4. Dale Patrick, *The Rhetoric of Revelation in the Hebrew Bible* (OBT; Minneapolis: Fortress, 1999), 81.

Of course, one of the most important of the methodological principles presupposed in collections of biblical law has to do with kingship. Although the "kingdom of God" is important to New Testament as well as Old Testament thinkers, its manifestations in the present world are not clear. Can the word "king" still indicate something essential about the sovereignty of God in the modern world of faith? If not, what is its substitute? And, in either case, how is the metaphor for divine preeminence to be worked out as exactly and profoundly as it was in the instruments of biblical law?

Another key premise is holiness. Are we done with holiness in the modern world? If not, what is there still to be learned from the thoroughgoing meditation of the nature of holiness found in biblical law?

Yet another organizing principle is the concept of incarnation. Implicit in all of the biblical law collections is the belief that YHWH wants his spirit embodied in human community. The eschatological hope is that the human community will become a dwelling for the divine reality. Biblical law, however, did not think of this expectation in future terms. Each of its major collections seems to say, "See, the home of God is among mortals" (Rev 21:3). Their commitment to the desire for incarnation was worked out with a precision that warrants careful consideration in the contemporary situation. At the level of method, they still have much to teach about how to think about right relationships between God and the human community and how to put those relationships into practice.

Further Reading

This list classifies many of the monographs and essays written in English that appear in the notes to this book. The focus is on legal discourse in the Old Testament/Tanakh. Generally available commentaries and entries in Bible dictionaries or encyclopedias are not included, nor studies quite limited in scope. Readers wanting a full classified bibliography for biblical and ancient Near Eastern law should consult John W. Welch, "Biblical Law Cumulative Bibliography," *The Ancient World Online: Institute for the Study of the Ancient World* (2014).

Surveys of Biblical Law

Barmash, Pamela, ed. *The Oxford Handbook of Biblical Law*. New York: Oxford University Press, 2017.

Berman, Joshua. "Supersessionist or Complementary? Reassessing the Nature of Legal Revision in the Pentateuchal Law Collections." *JBL* 135 (2016): 201–22.

Crüsemann, Frank. *The Torah: Theology and Social History of Old Testament Law.* Minneapolis: Augsburg Fortress, 1996.

Falk, Ze'ev W. *Hebrew Law in Biblical Times: An Introduction.* 2nd ed. Provo: Brigham Young University Press and Winona Lake: Eisenbrauns, 2001.

Greenberg, Moshe. "Some Postulates of Biblical Criminal Law." In *Yehezkel Kaufmann Jubilee Volume: Studies in Bible and Jewish Religion Dedicated to Yehezkel Kaufmann on the Occasion of His Seventieth Birthday,* edited by Menachem Haran, 5–28. Jerusalem: Magnes, 1960.

———. "More Reflections on Biblical Criminal Law." In *Studies in Bible, 1986*, edited by Sara Japhet, 1–17. ScrHier 31. Jerusalem: Magnes, 1986.

Greengus, Samuel. *Laws in the Bible and in Early Rabbinic Collections.* Eugene: Cascade, 2011.

Gesundheit, Shimon. *Three Times a Year: Studies on Festival Legislation in the Pentateuch.* FAT 82. Tübingen: Mohr Siebeck, 2012.

Gilmer, Harry W. *The If-You Form in Israelite Law.* SBLDS 15. Missoula: Scholars, 1975.

Jacobs, Sandra. *The Body as Property: Physical Disfigurement in Biblical Law.* LHBOTS 582. London: T. & T. Clark, 2014.

Knight, Douglas A. *Law, Power, and Justice in Ancient Israel.* LAI. Louisville: Westminster John Knox, 2011.

Patrick, Dale. "Casuistic Law Governing Primary Rights and Duties." *JBL* 92 (1972): 180–84.

———. *Old Testament Law.* Atlanta: John Knox, 1985.

Sonsino, Rifat. *Motive Clauses in Hebrew Law.* SBLDS 45. Chico: Scholars, 1980.

Strawn, Brent, ed. *The Oxford Encyclopedia of Bible and Law.* New York: Oxford University Press, 2015.

Varšo, Miroslav. "Interest (Usury) and Its Variations in the Biblical Law Codices." *CV* 50 (2008): 223–43.

Weingreen, Jacob. *From Bible to Mishna: The Continuity of Tradition.* Manchester: Manchester University Press, 1976.

Wells, Bruce. *The Law of Testimony in the Pentateuchal Codes.* BZABR 4. Wiesbaden: Harrassowitz, 2004.

———. "What Is Biblical Law? A Look at Pentateuchal Rules and Near Eastern Practice." *CBQ* 70 (2008): 223–43.

Westbrook, Raymond. *Property and the Family in Biblical Law.* JSOTSup 113. Sheffield: JSOT, 1991.

Westbrook, Raymond, ed. *A History of Ancient Near Eastern Law.* 2 vols. HdO 72. Leiden: Brill, 2003.

Westbrook, Raymond, and Bruce Wells. *Everyday Law in Biblical Israel: An Introduction.* Louisville: Westminster John Knox, 2009.

Law and Biblical Religion

Anderson, Cheryl B. *Women, Ideology, and Violence: Critical Theory and the Construction of Gender in the Book of the Covenant and the Deuteronomic Law.* JSOTSup 394. London: T. & T. Clark, 2004.

Bennett, Harold V. *Injustice Made Legal: Deuteronomic Law and the Plight of Widows, Strangers, and Orphans in Ancient Israel.* BIW. Grand Rapids: Eerdmans, 2002.

Berman, Joshua. *Created Equal: How the Bible Broke with Ancient Political Thought.* New York: Oxford University Press, 2008.

Boda, Mark. *A Severe Mercy: Sin and Its Remedy in the Old Testament.* Siphrut 1. Winona Lake: Eisenbrauns, 2009.

Brand, Miryam T. *Evil Within and Without: The Source of Sin and Its Nature as Portrayed in Second Temple Judaism.* Journal of Ancient Judaism Supplement 9. Göttingen: Vandenhoeck & Ruprecht, 2013.

Buss, Martin J. "Logic and Israelite Law." *Semeia* 45 (1989): 49–65.

Daube, David. "The Exodus Pattern in the Bible." In *Collected Works of David Daube*. Vol. 3: *Biblical Law and Literature*, edited by Calum Carmichael, 101–56. Berkeley: Robbins Collection, University of California, 2003.

Eberhart, Christian A. *The Sacrifice of Jesus: Understanding Atonement Biblically*. Minneapolis: Fortress, 2011.

Frevel, Christian, and Christophe Nihan, eds. *Purity and the Forming of Religious Traditions in the Ancient Mediterranean World and Ancient Judaism*. Dynamics in the History of Religions 3. Leiden: Brill, 2013.

Gerstenberger, Erhard S. "'. . . (He/They) Shall Be Put to Death': Live-Preserving Death Threats in Old Testament Law." *ExAud* 11 (1995): 43–61.

Heger, Paul. "Source of Law in Biblical and Mesopotamian Law Collections." *Bib* 86 (2005): 324–42.

Kaufman, Stephen A. "A Reconstruction of the Social Welfare Systems of Ancient Israel." In *In the Shelter of Elyon: Essays on Ancient Palestinian Life and Literature in Honor of G. W. Ahlström*, edited by W. Boyd Barrick and John R. Spencer, 277–86. JSOTSup 31. Sheffield: JSOT, 1984.

Klawans, Jonathan. *Impurity and Sin in Ancient Judaism*. New York: Oxford University Press, 2000.

Krašovec, Jože. "Is There a Doctrine of 'Collective Retribution' in the Hebrew Bible?" *HUCA* 65 (1994): 35–89.

Levinson, Bernard M. *Legal Revision and Renewal in Ancient Israel*. New York: Cambridge University Press, 2008.

Magdalene, F. Rachel. *On the Scales of Righteousness: Neo-Babylonian Trial Law and the Book of Job*. BJS 348. Providence: Brown University, 2007.

Oden, Robert A. "The Place of Covenant in the Religion of Israel." In *Ancient Israelite Religion: Essays in Honor of Frank Moore Cross*, edited by Patrick D. Miller, Paul D. Hanson, and S. Dean McBride, 429–47. Philadelphia: Fortress, 1987.

Patai, Raphael. *Sex and Family in the Bible and the Middle East*. Garden City: Doubleday, 1959.

Patrick, Dale. *The Rhetoric of Revelation in the Hebrew Bible*. OBT. Minneapolis: Fortress, 1999.

Scholz, Susanne. *Sacred Witness: Rape in the Hebrew Bible*. Minneapolis: Fortress, 2010.

Weinfeld, Moshe. *Social Justice in Ancient Israel and in the Ancient Near East*. Minneapolis: Fortress, 1995.

———. *The Place of the Law in the Religion of Ancient Israel*. VTSup 100. Leiden: Brill, 2004.

Subject Index

Index of Scripture and Other Ancient Literature